Tortured

Tortured

Abused and neglected by
Britain's most sadistic mum.
This is my story of survival.

VICTORIA SPRY

with Kate Moore

EBURY
PRESS

1 3 5 7 9 10 8 6 4 2

Ebury Press, an imprint of Ebury Publishing,
20 Vauxhall Bridge Road,
London SW1V 2SA

Ebury Press is part of the Penguin Random House group of companies
whose addresses can be found at global.penguinrandomhouse.com

Penguin
Random House
UK

This edition published by Ebury Press in 2015

www.eburypublishing.co.uk

A CIP catalogue record for this book is available from the British Library

ISBN 9780091960353

Printed and bound by CPI Group (UK) Ltd, Croydon CR0 4YY

MIX
Paper from
responsible sources
FSC® C018179

Penguin Random House is committed to a sustainable future
for our business, our readers and our planet. This book is made
from Forest Stewardship Council® certified paper.

For Ollie and Alfie and Milly
You will always have a place in my heart

AUTHOR'S NOTE

When I was less than a year old, Eunice Spry became my foster mother. When I was five, she adopted me, and became my legal parent. For eighteen years, I called her Mum. That is why, in this book, I still use that name.

Some people have criticised me for using the word instead of Eunice, now that everybody knows what she has done. Believe me, I know she doesn't deserve the title. I know she hasn't been one inch a good mother.

But some habits are hard to break.

She was just the only mum I ever knew.

PROLOGUE

I want you to close your eyes and imagine. Imagine a world where everything is not how it seems. Where toys are not for playing with. Where perfect parents are anything but. Where asking someone for help is just about the most dangerous thing you can do.

Imagine a world where the metallic bang of your mum unpacking tins of baked beans signals not your supper, but a weapon ready for wielding. Imagine a world where your mother brandishing a stick is not some make-believe game of pirates or spies, but something far, far darker. Imagine a world where the unmistakable sound of a bath tap running won't lead to a fun playtime, a child's laughter gurgling amidst the brightly coloured rubber ducks. Instead, you should listen out for the gurgle of a child's throat as she is held beneath the water's surface, time and time again, until she learns to feign death to make them stop.

Welcome to my world.

PART ONE

BAD GIRL

CHAPTER ONE

'Just *what* do you think you're doing?'

My hand shot back from the shiny silver can. My eyes dropped straight to the floor. I was only three years old, but already I knew to look down, look down, look down.

From beneath my lashes, I could see the tin cans all lined up on our red-tiled kitchen floor, like regimental soldiers: some tall, some short, some squat, and each in an identical silver uniform. Scattered around them were their labels. I had been peeling them off, one by one. Not out of naughtiness; perhaps curiosity. Perhaps because I wasn't allowed to play with any of the toys in the house, so I found my own distractions. The coloured labels, whether bearing the bright turquoise livery of Heinz baked beans, or the smiling face of a cat or dog, appealed to me somehow.

Sitting on the floor, I could feel Mummy's eyes boring into my back.

'Now I'm not going to know what's in what can,' she said crossly.

I dared to dart a glance up at her. My mother, Eunice Spry, was a short woman, but she towered above me now, her gaunt, drawn face blazing with anger, dark eyes piercing and cold. Suddenly, her hand whipped out and I felt a hard blow to the back of my head. I looked down again, quick as I could, my skull throbbing with pain. I didn't cry out.

I never did, anymore.

'Pick a can,' she commanded, in her thick Gloucestershire accent.

Confused, but knowing better than to question her, I reached out and picked up the one nearest to me. It felt heavy in my little hand. She snatched it from me and marched over to the kitchen table to open it.

'Sit in that chair. You are going to eat whatever's in this can. Eat it all up!'

The grinding noise of the tin opener filled the kitchen as its metal teeth bit into the lid. Silently, I walked over to the chair and, with difficulty, tried to clamber up onto its high wicker seat. Mummy grew impatient with my efforts. She came across and yanked my arm, pulling me high up in the air and then shoving me into the hard seat.

I sniffed and wiped my hand across my runny nose. I had a cold, again. I always had a cold. That was another thing Mummy was always complaining about; something else I could never do right. She would make me stand to attention while she tilted my head back and poured Olbas oil down my nose, holding me firmly when I tried to squirm away from the overpowering scent, every trickle of it stinging my senses. Somehow, even the whole bottle of oil poured down it only made my nose stream more.

Mummy pushed the open can in front of me. 'Eat it!' she ordered.

I peered inside. Jellied chunks of brown meat glistened, and a stench of cat food reached my poorly nostrils. Even the smell was enough to make me retch.

But I knew I would have to eat it. What I ate, when I ate and how I ate was something Mummy had controlled from the moment I'd been handed to her on her doorstep, at the age of ten months, borne into the sanctuary of a foster mother's home after my birth parents couldn't cope. Throughout my early babyhood,

I was later told, I lay ignored in my cot; never played with, barely fed or clothed, just lying on my back in a dirty nappy: placid, quiet, resigned to the fact that no one ever came.

As an adult, I don't blame them for giving me up. It was obvious they couldn't cope with me or my older brother, Tom, and so we were taken into care. Tom went off to another family – a family who also wanted to adopt me.

But that didn't happen. Instead, I went to Eunice.

'Eat it!' she hissed at me.

I picked up the fork she had thrown down on the table. My tiny fingers fumbled on the cutlery, but I was careful not to drop it – I didn't want Mummy to feed me. Though I didn't have a clear memory of it, some part of me instinctively recalled her force-feeding me when I was eighteen months old, the sharp metal spoon prising between my closed gums, blood streaming down my face. She used to pin me to the floor and shove the spoon inside.

'Get on with it, you autistic twit!'

I lowered my head and thrust the fork into the meat.

I wasn't autistic, but no one, not even the doctors, could convince Mummy otherwise. According to her, I was an autistic twit, a backward child; the most stupid girl she had ever come across. Mummy had two natural grown-up daughters, Judith and Rebekah, from her first marriage, and they were both bright as buttons. They had learned to read at the age of two. They had attended private girls' schools, spoke several languages, rode horses and played musical instruments. When I'd landed on her doorstep in December 1986, sometime after Mummy's second marriage had ended – she took the name Spry from that husband, but little else, and as he was never mentioned at home I only found out about him much later – I was withdrawn and solemn, and I didn't know how to work my little arms and legs because I'd never been encouraged to crawl or sit or play. Yet Mummy had instantly thought that God had sent her a devil child who simply *refused* to meet her high expectations. She was convinced I was autistic. Though social services had warned her that my development would be delayed because of my poor care, and the doctors pronounced me perfectly normal, she wasn't having any of it. She insisted on tests, diagnoses; she said I was stubborn and refused to learn. And when she beat me, she said that she was doing it to beat some sense into me.

I lifted the first forkful to my mouth. I retched again, but I forced it down. It was cold and slimy on my tongue, the jelly slippery and wet. It tasted vile. I managed a second mouthful, conscious that Mummy was watching me. With her dyed black hair pulled back in her usual tight ponytail, her expression was clear to see. She looked satisfied, somehow – and righteous. She believed in what she was doing; she believed she was absolutely right.

And I did, too. For I *had* been naughty; I was a bad girl.

I deserved to be punished.

Knowing this didn't make the punishment any easier to take, though. I forced another forkful of cat food into my mouth, fighting against the gag that convulsed my throat. Tears streamed down my cheeks, but I didn't make a sound, other than the rattle of my retching. In my three years on this planet, I might have been slow to learn how to build a tower of bricks, or how to walk on my own two feet, but one thing I had nailed was the art of crying in complete silence.

From another room in the house I could hear music playing. My five-year-old sister, Charlotte, was probably watching a Disney film. Charlotte was Mummy's adopted daughter. Unlike me, who came to her tainted and damaged, Charlotte had been in Mummy's care since birth. Mummy had in fact seen her born, and immediately coddled her in blankets and love, sweeping her back to our home at 24 George Dowty Drive to be cosseted and cuddled and spoilt rotten. Charlotte was a favourite. She had toys to play with and pretty dresses and her own room with Paddington Bear wallpaper and a bunk bed that Mummy had specially made for her.

Charlotte never had to eat cat food.

I couldn't help what happened next. As I swallowed down another mouthful, the vomit rose up the back of my throat and through my nose and spewed all over the kitchen table. I hiccoughed, the sick mixing on my face with my salty tears, my blonde hair stringy with it. Mummy and I both surveyed the mess.

'You are *such* a naughty child. No wonder Rebekah left. My beautiful Becky left because you were such a stubborn, naughty girl, from the moment you arrived. You've wrecked everybody's lives and you're still doing it, aren't you?'

It was my fault Becky had left our family – Mummy had told me many times. Just before I had arrived on Mummy's doorstep, her youngest natural daughter had gone to university, and at the same time she had written to the church we all attended, saying she could no longer come to the Jehovah's Witness meetings anymore. She was still in touch with us, she even popped in from time to time when she visited from university, but I had turned her worldly and that meant she was going to die when

Armageddon came. And of all the things Mummy told me I did wrong, every day, that was perhaps the one I felt most guilty about. Every day I lived with that guilt. Not only had I driven Becky out of our home, but I had damned her, too: she wouldn't join us at the resurrection.

Mummy looked in disgust at the vomit on the table before fixing me with a glare. 'You eat that sick up right now,' she said.

I wanted to shake my head. I wanted to scream and shout. But I had fought this battle before. So, instead, I lowered my head to the table and I lapped up my vomit, over and over again, doing just as I was told. Trying desperately to get in her good books. Trying hard to be a good girl.

And that's my first memory of living with my mum; my first memory, full stop. The cat food, and the sick, and her cold, commanding eyes, watching my every move.

CHAPTER TWO

Rat-a-tat-tat!

Judith banged on our neighbours' front door. We saw a curtain twitch, but no one came to answer her knock. With her lips curved into a thin, tight smile, Judith grabbed me by the wrist and yanked me back down the path and along to the next house.

We were on ministry for the church, going from door to door in our local neighbourhood, trying to encourage others to come into the Truth. It was a bitterly cold day, and my hands were bright red. I had no gloves, no hat. Shivering in my navy-blue coat, I rubbed my freezing fist against the constant trickle of snot coming out of my nose. My legs ached. I was still very little, and we had been walking for hours.

'Judith, why didn't you bring the pushchair?'

That was Sandy, who worshipped at the church with us. She had ginger hair and kind eyes, though I wasn't allowed to look at them. *Look down, look down*, that's what Mummy always said.

'She's lazy, she needs the exercise,' Judith snapped.

Judith was very close to Mummy. In her mid-twenties, she still lived at home. She loved her little sister Charlotte, but I knew I was an inconvenience to her. If I was sat quietly at the bottom of the stairs, she'd push me roughly out of the way. She was always rough with me – just as she was, now, as she bent down with a tissue to wipe my streaming nostrils. I squealed in pain as her fingers crushed my nose.

'How can you say she's lazy? Victoria's just a little girl,' Sandy protested.

'Mummy says she's lazy, and Mummy's always right,' Judith replied, serenely. 'She makes her walk up and down the stairs each night because she's lazy. And laziness is against Jehovah. "The lazy person has his cravings, yet he has nothing, but the diligent one will be fully satisfied."' She echoed Mummy in quoting scripture, and God's word, of course, was the last on the matter.

Mummy was always quoting scripture at me. She would push her face into mine and yell until she ran out of breath. I could see her right up close: her big, greasy nose with blackheads all over it; her sallow, dirty skin. She had yellow teeth and bad breath and her angry words would be accompanied by a noxious puff of air as she yelled about the 'rod of discipline': 'Do not hold back discipline. If you strike him with the rod, he will not die.'

Mummy was determined that we would be the perfect Jehovah's Witnesses, as a family. So we all had to study the Watchtower and rehearse the answers we might give in the weekly study groups at church. If ever I didn't pronounce a word properly, I was smacked in the mouth until my lips ballooned up like two fat sausages. The study groups themselves, which took place at different members' homes, were very intense – for me, at least. Mummy used to watch me like a hawk in case I got an answer wrong, which I often did because I was so nervous. I'd be punished for that later, at home: thrown into the living room, where the green curtains were always closed against the world, and beaten on the floor, while she stood on my throat to make sure no one heard me scream.

I think Charlotte quite enjoyed the meetings, though. After the Bible study, which she'd spend snuggled up close to Mummy on the sofa, there would be squash and biscuits for the children. I wasn't allowed squash, though; Mummy said I didn't deserve it.

One night, we were at a study group with Sandy. Though you were supposed to stick to the same group, Mummy didn't. We were always going to different groups – perhaps so that no one got too close. I was sitting on the floor and Sandy smiled down at me, catching my blue eyes with her kind ones. I quickly looked down … but it was too late; Mummy had seen. I felt her strong, scrawny hand come down heavily upon my shoulder, her fingernails blackened with dirt pressing hard against my coat. She squeezed: a warning.

Mummy had already had a clash with Sandy at the Kingdom Hall, our place of worship. When I was a very little girl, too young for me to remember, Sandy had smiled at me in my pushchair. Mummy had snatched up a blanket and draped it over my chair so that no such smiles would reach me, and my world was only dark. She had her eye on Sandy; she thought she was trouble.

It was very hot in the room, but Mummy wouldn't let me take my coat off. She had beaten me the day before, and I had bruises all down my arm. I grew hotter and hotter and redder and redder in the face. I wasn't allowed a drink, and I wasn't allowed to look at anyone. Suddenly, Mummy picked me up and started squeezing me tight. I went even redder as the air was crushed out of me. Mummy was a thin woman, but she was physically strong, and she used every sinew of muscle to crush me to her. Tears pricked my eyes and rolled silently down my cheeks.

13

'What are you doing to that child?' Sandy spoke up at last, the sole voice in a room full of witnesses.

'She's been diagnosed as autistic,' Mummy lied, so confidently, not letting her grip slip for a moment. 'This is what you have to do with them, squeeze them tight.'

I didn't say a word, but in my head I was willing Sandy to be quiet. *Please, don't*, I thought, *because she'll hurt me*; hurt me even more than she was already doing. Because any time anyone questioned her – not that it happened very often – it would be all my fault for getting her into trouble.

But, the thing was, hardly anyone did question her – for my mother was an intimidating woman, hard-faced and hard to please. She was manipulative, adept at playing whatever role suited the situation, whether aggressive or put-upon or sweet and innocent. And so, even though – unbeknown to me – my playgroup (which I'd attended only eight times before Mummy withdrew me from the class) had expressed concerns about my mother's 'harsh approach' to me, and the doctors had said she wasn't a suitable foster mother for me, and the medical reports said I never smiled, and health visitors were banned from the house, and even though I was spotted with an unexplained bruise on my face ... despite all of this, just after my fourth birthday, in January 1990, the official panel approved Mummy's application to adopt me, and the bureaucratic machinery started whirring to have me assigned permanently to her care.

Had I known about it, I wouldn't have had much of an argument against it. Mummy had told me all about my real parents: how my daddy was a murderer and my mummy was a psychopath and a drug addict – and how they never wanted me. (All of it was lies, but I didn't know that then.)

14

So where else would I go? Who else could possibly want a naughty, dirty, devil child like me?

'Torrie, come and play with me!' Charlotte called to me from the garden. It had been snowing outside, and the window in the kitchen showed a scene of perfect frosting all across the lawn.

I hesitated on the doorstep. It was freezing outside, and I didn't have any warm clothes or gloves, or a scarf to keep me toasty. Charlotte, in comparison, was bundled up like a Michelin man in layer upon layer of pink wool.

'Torrie, *now*!' she yelled.

In our house, whatever Charlotte wanted, she got. She was adored by everybody – including me. She was my sister, my sometime playmate; the girl I followed around, always desperately hoping that in so doing I would learn her secret. I looked up to her. After all, Charlotte always got it right; she was always in Mummy's good books. Maybe, if I could learn to be like her, I'd get it right, too.

'Come and play outside!'

I ran out to join her, on command. And we played together in the snow, two little girls messing about building snowmen and making snow angels. Charlotte was in charge of the game, and ordered me about, but I was used to that. She was bossy and domineering, but the only time I got to play was when she asked me to, so I did as she told me. Even though I always had to be the baddie to her angelic heroine, some playtime was better than none.

Before too long, though, the cold snow we were playing with had rubbed my bare hands red and raw, and I started crying because my fingers were so cold. I didn't want to play anymore.

'Mummy!' Charlotte stood stock-still in the garden, her imperious voice carrying into the house and bringing our mother rushing to her aid. 'Mummy, Torrie's not playing with me, she's not playing with me!'

Mummy seized me by the arm and dragged me inside, into the kitchen. I stared up at her in confusion – why wasn't she making me stay in the garden?

I soon found out. She opened the door to the big freezer, and thrust my hands into the ice box. 'Stay there,' she said, 'I'll show you cold fingers.'

And I did as she told me. As a little one, you don't fight back. I had been naughty, I hadn't played with Charlotte – I was a bad girl.

I knew this was the truth because the evidence was all around me, impossible to ignore. I saw how Judith and Charlotte were treated by Mummy: lavished with gifts, sprinkled with smiles and hugs and affection. Who was the odd one out? Me. It was my fault. So I meekly accepted that I didn't deserve her love. I always tried to be good enough, hoping, *maybe this time* … but I never was. And so, that afternoon, when Mummy took my shoes and socks off and told me to run around the snowy garden barefoot, I did exactly as she said.

'If you move, you'll get warm,' she told me, with perfect logic, as she slammed shut the back door and went to join Charlotte and Judith in the living room, where they were catching up on Mummy's beloved soap operas.

So I picked up my poor cold feet, and I ran, and ran, and ran, trying to find some energy from somewhere to keep on running through the winter night, trying to ignore the gnawing hunger inside me.

I was always hungry. Mummy told me you had to starve a cold – and I always had a cold. So I was always starving. I'm not talking a missed meal here or there, I'm talking for weeks on end, no food.

Of course, you can't survive that long without sneaking mouthfuls here and there, stealing the end of the bread or a snatched prize from the lowest cupboards in the kitchen, which were all I could reach. So, as well as being autistic, and lazy, I was also a thief.

I told you I was bad.

To be fair to Mummy, she tried to make the punishment fit the crime. If she caught me stealing food, she would tell me all about how, in Islamic countries, thieves would be punished by having their hands cut off. Yet even Mummy, despite her talents at manipulation, might have been hard-pressed to explain how a four-year-old lost a hand – and so she devised her own take on it.

If she caught me stealing food, she would summon me to the kitchen and turn on the hotplate. While it heated up, she would lecture me.

'In Arabia, they chop your finger off if you steal food,' she told me. 'They chop them off one at a time. Then they chop your hand off and eventually they cut off your arm. If you're going to keep stealing food, this is where this is going to go.'

In time – time enough for me to realise what she was planning – the hotplate was ready, glowing bright red for danger. Mummy took my hand and separated out my index finger from all the rest. With clinical precision, she pressed it firmly against the red-hot cooker and held it there.

Pulsating pain rocked through my body. Instinctively, I wrestled my hand out of her grasp and away from the searing heat that burned and burned and burned.

'Right,' Mummy said, 'you're going to have it held there for a minute now. Stop misbehaving!'

Mummy didn't understand that I'd moved because I was in pain; she thought I was deliberately going against her, being rebellious, not towing the line. She seized my finger and shoved it against the glowing hob.

Once again, I couldn't help but pull away.

Mummy looked at me with disgust and disappointment. 'Two minutes,' she said, unequivocally. If you went against her punishments, she'd always double the drill.

She took my hand for a third time, and pressed my finger to the searing heat.

'One, two, three …' she began to count.

The hotplate wasn't the only punishment for stealing food. She starved me so often, and I resorted to theft so frequently, that she would lash out with whatever was to hand. She pummelled me in the face with a baked-bean tin. She would make me throw up whatever I had eaten, so she could see the half-digested evidence in my sick. And then she would point to the clump of stale bread or whatever it was I'd managed to steal, and she'd say, 'You want to eat that, do you, madam? You want to eat that? Well, you get and eat that.' And I would gag and gag, and she would tell me I was weak-minded for gagging on my own sick. I would be crying and retching, and she'd say it was mind over matter: that I was weak, weak, weak.

One afternoon, though, she came up with a new plan that was different to all the rest. Mummy had locked me in Charlotte's bedroom as a punishment, a couple of days into a starvation sentence of three weeks. I can't remember what I'd done wrong;

it could have been anything, or nothing. I sat on the floor, staring up at the beautiful dappled rocking horse that Charlotte loved to play on, which I was never permitted to ride. My eyes drank in the toys piled high in the room. Dolls were my favourite. I had a big heart and I loved the idea of swaddling a baby doll in a blanket and kissing her and hugging her and loving her to bits. But I wasn't allowed to play with any of the toys. Sometimes, Mummy would present both me and Charlotte with elaborately wrapped gifts. We'd open them up, and Charlotte would be allowed to play with hers, but mine would be confiscated. Maybe one day I could earn it back, Mummy told me, if I was good.

My tummy rumbled, but my head was too full of hunger to focus on the forbidden treasures inside the bedroom. I listened carefully. The house was still and quiet. Maybe, just maybe, if Mummy had forgotten to lock the door, I could tiptoe downstairs and find something to eat.

I crept to the door and listened again. Silence. I tried the handle, and the door swung wide. After scampering down the stairs as quickly as I could, I snatched the end of the bread – what Mummy called the 'knobby' – from the bread bin, and ran back upstairs, my mouth aching to taste it. I crammed it in, my little hand tearing off strips at a time, and stuffing them into my mouth.

It wasn't long before Mummy discovered my crime. She came slowly up the stairs to Charlotte's room. I could hear each of her footsteps on each tread of the stairs, and I knew she would be coming for me. I stood up straight, and tried to look innocent.

The door opened. 'Where's the knobby?' she asked me, calm as you like.

'I don't have it, Mummy,' I said.

'*Mother*,' she instructed me coldly, 'I've told you before: "mummy" is common. You call me Mother.'

'I don't have it, Mother,' I said again, obediently.

In a flash, she grabbed me and slung me to the floor. I started to scream, but that was no good in a place like George Dowty Drive, where neat red-brick houses sat on a suburban street. Someone might hear me.

'Judith!' she called. My sister came rushing in. I tried to run, but Mummy grabbed me and flung me into the corner like I was a rag doll. I was four years old, and no match for her.

'Judith, stand on her throat, stop her screaming,' Mummy commanded. Judith, as everyone always did when it came to Mummy's demands, did exactly as she was told. She pinned me to the floor and pressed her foot, solid in its sturdy green boot, against my windpipe. The scream gurgled and died in my throat.

Mummy whipped my legs up, so I was lying on my back with my feet in the air. She vanished for a moment, and then she returned with a length of wood. Judith did carpentry – one of her many talents – so there were always bits of wood lying about the house. In fact, there were bits of everything lying about the house: Mummy was a hoarder, and the place was overflowing with stuff, piled high in every room against the curtains that were always drawn.

'I used to be a nurse,' Mummy told me now, chillingly, 'and I learned something in my time on the wards. Do you know what I learned?'

I tried to shake my head, but Judith's big foot on my neck stopped me from moving.

'I learned that feet don't bruise. So if I hit you there, nobody will be able to tell what I've been doing. Nobody will be able to see. No one will ever find out what's going on.'

I stared up at her in mute horror. And then she held my little bare feet still, and she brought the wood down firmly upon them.

'Do not hold back discipline. If you strike him with the rod, he will not die,' she intoned.

Pain rocked through me: dull, numbing, throbbing pain that travelled from the soles of my feet to my brain and back again. I tried to cry out, but Judith's foot kept the scream locked inside. Her foot shoved my head to one side so my cheek was pressed into the carpet, and I couldn't breathe, which made me panic deep inside. Mummy brought the wood down on me again, and again, and again. It was the worst punishment she had ever given me. It was the first time she beat me on my feet.

It wouldn't be the last.

CHAPTER THREE

I sat by the window, and tears streamed down my face. But I wasn't crying because of a beating, or because I was cold, or hungry.

I was crying because I missed my mummy.

She had taken Charlotte to Disneyland – without me, of course. I wasn't the kind of child who deserved to be taken to America to meet Mickey Mouse. And after all, being autistic, how could I possibly enjoy or appreciate the experience?

Every day that she was away, I sat by the window in Nanny's house, and I cried for my mummy to come home.

'Come on, now, Torrie,' my nan said to me, and I turned from the window to see her coming towards me with a brand-new dolly in her arms.

I loved my nanny. Spending time with her was the only bright spot in my life. She had a big heart, and she was kind and simple, nothing like her daughter. She and my granddad lived ten doors down from us in George Dowty Drive, in a humble red-brick bungalow. As soon as you walked through the door, it smelled of Nanny. That was the best smell in the world, a fragrance of fresh laundry and apple pie: clean and homely and warm.

At my nan's house, I was allowed to play with dollies. Nanny even bought some for me: every couple of weeks, she would collect her pension and go down to the post office and buy these porcelain dolls in outfits from around the world, and she would show me them. They lived in a suitcase on top of her wardrobe, and every time I visited she would show me them, hoping one day my mum would let me have them, that one day I'd be deemed good enough to enjoy the treat. My nanny knew that Mummy was strict with me, so she knew better than to let me keep the collection myself. She didn't give me the dolls to take home. Every time I played with them, she would give me a secret wink and whisper, 'Don't tell your mum.'

Nanny didn't know what was going on, not really. She didn't know the severity of it. She knew her daughter had strong beliefs and that she was strict, and she would sometimes even call her on it; she stood up for me. Charlotte never had to do chores, and my nan would say, 'Why is it always Victoria who's got to do all the chores? It's not fair, she's two years younger. Why can't you let Charlotte do some jobs?'

My mum would make some excuse, or tell Nan I had been naughty and was being punished, or get into a blazing row with her about it. When we got home, I would be beaten for causing tension in the family; for turning her own mother against her.

My granddad, like his wife, was lovely, too. He could be quite stern, but he used to lift me up onto his lap and call me his little ducky. He'd take the lid off his hip flask and jokingly dare me to smell it. I'd screw my nose up at the unappealing whiff that emanated from the silver flask and he'd laugh, a proper laugh that shook me on his lap as he cuddled me.

Mummy hated the fact that her father loved the little girl she so despised. And even worse was the fact they seemed to prefer me to Charlotte – or, at least, that Charlotte wasn't held up as the angel child Mummy knew her to be. For Charlotte had been raised to believe she was special, and that she was to have everything she wanted, so she was often demanding and bossy, which didn't endear her to my grandparents, though they had such big hearts they loved her just the same.

When Mummy saw me on Granddad's lap, she would pull me off and say, 'No, she doesn't deserve that.' She would order me to go and sit in the corner. 'Turn around and look at the wall.'

And Nan, bless her, would speak up for me and say, 'She hasn't done anything! Eunice, you're too hard on her.'

And another row, and another beating, would ensue.

But Mummy wasn't here right now. And my nanny had a very special treat for me.

'This is for you, Torrie,' she said, handing me the dolly. I barely dared reach out and touch it, but I trusted Nan. I looked up at her with my blue eyes round with wonderment, and she nodded at me reassuringly. So I took the dolly in my hands and stared down at her, drinking in every detail.

It wasn't a porcelain doll like those in the collection I could never keep. This was a rag dolly, soft and squishy. She had long yellow wool plaits, and a polka-dot pink top and skirt. I loved her the instant I set eyes on her.

'What are you going to call her?' Nanny asked.

I didn't hesitate. 'Katie,' I said. That was my nanny's name.

'I've made you this for her, too,' said Nanny, and she handed me a knitted doll's blanket made up of white and peach squares. No one had ever given me such a lovely present before. I carefully wrapped the blanket round Katie and hugged her to my chest.

'Thank you, Nanny,' I said, and she gave me a kiss on the top of my head.

From that night on, I slept with Katie by my side. I knew better than to let Mummy know what she meant to me. I learned how to hide her, under the stairs or twisted up in the bedding, and I tried not to show that she meant anything to me.

Mummy noticed the new addition to our family, of course. Those eyes missed nothing. When I told her that I'd named her after Nanny, she snapped at me disparagingly, 'God, you're so thick, you autistic twit! Why is it you've got to repeat names you've already heard, why can't you think of your own?'

I bowed my head and said nothing, as usual. Soon, though, I would have a chance to think on my own. That September, I was starting school.

Overbury School is a picture-perfect village school, set in a Cotswold-stone building on the southern slopes of Bredon Hill in Gloucestershire. In September 1990, Mummy marched me into my new classroom with strict instructions to speak to no one. The other children were worldly, she told me, and the Bible taught that 'bad associations spoil useful habits'.

She gave me a packed lunch to take with me, containing thickly pasted Marmite sandwiches. I hated thick Marmite sandwiches, but that was the way Mummy operated. It was like a game to her, like a war; it was a control thing. Mummy always had to be in control.

Yet that September, for the first time, I thought I might be out of that control, just a little bit. I was still very quiet, and I was so frightened of her that I tried to do what she said. Nevertheless, I found that, at playtime, another little girl might come up to say hello to me, or a teacher might bend down and give me a kind word as I sat on a bench on my own. I might smile back at one of the other children, or dare to look up to watch a game going on between the older kids.

Quite early on in the school term, I came home from school and Mummy was waiting for me.

'Get upstairs,' she told me. 'Take your shoes and socks off.'

I scurried to obey. We had a dirty green carpet on the stairs at George Dowty, and it didn't quite reach the landing – there was a little strip of bare wood at the top, where she now directed me to stand. She sat on the stairs below me, my bare feet in front of her face.

'Did you speak to anybody at school today?' she asked me. Her voice was calm and inquisitive.

I thought back to the little brown-haired girl who'd tried to involve me in a game that lunchtime. But Mummy hadn't been at school – there was no way she could know about that.

'No,' I lied. 'Nobody.'

She looked up at me. 'Don't lie,' she warned.

'Nobody,' I squeaked.

'Liar!' she roared. She raised her arm, and I saw she had a wooden chair leg in her hand. She brought it down on my toes, hard. I bit my tongue to keep from crying out, the pain almost shocking me into silence.

'No liar will stand in my presence,' she quoted from the Bible. She beat me again, tens of hard raps across my toes, until my nails swelled, red and bleeding. I looked down as the blood bubbled beneath them. Suddenly, I was glad to be standing on the wooden bit; there was always hell to pay if I ever got blood on the carpet.

'Get downstairs, you liar. We're going to wash your mouth out for telling such dirty lies.'

I walked gingerly down to the kitchen, my feet throbbing with every step. She stood me by the sink and grabbed the washing-up liquid. 'Head back,' she ordered. I tilted my head back, but I kept my mouth firmly closed. 'Mouth open,' she ordered. When I stubbornly kept it closed, my body fighting against the punishment even as my mind succumbed, she pinched my nose until I had to open my mouth to gasp for air. In an instant, she had shoved the plastic bottle between my lips, the teat jamming hard against my teeth. She squeezed firmly and glutinous lemon liquid squirted to the back of my throat. I gagged.

'Don't be so weak-minded!' she yelled at me. '*Drink*!'

I had no choice but to swallow, and then swallow again. She glugged it down me, the whole bottle. When I threw up in the sink, she made me eat my own vomit, and threatened that, if I was sick again, she'd do the same thing again with a bottle of bleach.

'Don't you lie to me ever again,' she warned. 'I've got a magic eye; I can see what you're doing. I've got a magic eye; I know *exactly* what you're doing.'

And every single day at school, she did. Somehow, she knew who I'd been with; if anybody had spoken to me. I never dared to speak to anyone ever again. As an adult, I've realised that she must have spied on me. As a child, I could only assume that what she told me was true: she had a magic eye, and she could see me at every minute of every hour of every day. She was an all-powerful, all-seeing being. I could never, ever get away from her gaze.

The school term drew on. Soon there was a chill in the air, and the classrooms began to ring with the excited chatter of children anticipating Christmas, and the imminent visitation of someone called Santa Claus.

As Jehovah's Witnesses, we didn't celebrate Christmas – or birthdays, for that matter. Several times Mummy had read me the riot act about the upcoming festivities. 'You're a Jehovah's Witness, you've got to stand strong,' she would say. 'You're only worthy if you don't join in.'

That December, there was a whole school assembly about Christmas. The teachers shepherded us all into the hall, and I followed meekly. If nothing else, Mummy had certainly taught me to obey adults and to do as I was told. So I joined in the assembly, and I even coloured in a Christmas bauble when we did festive arts and crafts in the afternoon.

As soon as I came out of school, clutching my Christmas decoration, I knew that what I'd done was wrong. Mummy's eyes … She was so angry. And I knew what was coming when I got home.

She flung me inside as soon as the front door was open, and I sailed across the hallway, just like my rag doll, Katie. Then she beat me around the floor, each blow emphasising her words: 'You. Are. Evil. The Jehovah God disapproves of anything to do with Christmas. You have just gone and coloured. In. A. Bauble.' She was absolutely livid.

So livid, in fact, that five days before Christmas 1990, records show that she withdrew me from Overbury to be educated at home.

No one was going to teach me a lesson better than her.

For some reason, though, I did go back to mainstream education, at least for a time. I changed schools to Northway Infant School in Tewkesbury, and Mummy's instructions about speaking to no one and keeping my gaze down were reissued. Not that I really needed to be told, anymore.

Unbeknown to me, Northway polished up her magic eye for her even more, because there was a Co-op car park that backed onto the playground there. Mummy used to park there every day and watch me. I didn't know she was there, all I knew was that she always knew exactly what I'd been up to.

Mummy was still keeping up the starvation punishments. At school, I found the temptation of the other children's lunchboxes too great, and I started pinching food from them because I was so hungry. Mummy, of course, got called in. And I was punished not only for stealing fruit, but also because I'd made her look bad as a parent; I'd humiliated her. For Mummy, who always strived to appear better than any other mother, any other family, this was an unforgivable sin.

She told me I was to come home for my lunch from now on but one lunchtime, when I got back to George Dowty Drive, there was no one there: she'd forgotten about me. I sat on the doorstep for a while, waiting, unsure if I'd be in trouble if she came home for me and found I wasn't there. Eventually, I ran down to my nan's, but she was out, too. I headed back to school in the end, quite late, and innocently explained, 'Mummy's not in.' They asked me if I'd had lunch, so I said no, and they gave me a school dinner.

I was kicked around the hallway floor for that. 'How *dare* you tell people I'm a bad parent!' she ranted. My lips ballooned as her boots collided with my face. She kept me home from school the next day, and on any other days when the bruises were too obvious. She was a clever woman, my mummy; she always knew how far she could go.

One morning, we were late for school. As usual, it was my fault: I had wet the bed. I was always wetting the bed, plagued by nightmares about Satan coming to get me. He would come down the driveway and through the hall and up onto the landing, coming to snatch me and take me out the window. Every time there was a thunderstorm, I thought Armageddon had arrived. And, especially as I grew older, Mummy would show me horror films where people died, one after the other in bloody, violent scenes, and she'd say, 'Go and make sure you pray to God because you've been really naughty today and you might not be here in the morning.' On this particular morning, Mummy marched me down to school with the sopping-wet, urine-soaked sheet, and she held it up in front of my entire class.

'This is why we're late. This is what this dirty child has done,' she announced.

I hung my head in shame and humiliation – but I had only myself to blame. Mummy had been trying to stop me from wetting the bed for as long as I could remember. As with all of my development, I was slow to learn. Slow to be potty-trained, despite the fact that she would tie me to my potty all day; despite all her best efforts in that field. If ever I had an accident, she would rub my face in the wee on the floor and then wipe my wet knickers all over my face and shove them in my mouth. I'd have to sit there with my soaking knickers in my mouth, as a punishment.

As I got older, and the bed-wetting continued, she'd make me drink her wee in retribution for my crime. She'd pee in the toilet, a dark, dark wee, and then summon me over to drink it. She'd get a cup and I'd have to dip it in the loo and then swallow it down. And I'd gag and I'd cry, and I'd spit it out, but the more I spat it out, the more she'd say it had to be done, there were no two ways about it.

It didn't stop me wetting the bed. Instead, I had more nightmares than ever, and on more and more mornings I woke up with a sinking feeling at that tell-tale cool dampness on the backs of my legs. Mummy would rant and rave, and call me an attention-seeker. And one Sunday, she had had quite enough.

We got dressed for church as usual. Judith and Charlotte were done up to the nines, in smart frocks scattered with bows, and even pretty bonnets tied around their smiling faces. They looked like a double act: two Little Bo Peeps. I struggled into my charity-shop clothes, which were dirty and ragged, and always too small or too big – usually too big, for the starvation punishments had made me into a scrawny little girl, skin and bone within a hand-me-down coat.

When we were ready, Mummy made me turn around and pinned a handwritten sign on my back. And then, together, we walked to the Kingdom Hall. We came in late, and sat towards the back. Sandy was in the row behind me. I sat quietly, with my head down, and she could see each word on the sign writ large and clear.

This child is evil. She's an attention-seeker. Do not look at her or talk to her.

For Sandy it was the final straw: she rang social services. *Something*, she thought, *had to be done about this woman.*

CHAPTER FOUR

Social services rang Sandy back, two weeks later. They said they had investigated, but felt there was no problem, before adding: 'What do you expect us to do? We're short on foster mothers.'

I can remember social services coming round to call on Mummy and me – not because of Sandy, necessarily; they came quite frequently. A social worker would come and knock on the door of George Dowty Drive, as I sat inside in the cold kitchen, listening to the exchange on the doorstep of the house; or they would phone, and I'd hear my mother's end of the conversation. Each time they came I dreaded it, because Mummy would say I had caused trouble in bringing them to her door, and she would beat me for it.

It was never convenient for the social workers to call in. 'I'm on holiday that week,' Mummy would say, brooking no argument, if they phoned in advance to schedule a visit. Or, 'No, I'm sorry, now is not a good time. You'll have to come back later,' if they turned up on the doorstep unannounced. She'd say it with the door open only a sliver, not showing them anything of our world.

Of course, 'later' was never good either, for one reason or another. I'd sit listening to these exchanges, with bruises all over my body, and I'd wonder why they weren't coming in … but I knew why, really: my mother. My mother and her manipulation. They were intimidated and they were subtly influenced. Nobody could wrap social workers round her finger better than my foster mum.

Yet she wouldn't be my foster mum for much longer. Her application to adopt me was gaining pace. There was a severe setback to her plans in December 1991, though, when my social worker suddenly told Mum that she would not support the adoption due to 'concerns' she held about Mum's care of me – and instead instigated a six-month assessment of my care.

But this was my mother they were dealing with. She simply refused – once again – to see the social worker to allow the assessment to be carried out. I also found out, much later, that social services were late in delivering their file on me to the judge overseeing the adoption process; they simply didn't get the file in on time.

And so, just one month after that official concern was raised, my adoption was formally approved. Eunice Spry was now my legal mother – and I was on my own.

Tick-tock, tick-tock, tick-tock.

The clock sounded loud in the hot, mustard-coloured Volvo. Alone, I sat in the car, watching the farm outside the window, where families had come to pick their own fruit for simple summer suppers. I could see them smiling and laughing as they milled about the open barn, where the farmer, John Drake, weighed their produce and bade them a good day. We were in Eckington, at a thirteen-acre farm near the border of Worcestershire, a nine-mile drive from George Dowty. Looking at the families happily dashing about in the fresh summer air, it felt a lot further away than that.

Mummy and Charlotte had gone to pick some strawberries, but I'd been left behind in the sealed car. I sweated in the sunshine. *Tick-tock, tick-tock, tick-tock.* Suddenly, I heard the suction of the car door as it opened: Mummy had returned. She had a funny expression on her face. I was soon to learn that she had made a new friend in John Drake.

After that, we started going over to the farm quite regularly, Charlotte, Mummy and me. Mummy would go over and cook supper for John. He was a much older man, who had been diagnosed with lung cancer, and he was unmarried and lived all alone in this great big farmhouse, on all these acres of land, with all this money in the bank. Mummy went straight through that door and wormed her way inside.

I remember him as a gruff but quite kind-hearted man. There was a sandpit outside the big barn and he used to hide Mars bars in there for us kids. Of course, if ever I found the chocolate, Mummy would snatch it off me and say, 'That's not for you, that's for Charlotte.' And Charlotte, not knowing any better, would toss her dark hair over her plump shoulders and giggle as she reached for the treat. She was allowed to go for a ride on the tractor with John Drake, but I wasn't. But I didn't resent it, I accepted it: I sincerely believed that when Mummy said I didn't deserve it, every word was true.

The farmhouse was a very old, red-brick Victorian house that was just off the main road. Though the farm was set in rolling countryside, the house itself was just at the edge of the village, opposite a playgroup and another house; it wasn't in the middle of nowhere. Very tall, with five bedrooms, it had old-fashioned sash windows that would rattle in the wind. It had an old man's smell, and was always very cold, as there was no heating.

The kitchen was the only warm room, as John Drake kept his cream Raeburn lit with glowing coals. He'd sit beside it in the evenings with his newspaper, and he had a traditional butter dish that he kept on the kitchen table. We'd come in, Mummy would cook him a meal, and I'd watch his little Jack Russell dog as it lay on the red stone kitchen floor beside him.

I loved dogs. We had a little terrier called Meggie, a yappy little thing, but I never warmed to her for some reason. Other dogs, though, I simply adored. I loved the way they'd meet my eyes when I looked down, and never seemed to judge. My favourites of all were Labradors. What I wanted, more than anything in the world, was a Labrador dog of my own.

One evening, as I watched John begin to tuck into his supper, my hungry, growling belly spoke through me. 'Mummy, I'm hungry,' I said, almost before I knew that I'd opened my mouth.

John Drake tried to give me something to eat.

'No, no,' interjected Mummy. 'She's not to have it.'

'Come on now, she's only little,' he protested.

'No,' Mummy said firmly. 'She is not to have it.'

John looked into those cold, insistent eyes of hers, and he found himself sitting back in his seat and relenting. A hacking cough, a symptom of his cancer, wracked his ravaged lungs as he let the issue lie.

When we got back to George Dowty Drive that night, Mummy grabbed me by the hair and smacked my head against the door.

'What are you doing, asking strangers for food?' she hissed at me. 'You are such a rude little girl.'

Being so young, I didn't know it was bad etiquette to ask for something to eat in another person's house. As usual, she didn't like the fact that I had made her look bad, like a bad parent.

She'd hated being put on the spot and shown up. Looks were very important to Mummy. Not physical looks – she never wore make-up, that was worldly, and she never looked clean or smart – but it was so important to her to be seen to be the best: the best Jehovah's Witness; the best mother, raising her charming, adopted daughter and this awkward, autistic child. What a giving woman she was.

As Jehovah's Witnesses, we rarely had parties, as birthdays were never celebrated, but I remember a girl at the Kingdom Hall having a children's party once when we were small. Her name was Jo. She was a few years older than Charlotte and me, and she had black curly hair; she was very pretty. Charlotte and I were both invited to the party, and Charlotte went in and played while I was left outside in the car. Jo's mummy, Ann, came out and passed me a present through the window. I thanked her numbly, knowing that Mummy was going to go mad. And she did. She went mad at Ann, she went mad at me, and the other Witnesses looked at her aghast. People knew she was odd and they knew she was batty, but she was such a forthright, intimidating, righteous woman that somehow no one ever confronted her. Not the Witnesses, not social services, not the doctors, not even the school.

I can't think what possessed me, because I had never been anything but obedient, and I truly believed Mummy was doing as she did with the best of intentions – to try to make me good. Nevertheless, one day I decided to take matters into my own hands. In my time at school, I had learned to hold a pen and form my letters. It was a very basic scrawl, but I could write in big, babyish script. And I used my newfound skill to ask for help. I collected some envelopes from the hoard of stuff stacked up in every room in George Dowty, and I wrote on them, in painstaking letters.

Will you be my new mummy?

My plan was to post them through my neighbours' doors, through the letterboxes of the semi-detached red-brick houses along George Dowty Drive.

But I never got the chance.

I'd hidden them under a piece of loose carpet on the stairs, and Mummy found them. At first I didn't know. In our early days together, her punishments would be performed in anger. She would lash out, striking me across the back of the head or across my feet with barely controlled rage, but she was starting to be calmer now. She found the envelopes, and she brooded, and mulled over my punishment. When she was ready, and only then, she came and found me. She was very calm. Chillingly calm. She picked me up by my blonde hair, picked me up until it was tearing at the roots, and then threw me back on the floor.

'You sly, disloyal scumbag,' she said, serenely. And I knew then she'd found the notes.

She threw me into the kitchen, and then she started kicking me. In the head. In the stomach. In the back. In the face. My arms instinctively went up to protect myself, but she pulled them down roughly and kicked me twice as hard.

'Stop trying to get one over on me,' she said. 'Stop retaliating. You've brought this on yourself so you can take your punishment. You autistic twit.'

Kick. Kick. Kick.

'Not even your biological parents wanted you. They couldn't stand the sight of you, that's why they gave you to me. "New mummy"? Don't make me laugh. No one else would want you. If your own parents didn't, no one else will.

'Get up!'

The abrupt cessation of her kicking threw me.

'I said, *get up*!'

She yanked me by the arm and dragged me over to the sink. Once again, her dirty fingers tangled in my hair and tugged it, driving my head backwards, while with her other hand she grabbed at the washing-up liquid always within easy reach at the sink.

'Open your mouth.'

She began to pour the bottle down me. I was gagging and choking, tears streaming down my face, bubbles foaming at my mouth. I heaved and retched, just waiting for that familiar sensation of the sick rising from my stomach, but she thrust her face into mine and screamed at me that, if I was sick, she'd do it all over again. I swallowed hard, the lemon, chemical taste all over my tongue making me gag, but I kept it down. Just.

'It's all in your head, this being sick. Stop being so weak-minded. It's mind over matter. Now swallow the rest,' she told me.

She lifted the bottle to my lips and poured the rest of it down. I swallowed, and swallowed and swallowed. Then she threw the bottle in the sink, and threw me to the floor. Kick. Kick. Kick. This time she concentrated on my mouth. She kicked me in the mouth until she'd chipped a tooth and my lips were a bloody mash, sore and swollen and misshapen on my face.

But she hadn't finished yet. This was a bad punishment, for I had been a very, very bad girl. Daring to ask for help? Daring to suggest that I *needed* a new mummy? She was the best mummy for me, she was trying to help me; no one else would help me like she could. After all, as she told me over and over, 'Whoever holds back his rod hates his son, but the one who loves him disciplines him diligently.'

She commanded me to run up and down the stairs. I bowed my head and scuttled past her as I dragged my beaten, bloody body up and down, up and down. She stood in the hallway and watched me for a bit. My sisters were probably in their own rooms; in their own worlds. They never came out to see what was happening. It was normal in our lives that I would be disciplined; they'd have been more likely to stick their heads round their doors, with shocked expressions on their faces, if they heard Mummy being nice to me.

'Faster,' she said now. Then she turned and went into the living room, and put on the TV.

It was naughty, I know, but once the TV had been on for a bit, its volume turned up loud, I sat down on the top of the stairs to rest. I felt so exhausted, I couldn't carry on.

Yet that wasn't my biggest error. My biggest mistake was falling asleep. I woke to the sensation of falling, falling … falling down the stairs.

'You are a sly and evil child,' she told me coldly, as she threw me down. I landed in a heap, in a tangle of bruised and tender limbs, but it didn't hurt as much as the beatings before. I counted myself lucky – for now.

And then, for the rest of the night, she made me sit on the 'invisible chair' against the inside door of the living room, where she could see me, because she said she couldn't trust me to do it alone.

The invisible chair is a torture position. I don't know how Mummy knew about it – she often read books about the Nazi regime and serial killers, so perhaps she discovered it in one of those. I had to stand with my back against the wall, my feet a short distance in front of it, and slide down the wall until my thighs were parallel with the floor. Within minutes, my muscles started to burn. My feet slipped from the sweat collecting on my soles. But of course moving wasn't allowed; she'd hit me if I moved.

I stayed there for the rest of the night, just as she commanded.

'You stay there so I can watch you,' she said, 'watch you with my magic eye.'

My mother was all-powerful, all-seeing. And this life was all I knew.

I never tried to get a new mummy after that.

I wasn't sure there was much left of me to mother.

CHAPTER FIVE

In the distance, I could hear the strains of a folk band playing, the music carrying in the still night air to where I stood on a plastic mat inside my mother's caravan. Every now and again, the dark room was lit by the beams of revellers' torches as they made their way back to their tents at the folk festival, their happy voices chiming with those of the singers.

Mummy and Judith regularly attended folk festivals, and barn dances. Always Mummy would brag about how nobody else could dance quite like her. Sometimes, they would leave me behind with my nan when they went camping, but it was a regular hobby, and frequently I would find myself climbing up the steps to the caravan, entering its narrow, thin frame and trying to make myself as unobtrusive as possible.

Unfortunately, my sleeping body didn't realise I wanted to remain inconspicuous. I was a snorer; a loud, throaty snorer, whose adenoidal rattle would sound even louder in the small confines of the caravan. And so, when night fell, a familiar scene would play out.

'Mummy, Torrie's snoring, I can't get to sleep,' Charlotte would whine, and I'd wake to find my mum's fingers pinching my nose. She'd drag me out of bed and force me to stand awake, all night, on a clear plastic mat. My legs would ache, my calves would burn, but if I cheated, and leaned against the rickety wall of the caravan to take some of the pressure off my exhausted limbs, Mummy would snap from beneath her duvet in her warm bed, 'Get up, I can feel you leaning! Get up or I'm coming over there …'

In the daytime, I was dead on my feet, so fatigued from staying awake all night that I'd be falling asleep, and Judith would say, 'Oh God, get her out of my sight, lazy child! Put her to bed.' Mummy would let me climb into bed, and then she'd stand over me, watching.

'If you're not asleep within one minute,' she'd say, 'you can get back up and stand because you're obviously not tired enough.'

I'd squeeze my eyes shut, and will myself to go to sleep, go to sleep. But no matter how hard I tried to convince myself to fall unconscious, my brain was all too aware of her standing over me, and my body seemed to get tenser and tenser rather than more relaxed.

'You naughty girl,' she'd say, when sixty sluggish seconds had passed without me dropping off. 'I told you to go to sleep and you didn't. Now you can get back up and stand.'

And I would swing my little legs round and obediently go and stand on the mat, my bare feet cold and frozen, my legs already protesting at the long night ahead. Yet the most painful thing of all was my heart: for once again I had been naughty, and disobeyed my mother. She had told me to go to sleep, and I didn't. Just like she always said, I was a very, very naughty girl, and knowing that made me hang my head in shame.

Back at George Dowty Drive, Mummy was fixated on my sleeping. I snored there, too, and I would keep Charlotte awake. That simply wouldn't do. Mummy would strip my clothes off and make me stand all night – sometimes outside in the shed, which was full of junk, or just outside her bedroom doorway, where she could keep an eye on me. She'd fall asleep, and I'd stand there on the green carpet of the landing, listening to the house settle in the darkness, hearing her snores as she slept, and imagining Satan coming to get me, hiding behind every stack of junk that littered the house.

I was so tired. I did chores all day: caring for Meggie the terrier and our five cats, doing the laundry, learning how to cook spaghetti Bolognese just the way Mummy liked it. And I was hungry. My tummy rumbles would join in the lullaby of her snores and, much as I tried to fight against it, I always found I couldn't: as I stood on the landing, I'd feel my head lolling ... and snapping back up; lolling ... and snapping back up again.

Eventually, I'd slump to the floor, onto the green carpet that stank and was filthy, and nestle my little body between the piles of stuff. My eyes would close; and I let them, in the end. I knew what was coming if she saw me asleep, but I was so tired I just didn't care.

One evening, in the middle of the night, I woke from a deep, deep slumber in the doorway to find myself being dragged across the landing by my hair. Mummy booted me viciously off the top of the stairs – for disobeying her orders to stay awake. I tumbled all the way down, a tangle of limbs. She did this punishment often, and so violently that picture frames would come flying off the wall where I smashed into them.

But this time was different. This time, I rolled into a big, full-length mirror at the foot of the stairs.

It shattered all over me, a broken kaleidoscope of silver knives that sliced into my naked flesh and scattered over my hair like confetti. I lay stunned, not daring to move for fear of being cut further, deeper, harder.

Mummy looked aghast from the top of the stairs, and then rushed down to me. She flung me into the hallway, kicking me around the hall until my mouth was swollen and bloodied.

'That was my favourite mirror!' she shrieked. 'You autistic twit, you have broken my favourite mirror! Most children would have stopped themselves falling right to the bottom of the stairs, but oh no –' and here she kicked me harder '– you're not *normal*. You *autistic* twit. Other children would have stopped themselves falling.'

My 'autism' was to blame for a lot of things I got wrong. As Judith had revealed to Sandy, when she told her about my mum's punishment for me being lazy – and I knew I was a lazy child, for I would often yawn throughout the day – another of my daily tasks was to run up and down the hallway or the stairs of our house. One afternoon, Mummy told me I wasn't doing it right.

'Run down the hallway *properly*,' she screamed, 'the entire hallway. Don't stop.'

And so I ran, all the way down the hallway – and I didn't stop, just as she'd said. I ran through the glass door at the end and I kept on running down the road; the broken glass having cut my skin to shreds, my face, legs and arms oozing bright scarlet.

'You autistic twit,' she hissed at me, after she'd run down the road to catch me. The disappointment was heavy in her deep voice. 'Only autistic children would do that – because they take things *very* literally.'

She couldn't see I did it because I wanted to please her so very badly. I wanted to do anything she said, if it would spare me a beating; I hated getting beaten.

Running up and down the stairs soon became a nightly occurrence. I had fallen asleep in the doorway of her bedroom one too many times, and so she decided I needed something to occupy me through the long hours of the dark night. She said she couldn't trust me to stand up all night; I was a sly child, an evil child, a liar and a thief.

And this sly child, I'm ashamed to say, proved her pronouncements right once more. To begin with I would follow the punishment, my feet pounding up and down the stairs, relentlessly, my legs dragging with tiredness and hunger. I would hear her fall asleep, and my brain would buzz with the usual frightened question: 'Is she asleep or is she only *pretending* to be asleep?' Because I'd been caught out that way before.

In time, once I was almost sure, as sure as I could be, that she was truly asleep, I would sit at the bottom of the stairs and bang my fists on them to make it sound like I was still running. It was naughty – *so* naughty, I knew – but I simply didn't have the energy to keep on running, not for the hours and hours and hours ahead. So I'd sit, and I'd bang, throughout the night, even while she was snoring – because she might just have been playing make-believe. If I heard her stir, the banging at least gave me a chance to get up and run, run, run once more.

I was so tired; it was perhaps just as well that Mummy had withdrawn me from school for good, to be 'home schooled'. There was no way I'd have been able to stay awake in class, or focus on learning how to read and write any better than I already could. I was now in her care for home schooling permanently, as was Charlotte. My world shrank to the red-brick walls of George Dowty Drive, and I no longer had any contact with anyone outside the family, outside of the Kingdom Hall.

To begin with, Mummy did go through phases of teaching us. She'd summon us to the living room, and try to teach me maths and English. Maths was the worst. Mummy always said, 'Intellectual people can do maths,' and she was determined that I would get it right. It was torturous: she would throw these great long divisions at me that I'd have to calculate and then multiply and do this, that and the other with and it was all just going over my head; I couldn't get it. And she'd kick me around that stupid head of mine, kick me hard in my ears and nose and mouth, and then say, 'Sorry, but you've made me do this; I've had to beat some sense into you.'

My English lessons weren't much better.

'Describe your sister Charlotte.'

'Um, she's pretty.'

'Describe her dress.'

'Er, it's pretty.'

That wasn't good enough for a six-year-old child – certainly not a six-year-old child in my mother's care. My lack of imagination and description would provoke a violent attack: 'You're so autistic and thick, if Hitler was around he'd have killed you off!' She'd rant and rave and lash out – but the more she shouted, the less I found I was able to learn. It was like my brain iced over, and I became an impenetrable frozen fortress, where none of her words, whether helpful or hurtful, could reach me in our 'classroom'.

'You are so thick; you are such a thick child. Look at Charlotte, she's getting it. Look at Judith and Becky, they went to private schools, they *excelled*. But you, you autistic twit, you can't think of a single word other than "pretty"?' Her hand lashed out and hit me round the back of the head. 'You are so *stupid*!'

I knew she was right. The evidence was right there before me: in Charlotte's bright eyes and nodding head, always being praised; in Judith's accomplishments as a carpenter; even in Becky's absence, away at university and building her own, independent life. I never measured up to any of them, I never picked things up quickly enough; I was always too slow. I was convinced I was on the scrapheap, not even second-best.

Mummy loved to hit me round the back of the head; she did it often, just because. My absolute favourite place at George Dowty was a little cubbyhole in the kitchen, where the big breezeblock bricks of the walls would fence me in and keep me safe, as I stood tucked down between the kitchen table and the door, our big industrial oven hanging over my head as additional security. The kitchen was half-renovated, so the bricks were cold and exposed, but I felt safer there than anywhere else. With my back to the oven, there was no way Mummy could come up behind me and whack me on the skull, which she frequently did as she was passing by me in other parts of the house.

I spent a lot of my time, once the attempts at lessons ended, standing in that cubbyhole. Or I'd be ordered to sit at the top of the stairs; or in Charlotte's room, as long as I didn't play with the toys. Anywhere that was out of the way. With my nose still streaming, day after day, Mummy would tell me I was a weakling for having a cold and that I couldn't take part in whatever the others were doing. So I'd sit and listen to their loving voices from wherever I'd been banished, as Mummy chatted fondly to Charlotte, or let her play with her toys downstairs; the happy sound of Charlotte's laughter only serving to emphasise how very bad I was in comparison. Mummy only seemed to bother with me when she was beating me – or when she might sit me in front of the mirror, my hair tangled round her wrist so she could use my own head as a weapon, and question me as to who I was.

'What are you?' she would say.

'An autistic twit,' I'd respond automatically, 'a sly bitch. I'm backwards. I'm thick. I'm evil.'

Even though I was parroting her own words back at her, often I'd get it wrong … somehow. When I did, she would jerk her hair-tangled hand forwards, roughly, so my forehead would smack into the mirror with a solid *clunk*. '*What* are you?' she'd say again. I'd stare at my reflection, but I wouldn't see big blue eyes and bright blonde hair and a little six-year-old face.

I'd see the scum of the earth.

One day, in my timeless, never-changing world, something *did* change. One of my teeth – one that Mummy had not knocked out with her kicking feet – started to wobble in my mouth. I wobbled it and wobbled it, experiencing the queer sensation of its looseness in my mouth, a looseness that was entirely natural. And the looser it got, the more and more excited I became.

Because I knew: when you lost a tooth, you got a visit from the fairies.

And I loved fairies. I was a girlie little girl – full of love for Katie and my nanny's dollies, besotted with the pretty dresses and hair clips Charlotte wore – and the idea of magical creatures who fluttered about on silver-tipped wings and were elfin-faced and good-hearted and wore dresses made from morning dew and spring flowers was just about the most exciting thing I'd ever heard of. Charlotte, being two years older than me, had received many visits from the tooth fairy, and I'd watched with wonder as she squealed in delight at the gifts and money that magically appeared beneath her pillow whenever she lost a tooth. I believed in fairies to my very soul, and the idea that I too might now receive a visit from them sent my finger straight to my mouth to wobble, wobble, wobble my tooth from its bearings.

At last, it fell out, and I showed it to Mummy with an unfamiliar touch of pride, my blue eyes twinkling a little with delight. I loved the fairies so much; I was *so* excited.

Mummy smiled – a narrow smile that didn't quite reach her eyes. 'Well, you can leave it under your pillow,' she said, 'but I don't think your fairy's very happy with you.'

My heart sank. Of course, Mummy was right: I was a naughty girl, a liar, a thief, so disobedient I was punished every day. I had hoped that the fairies, being magical and so good themselves, not to mention so beloved to me, might see how very hard I was trying to be good and reward me, but Mummy's words made perfect sense.

That night, nonetheless, I put the small white tooth underneath my pillow, and hoped. Mummy let me sleep that night, and in the morning, when I woke, I lifted up my pillow with trepidation, and a shaky faith. Had the fairies come? Had they flown about me as I slept, their silken wings flapping over my face, making my blonde hair stir in the breeze? Had my love been returned?

My breath caught in my throat. There, lying on the mattress, was a little blue card. I reached out and touched it, my fingertips searching over its surface for fairy dust. *This came from the fairies*, I thought, *this is a special message just for me.*

I opened it up.

We've taken your tooth, the fairies wrote.

I glanced down at the mattress again. It was true! They had: the tooth had vanished, borne away by dozens of fairy wings, carrying their heavy load back to their woodland home.

The note continued.

We've taken your tooth, but you're such a naughty girl, you're not getting anything.

My heart didn't fall this time; I wasn't even disappointed. Instead, I nodded to myself, sadly. I understood. So I tucked the little blue card back in its envelope and kept it safe, bound up with Katie and her blanket: my special things.

The note was from the fairies, after all. It was still exciting, and magical, and I knew it wasn't their fault they couldn't leave me anything more: it was *my* fault.

More than ever before, I knew I would have to try harder to be good.

CHAPTER SIX

I experienced another change at the age of six; another sign that I was growing up. We had gone round to my nan's and I was enjoying being in her lovely-smelling home, as well as the chance to sit on her sofa, rather than the floor. Mummy always told me I didn't deserve a chair to sit on, but Nan would let me clamber up onto the squishy couch without a murmur of disapproval.

We even had a film on. We were watching *The Sword in the Stone*, and I was entranced by the antics of Merlin the wizard and the plucky heroism of young Arthur.

A loud burp interrupted the animated proceedings on the screen. That was my uncle Phil, Mummy's brother, who was sitting next to me on the sofa. He looked a little bit like her, but he had quite a big broad face, whereas hers was thin and drawn. He had bloodshot blue eyes and dark short hair and stubble that pricked his cheeks with a permanent shadow.

'Come and have a cuddle, Torrie,' he slurred at me.

Uncle Phil was always slurring his words. Nan and Mummy didn't talk about it, but I'd seen him drinking foul-smelling stuff constantly, stuff that smelled like the inside of my granddad's hip flask, only worse. He himself smelled bad, too. Like Mummy, he rarely, if ever, showered or bathed, so every time he called me over for a cuddle, I'd have to brace myself for the stink of being near him, the stench of weeks-old BO and cheap alcohol.

Obediently, my eyes still glued to the screen, I reluctantly shuffled over, responding to the adult command. Uncle Phil always wanted cuddles. Strangely, for a little girl so lacking in love and affection, they weren't cuddles I enjoyed. There was something a little bit off about them; they didn't seem genuine, somehow. Not like the cuddles from Nan and Granddad, where they would sweep me up carelessly in their arms and squeeze me tight.

Uncle Phil cleared his throat, and I felt his stinky breath on my shoulder, hot and heavy and fast.

'There's a good girl,' he said, as he put his arm around my shoulder and rubbed my skin with his big hands. Uncle Phil had the biggest hands I knew, with great thick fingers at the ends of them, meaty and wide. His hands were calloused and incredibly dry. It was like being rubbed with sandpaper as he ran his fingers up and down my skin. I tried to ignore him and concentrate instead on the special treat of the Disney film (I loved Disney films, but I only ever got the chance to watch them at my nan's).

Suddenly, I felt Uncle Phil lifting me up. Charlotte, her nose inches from the screen, the best seat in the house, didn't move an inch as he scooped me up and carried me out of the room. I didn't make a sound, either. I was a very quiet little girl. I had no confidence or courage to speak, and I certainly wouldn't say a word to an adult, especially one who had Mummy's ear.

Uncle Phil took me into the bathroom in the bungalow. He set me down on the tiled floor and turned to lock the door. When he faced me again, he had a big bulge in his trousers. I looked up at him and he looked down at me, his breaths still coming thick and fast. I could see his chest heaving with them.

Uncle Phil beckoned me over to him, and then he reached out and started rubbing me between my legs. Now I was confused.

I knew this didn't seem right, but I didn't know what it was, or what was happening. I just didn't get it.

Uncle Phil put his hands inside my trousers, and groaned. He was trying to push his fingers up inside me. It wasn't painful, as I remember, just humiliating and bewildering. What was he doing? It felt very strange.

Suddenly, he released me to move his hand to his own trousers. He slid them down, along with his pants, and showed me his pink, dirty-looking willy, which was sticking straight out from his body and quivering.

'Touch it,' he said. He wasn't slurring his words anymore. In fact, he looked more alert than I had ever seen him, his blue eyes burning with a weird intensity. 'Touch it,' he said again, more urgently.

But before I did, he gave a cry and white stuff spurted out the end of it, and dropped stickily to the floor.

Uncle Phil stood there for a moment, panting hard, and then he spoke to me again. 'Mop it up,' he said.

Now that was an order I could understand. I went to the toilet and spooled out some loo roll, and scurried back with it to wipe up the gummy mess on the floor.

'There's a good girl,' Uncle Phil said again, and he put away his willy and did up his trousers. And then we went back and watched the rest of The Sword in the Stone.

After that, every time I saw him he would try to get me on my own to touch me or to wank his willy hard in front of me, my big blue eyes round and uncomprehending as he showed it off to me with evident pride. It was difficult for him because there were often people around. If he got me alone, he'd ask me to take my top off and then he would touch me, his big, dry hands on my white skin, smelly and unclean; the whiff of cider or whisky on his breath. But I didn't really understand what was going on. I was lucky only in one sense: Uncle Phil wasn't around much in our lives. He would dip in and out, like an evil cameo in the horror movie of my childhood; a bogeyman who was all too real.

It was after these encounters with Uncle Phil, with those filthy fingers of his, that I longed to be able to have a good wash and clean the stink of him off me. But washing wasn't something that happened very often at George Dowty Drive. Personal hygiene, for all my mother's longing to be the best, didn't rank highly among her list of priorities. While she believed herself to be spiritually clean, being physically clean clearly didn't correlate for her. She would only have a bath about every three months, and I wasn't ever allowed to have one, too.

You'd think those rare baths would be welcome novelties – moments where my mother's natural scent and bad BO was replaced by sweet-smelling perfumes and bath oils, or at least a smell of clean rather than dirt – but seeing the bath full of water obviously gave her an idea; she was, after all, endlessly inventive with her punishments. And so, instead, bathtime became one of the most terrifying experiences of my entire childhood.

I remember being stood on the landing, on that green carpet, hearing the bath fill up. And it was just the most awful thing: being stood there, hearing that water, ready for you. Just awful. I'd stand there crying, the tears rolling silently down my cheeks, knowing what was coming, and knowing there was nothing I could do to make it stop.

I'd have to wait outside. When the bath was full, Mummy would call me in.

'Take your clothes off,' she'd say calmly, with almost a military tone, as though we were running through a drill and she was putting me through my paces. I'd slip out of whatever ragged clothes I was wearing and stand submissively beside her, the tears still falling, washing my face wet.

That didn't really matter, though, because it was about to get much, much wetter.

Once I was nude, Mummy would seize me and force my head under the water. If she'd had a bath, it would be grimy with her scum and a bit warm. Much more often, though, she'd run the bath deliberately to drown me, and so then it would be cold. She'd hold me there, my face beneath the surface, her hand unrelentingly firm upon my head, her fingers tangled in my hair.

In no time at all, my lungs would burn to breathe and my body would start kicking back, fighting to escape her unyielding grip. Of course, that was fighting back; that was being disobedient. My mother would hold me still, submerged in the water as my hands flailed and splashed with frantic strength. And eventually, too soon, always too soon, my mouth would automatically open with a desperate need for air and my throat would fill up with the bathwater. It would flood my mouth and gums and teeth and wash all the way down my airway, cutting off my breath until my brain felt as if it was going to explode. And just when I was on the point of blacking out, when my limbs had stopped thrashing and my body weakly slackened, giving up, giving up the fight, my mother would raise me up and throw me down on the bathroom floor as I gasped for air, my lungs on fire, the stale air of the bathroom the sweetest I had ever tasted.

The whole thing took place in silence, apart from the splashes that might just as easily have been caused by any enthusiastic child having a bit too much fun in the water. That was why it was a perfect punishment for the suburban house on George Dowty Drive: no one can hear your screams when your face is buried in a bathtub.

People always ask me: 'What had you done?' They want to believe there was some misdemeanour that set her off, some heinous act that provoked her to go to such extremes. Not to say that it was my fault, or that I deserved to be punished in that way, of course, but they want to plot the events, cause and effect: you did this, then she did that …

But it could be anything, or nothing. I know that's hard for people; they like to think something horrendous must have happened. It might have been that I'd not cleaned the animals out properly. Or I hadn't cooked her tea exactly as she wanted it. Or I'd fallen asleep. Or I hadn't played what Charlotte wanted to. Or I didn't learn something quickly enough. It could have been any of those things – or just because I was there, and in the way.

There is one particular bath that stands out from this time, though, from when I was six. It stands out because there was no drowning. Instead, my mother bathed us little girls in perfectly tepid water, not hot enough to scald, not cold enough to chill, and then dried us off and dressed us in flannel nightgowns that I'd never seen before. Mine was cream with Winnie the Pooh pictures on it. I remember standing on the landing, lined up with Charlotte as Mummy bade us both good night, and looking down in confusion at my cosy nightie, my body feeling so unlike mine: warm and clean inside a well-fitting garment.

Yet there was a reason for Mummy's sudden staging of the perfect childhood bedtime routine. For there was another little girl lined up with us on the landing that night. She had dark gypsy curls that tumbled down her back, green eyes that blazed with personality, and she was dressed in a matching nightgown to Charlotte and me.

Mummy had found a new little soul to save.

CHAPTER SEVEN

The little girl's name was Alloma. She first came into our lives as a temporary foster child. When her mummy went into hospital for an operation, and a foster parent was needed to look after her daughter, it was Eunice Spry who stepped into the breach. That first stay was short, and Eunice was on her best behaviour.

But Mummy never forgot her new little charge. So when, a short time later, Alloma's mummy was struck down with meningitis when she was five months' pregnant with her third child, and she was once again taken into hospital, this time to intensive care, it must have seemed to Mummy like a gift from God.

And to Alloma's mother, Mummy herself seemed Heaven-sent. Here was a woman who already had four daughters under her wing, two of them fully grown and flying; a woman who was a trained nurse and a foster parent approved by social services; a woman who could sweep into her family's life and through sheer force of personality make everything seem OK. Alloma's granny had bumped into Judith at the supermarket shortly after the meningitis struck, just as things were starting to unravel; as Alloma's daddy kept a bedside vigil and found childcare a challenge too far. Alloma's granny wondered if Eunice was still fostering, and Judith said yes. And in no time at all, Mummy had bustled in and, in a private fostering arrangement this time, welcomed Alloma back to George Dowty Drive. Her little brother, Damon, went to a different foster family – for now.

I remember Alloma arriving in our midst. She was only a year older than me, yet she wasn't like any other little girl I had ever known before. She had a spark about her, and a confidence that came from having parents who loved her dearly; she was outspoken and high-spirited. I was too shy and quiet to speak to her much, but I watched her self-assured chatter with my blue eyes out on stalks, and I enjoyed having her around. Not least because – unbeknown to me – Eunice was on a charm offensive with Alloma's parents, which meant that all three of us girls would be taken out on day trips. In addition, with more people coming and going in our lives, she had to be a bit more careful about where and when she hurt me, though the punishments didn't stop.

I can remember the three of us going swimming. I had bruises on my body, and my toenails were black from beating, but I was so excited to be allowed to go on the trip. Alloma and Charlotte ran off to play together; Mummy wanted Alloma to settle into her new home, and Charlotte was an unwitting player in making her feel comfortable and at ease. With both of them feeling entitled to the treats she was showering them with, they had a natural bond. I didn't feel jealous of it. To be honest, outings like the swimming trip were so exceptional in my life that I wasn't really with it. I just felt very confused.

Alloma slept in Charlotte's room, in the room with the Paddington Bear wallpaper and the bespoke bunk bed. And some of the happiest times in my childhood happened in those few months when Alloma first moved in. Mummy was still going over to the farm regularly to look after John Drake, whose health was in decline, and sometimes she would leave us at George

Dowty while she drove the nine miles to visit him. Charlotte, Alloma and I would drag out Charlotte's dressing-up box full of Mummy's old clothes and put on 'Don't Cry for Me, Argentina', and we'd dress up in these funny outfits and dance around. Or we might go over to my nan's house and watch Disney movies together. We all had our favourites. Mine was *Beauty and the Beast* – though I could never watch the scene of Gaston and the Beast fighting on the roof; it frightened me too much. I adored Belle, however, with her kind eyes and her good heart, and I guess the storyline appealed to me. If a wonderful princess like Belle could see the beauty inside the horrible Beast, maybe one day someone might just see a flash of beauty in such a horrible child as me.

Alloma, in contrast, loved Jasmine from *Aladdin*, with her skimpy dress and her heavily made-up eyes. That was just one difference between us, but there were many. Alloma was seven, and she'd lived properly in society: gone to school, had a proper family life. She was definitely what my mother termed 'worldly'. It was strange for me, having her around, because I didn't really know how to make friends. I just felt happy to have someone else in the house – and soon our little brood grew even bigger.

Alloma's mummy was still in hospital, and things had taken a turn for the worse. A lumbar puncture in her spine had gone wrong, and she required further long-term medical care in hospital, as well as facing the rest of her life in a wheelchair. I don't know who it was that suggested Damon joined us at George Dowty Drive, but I can guess. At any rate, it wasn't long before a happy-go-lucky three-year-old boy picked his way through the junk-ridden rooms of our house, and we gained a little brother.

Damon was a boisterous boy. Like his sister, he had complete confidence. He was cheeky with it, and he was quite sweet. He too had inherited the family's dark curls, and he and Alloma looked like two peas in a pod.

With the two children firmly in her grasp, Mummy stepped up her campaign with their parents (Alloma would later say she groomed them). Mummy would suggest they weren't capable; that she could give the kids a better life. She'd lie about the opportunities she could provide for them; she'd manipulate and charm and exploit. She played on their emotions – their guilt, their hope, their fear – and she kept her eye on the main prize: the unborn baby still growing inside Alloma's mummy's tummy. When Adam was born, in September 1992, he went straight into Mummy's care. Such was the completeness with which she had manipulated her way into the family's lives, she even saw him born.

I remember going into hospital to visit him. He was a poorly baby, born with a cleft palate, and the pregnancy can't have been easy with his mother so ill. Mummy told us all that his parents were drug addicts and drug dealers and that the baby was born addicted to drugs: more lies that we swallowed down without question. Damon, understandably, became very scared of his real mum and dad. Mummy told him they were evil, and he was only three. He wouldn't cuddle them anymore on his increasingly rare visits to see them; he would cling to Mummy instead, and she would smile above him, making eye contact with his real mother as if to say, 'You see? Your children are better off with me.'

My first glimpse of Adam was of this tiny newborn in an incubator in the hospital. Naked, he had only a blanket over him, but the thing that struck me most were the tubes that snaked across him. He looked so vulnerable and frightened, his miniature hands and feet waving in the air and the tubes holding him in place, the machines they were connected to beeping mechanically all around him. I just wanted to pick him up and take care of him. From the word go I loved him; I thought he was amazing. I looked at his perfectly formed little body in the incubator, and all my love of dollies came to the fore. *That's a real one*, I thought.

Later, back at George Dowty Drive, Mummy told us he was coming to live with us. And I remember her saying, 'If you ever touch him, you've got to wash your hands because he's such a poorly baby.' Only a short time later, Judith came in with him in a baby carrier; he was dressed in a Babygro with a cream blanket on him. What a lamb.

Caring for Adam soon became my main job at home. And not just to keep an eye on him: I would change his nappies, bath him, put him to bed in a crib in Mummy's room, sterilise his bottles, check the temperature of his milk and then feed him. His cleft palate meant milk often shot straight out of his nose and my heart would go out to him. My little six-year-old arms would cuddle him close and I'd tell him that I loved him.

For Mummy, the picture-perfect family had landed in her lap, and she was at pains to show the world how impeccable her mothering was. She made us all matching clothes to wear to the Kingdom Hall, like we were the von Trapps or the Waltons or something, all handmade on her sewing machine. I can remember standing in Charlotte's room, ready to be measured up, Mummy's cutting words as sharp as her scissors as she said, 'You've got no figure. You're not going to be very pretty at all when you grow up.

You'll never be able to wear nice clothes like Charlotte. A runner bean, that's what you are – you'll never be a proper woman.'

And she was right: I was like a runner bean; very, very thin with no bum or puppy fat on me whatsoever. Her starving punishments had seen to that. Yet, for once, her words didn't really bother me; I was still an innocent and, especially in my life, what I looked like was the least of my worries.

Our visits to the Kingdom Hall now required us, more than ever, to perform to the best of our abilities – better, in fact. One week, Mummy became determined that we would all learn the song 'Jesus Christ's Death' off by heart, so that when we went to the meetings at church, everybody could see her kids didn't need a book; that our family was so devout and Mummy such a good mother that we all sang from the heart and from memory; that we were the best.

She made us all line up in the kitchen and sing it to her: a rehearsal to be the flawless Jehovah's Witness children she had in her mind's eye. Charlotte and Alloma picked the song up right away; I don't remember Damon being there. But, hard as I tried, I just couldn't get it. Maybe I was a bit thicker than the others – that was certainly what I thought at the time – or maybe the age difference played a part, or perhaps the fact that I used to shut down mentally whenever I tried to learn something new, frozen in fear, was the overwhelming factor. Whatever it was, those lyrics would not stay in my head.

'Sing,' Mummy commanded, her dark eyes watching us all closely.

Charlotte and Alloma started up the melody beside me, their high-pitched voices crooning out the words. I mouthed along beside them, desperately hoping she wouldn't notice I hadn't picked it up. Some hope.

'Victoria, sing it on your own,' she ordered.

Of course, I couldn't do it, so she sent the others out and went to get a baked-bean tin from the cupboard. She smashed it into my mouth, over and over, and pounded me around the head with it, bludgeoning my ears. I stood there and took my punishment, tears rolling down my cheeks. I was so sad I had let her down; I was always such a disappointment to her, and it broke my heart.

She looked at me when she'd finished. She'd properly lost her temper, enraged that I wasn't picking it up, and she hadn't controlled herself. I lowered my eyes, my lips throbbing and bloody; ears still ringing.

'Now, what are we going to do about the meeting?' she said, disappointment dripping from her words. 'Your lips are going to be all swollen up; people are going to ask what's going on.'

Nevertheless, we still went to church. Mummy always had some excuse, my autism being a favourite: it made me clumsy, she said, and I would lash out in illogical anger, driven by my condition, and hurt myself. Mummy could always explain anything to anyone.

She hadn't given up on trying to get me officially diagnosed as autistic. A medical report from that time registered a concern that she might have been giving me Valium obtained from a neighbour – so she could take me to the doctor and pass off my drugged state as autism. But the doctors, to Mummy's frustration, weren't playing ball. No one followed up on the Valium allegation, though. Or, if they did, Mummy somehow managed to manipulate her way out of it, as usual.

And she certainly had social services wrapped round her little finger. She had performed the part of caring foster parent admirably – to them, to Alloma, Adam and Damon's parents, and even to the children themselves. She may have occasionally punished the older two with a slipper on their backsides, or twisted their arms, but corporal punishment wasn't a crime. My new siblings had no idea of the other punishments she had up her sleeve; not like I did. For months, then years, Mummy played her part, patient as the saints she so devoutly worshipped, just biding her time, and waiting … waiting … waiting.

By December 1993, her job was done. My siblings' parents signed away their rights, and at last Mummy had legal parental responsibility for all five of us. And from that moment on, any involvement with social services ceased.

The picture-perfect family was well and truly under Mummy's control – for good.

CHAPTER EIGHT

Adam was the apple of my mother's eye. She had, if you recall, seen him born into this world – just as she had Charlotte. And, like my big sister before him, this lily-white child, untainted by any worldly filth, became a favourite. Mummy spoilt him rotten, and kept him close, having him sleep with her in her bed every night, giving him everything money could buy, and letting him get away with murder.

It was never Adam's fault if he misbehaved. As his carer, it was mine. He never faced any consequences for his actions. If he threw something at my head, or smashed his toys, or broke a window with a violently hurled toy car, it was me who would receive a beating. 'You are a child of Satan, you autistic twit,' she would yell, 'any other child would have caught the toy before it damaged anything.'

When I'd give him his bath at night, he would chuck buckets of water over the side. The more I told him not to do it, the more he did it. He could already sense, even as a toddler, that I wasn't someone to be listened to. And he thought it was funny. So he kept on doing it, until the fawny carpet in the bathroom turned a black, manky colour, and the ceiling underneath the bathroom was all damp, the lights hanging off it.

Nonetheless, Adam and I became very, very close. I loved him with all my soul. I could see he had an honest, open heart, and it wasn't his fault that Mummy was bringing him up to be a child-king, above the law, reigning above the rest of us in the household – all of us except Charlotte, who remained a favourite.

I thought he was sweet-natured, and he and I would spend almost every minute of every day in each other's company; Adam playing whatever he wanted to, and me looking after him.

We became even closer in 1994, when we both ended up sharing a ward in hospital. Adam was having an operation to fix his cleft palate, which Mummy attentively organised; a far cry from the days when she wouldn't bother to attend my immunisation appointments when I was a baby. Adam was booked to go into hospital, and Mummy asked the doctors if they might take a look at my ears while they were at it. Not out of parental concern, of course, but because I'd recently suffered very bad hearing loss, and was bleeding from both ears; she was worried there might be hell to pay if it was anything serious or life-threatening. She told them Damon had kicked me in the head – 'boys will be boys' – when, really, it was her own boots that had done the damage; her boots, and the regular poundings around my head with the shiny silver baked-bean tin.

The doctors inspected me, and agreed to operate on my 'cauliflower ear'. I didn't say a word to anyone during my stay in hospital, nor in any of the doctor's appointments. Mother had trained me well. She was always telling me to look down whenever we saw doctors, to support her claims that I had autism, and threatening to beat me if I didn't obey. She did all the talking for me, and the Mummy they met was a creature I had never before encountered, who had a funny purr in her voice as she cooed over me and faked concern, and who stretched her thin lips into something approximating a smile.

Back home after the operations, life continued. Alloma was still going to school, and I would sometimes watch her from the window, as she attended a local primary school whose playground backed onto George Dowty Drive. I wondered what it was like, and I could even have asked her, had I the confidence, for she and I were increasingly thrown into each other's company these days. She had been banished from Charlotte's bedroom for some misdemeanour or other, probably talking back, and so Damon, Alloma and I now shared a room, a tiny room, which had only a single cheap chipboard bunk bed in it; so one of us always slept on the floor, beneath a dirty duvet. It was more like a cupboard than a room – Mummy had put up a fake wall to create it, so there was nothing in there but the bed and the bedding. I called it the brown room, and it was dark and cold and small. There were no toys in the brown room; but then, Mummy had said we didn't deserve toys.

Alloma was in her bad books more and more often these days, or so it seemed. It was usually because she dared to challenge Mummy's authority with that vibrant, sparky self-assurance she had. I couldn't understand it. Mummy would tell her to do something, and she would speak up and say no; or Mummy would tell her not to do something, but Alloma would do it anyway. That was just her: she had a fighting spirit. And Mummy would smack her to discipline her, or pull her lips down hard over her teeth, so that her teeth would cut into the tender gums and make them bleed. I couldn't comprehend why she would talk back – it meant she was going to get hurt twice as much, and I couldn't fathom why she'd want to get herself hurt.

I myself never thought about speaking up. I'd been brought up to have no opinions, no options; no character. I thought I was a nobody, and that whatever anyone else said was right, and

I'd best go along with it; I knew no other way. And watching Alloma, feisty and determined, trying to stand up for herself but being beaten all the same … Well, that showed me with crystal clarity that there was no way of winning. Best to keep your head down, and get on with it.

One afternoon at George Dowty, I was doing just that, getting on with my chores and feeding the cats. I lined up the bowls for the five of them, and they wound around my legs, velvety and soft. I got a clean fork from the drawer and spiked the cat food from the tins into the bowls, and then bent down to pop them on the floor. The cats started to eat.

Wallop! Mummy's hand smacked the back of my head as I crouched on the floor next to the cats. I cowered, firmly keeping my hands to my sides, in case she saw them move and accused me of 'fighting back'.

'You never use your brains, do you?' she shrieked. 'Why have you used a clean fork to feed the cats? You should have used a dirty one from the dishwasher. That's it! You're too thick, you don't deserve to be fed. No food for six weeks.'

I was used to that, of course. So I went about my days as usual: chores and looking after Adam, and then the torture of watching everybody else eat dinner while I was banned from consuming anything. Everybody would be told I had been naughty and wasn't allowed any tea, and I would hang my head in shame. I would watch Mummy eat, her mouth opening wide as she shovelled in a forkful of spaghetti Bolognese, the white pasta flicking against her lips and the meaty red juices spilling down her chin. I would watch her and I would visualise myself eating each mouthful, trying to imagine the texture of the mince on my tongue, and the slippery snakes of the spaghetti … My mouth would fill with saliva, and I'd swallow down the empty spit.

I'd go about my usual survival techniques, too: sneaking a knobby of bread here and there, stealing a tin of tuna, or something frozen from the freezer. I got so good at slurping out corner yoghurts from their packs, learning how to peel back the packaging just so, so it didn't look like it had been opened, that Mummy used to complain to the shop – rather than me – about the missing yoghurt.

And then, one afternoon when I'd been banished to Charlotte's room, I hit the jackpot. I found several boxes of chocolates piled up among the toys. Very naughtily, I ate a whole tray of the chocolates. A whole tray. And then, being the sly child I was, I put the empty layer at the bottom of the box, and the full, untouched layer on the top, to make it look as if I hadn't eaten them.

What was I thinking? I might have been eight years old, but I was still as foolish as ever. A mummy with a magic eye was never going to fall for that trick and, sure enough, before too long, she discovered the missing chocolates. It was October 1994, and it was the night of the Mop Fair.

The Mop Fair was always a big excitement in our house – in the whole town of Tewkesbury, in fact. It was a two-day festival with funfair rides and traditional games, and stallholders selling all kinds of wares. We had gone to it even before the others came, and I had happy memories of being out of the house, enjoying the pretty lights and the nice smells. The fair was that very night, and we were all looking forward to the occasion.

'Victoria, Harriet, Christopher!' my mother called, and Alloma and Damon and I came running.

For that was another thing Mummy had done, since the picture-perfect family became her own: she had actually changed Alloma and Damon's names. She was wiping the slate clean, trying to remove all traces of the life they had known before. She was just like, 'We'll change that name,' as though the children were dogs, animals. She'd done it to me, too, though of course I was too young at the time to remember. My real parents named me Sarah when I was born, but when I came to Mother, she called me Victoria, and that is the only name I've ever known. Damon, as he was, uses the name Christopher now, so I'm going to use that name for him from now on. Alloma was always 'Harriet' to me growing up, but she prefers Alloma, so I'll stick to that for her.

Alloma, Christopher and I came running in and lined up for Mother, three little soldiers reporting for duty. Mummy had a thick wooden chair leg in her hand.

'Take your shoes and socks off,' she told us all, and we hurried to obey. Christopher and Alloma hadn't been asked to do this before, but they knew by now that when Mother told you to do something, you didn't do it at your peril. They were quicker than me at slipping off their shoes and peeling off their socks. Perhaps I tarried because I knew what was coming next: Mummy and I had danced these steps a hundred times before.

Once we all had bare feet and were lined up neatly in front of her again, Mummy started her interrogation.

She questioned me first. 'Did you do it? Did you eat the chocolates?'

And, knowing I would be punished whatever I said, I lied. I'm ashamed to say I lied. 'No, Mother,' I said quietly, 'it wasn't me.'

Mummy fixed me with a glare, with those eyes that always seemed to penetrate right through to my dishonest soul, and then she calmly brought the heavy wooden chair leg down upon my toes. There was a dull thumping sound as the weapon connected with my flesh. I screamed; I couldn't help it, but I tried my hardest to keep it a quiet one.

Then she moved along the line. And this might sound naïve, it might sound foolish, but I swear, I didn't know what was going to happen, I truly didn't. She had never before hurt my brother and sister too badly, and I honestly didn't think she was going to do so this time.

But I was wrong.

'Did you do it?' she asked my sister.

'No, Mother,' said Alloma, telling the truth.

And Mummy brought the chair leg down upon her feet, and the blood started welling beneath her toenails.

'Did you do it?' she asked Christopher.

'No, Mother,' replied my little brother, who was then only five years old.

His feet, too, were pounded with the wooden stick. Again and again.

I know I should have owned up; I know I should have done. I know, I know. But I was scared stiff, and in shock, and the beating was so painful that all my thoughts went on trying to stand up straight, so she didn't beat me more for shirking the punishment, and on trying to keep my screams locked in, so silence would reign on the suburban street.

I will never, ever forgive myself for not speaking up.

For it was my fault they were beaten, that first, awful time, and that is something I will have to take to my grave.

Afterwards, she made us squeeze our bloody, swollen feet back into our shoes, and we still all went to the fair. I could barely walk, each step sending painful shockwaves up my spine. Alloma and Christopher limped along beside me as Mummy paraded us around the fair. And we followed Adam and Charlotte as they went on all the rides, and ate candyfloss pink as Charlotte's pretty dress, and we bit our tongues to keep from crying out with the pain.

Yet my heart hurt even worse than my feet. I was remembering something my mother had told me. About how Judith and Rebekah were perfect, and how Charlotte was an absolute angel. And how it was only when *I* came along that things changed – that *she* changed. That it was me who had turned her like this.

My mind whirred with an unstoppable cinematic reel of the beating. Seeing Christopher's little face crumple and cry out. Watching Alloma's fiery green eyes widen in shock and hurt, and then go dull, losing their spark as the chair leg came down again and again on her feet. And knowing, with each cry, and every blow, that it was my fault. Not just for lying, or for not owning up – but because I had turned her. I had made Mummy the way she was.

I had never felt so guilty, or such a bad, bad girl.

CHAPTER NINE

'Out of the car,' Mummy said, and the three of us scurried out from the big minivan she now used to ferry us around. I lifted Adam, aged two, down from his car seat. 'Charlotte, come with me.'

Mummy headed inside the farmhouse with Charlotte. The rest of us remained outside, in the sprawling grounds of the farm, where various outbuildings were dotted around the place. The one good thing about the farm was that, because it was so big, we could sometimes disappear from Mummy's sight. We never got lost – partly because we'd be too scared not to be able to return on time when Mummy hollered for us, but mostly because we now knew the grounds inside out and backwards. We were frequently over at the farm now, staying for weeks or months at a time, as Mummy nursed John Drake in the final days of his life.

She had taken Charlotte inside because she was determined that she would be his favourite. Hadn't he known her since she was just a young girl? Hadn't he always treated her, with tractor rides and Mars bars hidden in the sandpit? Wasn't she totally adorable? Mummy had a masterplan and never failed to show off her adopted daughter to him at every opportunity.

For the rest of us, being on the farm was a strange, chaotic existence. There was no bedroom for us three devil children, as we now were to her, lumped together in an unholy trinity of wickedness, so we simply slept on the floor. Mummy kept odd hours, and we would flit between the farmhouse and George Dowty, rootless creatures with no routine. I can remember being sat outside in the minivan until two or three in the morning, waiting for her to be ready to leave, and then driving back to George Dowty, where she'd demand we make her a bacon sandwich before she went to bed.

Alloma was always with us now. Shortly after the night of the Mop Fair, Mummy had withdrawn her from mainstream school, so she could be 'educated' at home with the rest of us. And with the farmhouse now taking up so much of our time, we stopped going so regularly to the Kingdom Hall. Mummy lost none of her religious fervour, though. When she beat us, she would often quote the scripture she was so fond of. She would still tell me I was sure to be killed at Armageddon; she would describe how the birds were going to come down and peck out my eyes.

My eyes were something Mummy now included in her punishment repertoire. She'd come up close to me and poke me right in the middle of my scared blue eyes. I'd close my eyelids as she stabbed at me with her finger, an involuntary reaction, but that would be wrong; that would be bad; that would be being disobedient.

She also took to pinching my windpipe, squeezing it between her forefinger and thumb. I'd struggle to breathe, and she'd say with disgust, 'You're such a weak-minded person! Breathe, calm down and breathe. You can breathe, you can breathe.' Her mind games were worse than ever before.

Because, with three 'bad' children now at her disposal, she started to play us off against each other. Already I felt a bit of an outsider in our trio – Alloma and Christopher were natural brother and sister, after all, and their bond was watertight; at least, that was the way it seemed in the beginning. I didn't resent their closeness, for two reasons. Firstly, someone as worthless as me didn't deserve any kind of friendship. Honestly, that's what I thought. Secondly, and more importantly, the way they were being treated was all my fault so *of course* I was on the outside.

It didn't take long for Mummy to break us, and turn us all against each other. When you're starving hungry, as we so often were, you will succumb to the pressure and dob in another child. To avoid a beating, you might accuse your sibling of being the guilty party in whatever crime she had created. If you were in Mother's good books, you would do anything – anything at all – to stay in them, even if that meant betraying your brother. None of us is proud of it but we all did it, time and time again.

Only when we thought we could get away with it would we help one another: throwing Christopher a bit of bread if he was on starvation; bandaging each other up after a bloody beating; the others not telling when I wet the bed; sharing a look that said, 'I understand.' When it really mattered, we tried to be there for each other; but more often than not we were against each other: sometimes physically, always psychologically. Mummy would dress Christopher in girls' clothing and we'd all stand round and point and laugh at him, the threat of a beating if we didn't ever-present.

One afternoon, I was at George Dowty with Judith and Adam when the phone rang. Mummy didn't like Adam to be around the farm too much at that time: John Drake was dying, and she didn't want him in the unnaturally silent house, its sickly air pierced sporadically with the staccato sound of John's hacking coughs. As my main job was to follow Adam wherever he went, I went with him to stay at George Dowty for a few weeks. In a sign of how close we were, Adam had even started to call me his 'little mummy'.

The phone rang, and Judith answered it. It was Mother, ringing to let us know that John had finally died.

When the will was read, a short time later, it turned out he had left everything – the farmhouse, the grounds, the money in the bank – to Charlotte, which of course meant that it had fallen neatly into Mummy's clutches. She had a brand-new dominion to call her own, and she wasted no time at all in asserting her authority.

The barn door slammed shut, and the three of us sat down in its pitch-black interior, hearing the click of the padlock on the outside as Mummy locked us in. It was bedtime, such as we knew it.

These days, we were often not allowed even to sleep inside the farmhouse, wrapped in a filthy blanket on the floor. Mummy was renovating the place, building an attic bedroom for herself and Adam, creating a vast playroom for him that would soon be chock-a-block with Lego and cars and games, as well as a princess bedroom for Charlotte, pretty in pink and more suited to a toddler's taste than that of a soon-to-be-teenage young woman. Mummy abused Charlotte and Adam in a different way, keeping them young, babyish and totally dependent. As for us devil kids, she cut us loose into the night. With so many outbuildings to choose from, now she could easily make us sleep outside, in the cold and the dark – and with the rats.

I hated the rats. The barn was cavernous, and its high ceiling would echo with the noise of their scratchy little paws as they ran here and there in the dark. A rat's smell is very distinct, and it used to frighten me to death when my nose picked up their tell-tale stench. I couldn't see what was going on, but I could hear them, and my heart would pound with fear. We kept chickens on the farm, and too many times to mention I had come across a half-eaten, half-dead chicken being gnawed by rats. I'd seen the destruction they could cause, too: the chicken's bloody entrails staining the ground, the rats' twitching little whiskers and sharp, sharp teeth. Vile creatures, they swarmed about the grounds and the outbuildings like something out of the Armageddon Mummy was always describing to us: a plague of rats.

The chickens weren't the only new addition to our ever-expanding menagerie of animals. We'd always had cats at George Dowty, and a characterless terrier called Meggie, but our collection of 'pets' had since ballooned. Now, we kept rabbits and hamsters and guinea pigs; we also had a duck called Queenie, a snake called Sequin *and* a parrot named Oakie. Most of the animals lived in cages; we'd keep them in the kitchen at George Dowty, under the kitchen table, and the house was rank with their droppings. At the farm, we had taken on two pigs, too: Bessie and Bunty. Alloma cared for them, and I think in some ways she had a closer relationship with those pigs than she ever did with us. We all needed something to keep us sane. I had Adam, with his picture-perfect baby-blond locks and fat toddler arms, and I still had my dolly Katie, too: that beloved long-ago present from my nan.

Yet even that wasn't sacrosanct to Mummy. Of course it wasn't. One day at George Dowty – for we were still doing our flits between both properties, seemingly with no rhyme or reason – she grabbed Katie from my arms and flung her in the oven: punishment for me eating something I shouldn't have. Katie went up in bright burning flames; I could only watch in horror as my friend was burned 'alive'. Mummy – more to save the oven than Katie, I think – pulled her out again and ran the cold tap all over her blackened polka-dot clothes and her singed yellow plaits. She threw the sodden, smelly mess into the back garden and slammed the door shut.

Later, I snuck outside and found her, discarded on the lawn in a heap of wet ashes. She half-smiled up at me with what was left of her face, a friend to the last, and I washed off the burn marks as best I could, dried her off and took her back inside. The world might have abandoned us children, but I was determined never to abandon anyone I loved. I knew only too well how it felt to be alone.

The world did show a passing interest, though, from time to time. My nan would sometimes stop by the farm, though only ever on tightly controlled visits Mummy had scheduled, and Mummy's 'home schooling' also required some inspections – inspections for which she received plenty of warning, so she had more than enough time to prepare. My mother was a master of deception; she had a degree in manipulation. Her plan was to dazzle the inspector as soon as she walked through the door – and it worked.

We would be kept busy for weeks beforehand on the subterfuge: not on actual schoolwork, but in tidying up the filthy rooms, in hanging up geography maps on the walls, and in displaying model boats and other hallmarks of what my mother termed 'alternative education'. The biggest effort, though, was put into drilling us kids on what she called 'protect Mum' mode. What do you do if you get asked about your life?

First and foremost, we were to avoid eye contact and look at the floor. But then, at other times, she wanted us to look at her because, if we didn't, they might suspect something. Sometimes she'd say, 'Be convincing, look people in the eye.' The instructions were confusing, and I was forever thinking, *Am I going to get this wrong? Am I going to mess this up?*

Most importantly, if ever we might be asked about punishments, we would have to say something like she only ever smacked us on the bottom, and only if we'd been very bad indeed. Or that we weren't given pudding after dinner, or weren't allowed our weekly magazine, or penny sweets. Mummy was clever: if we were never punished, according to our well-rehearsed answers, then that would also look off. She had the whole thing down to a fine art.

In the inspector would come. And Mummy would wow her from the instant she came inside – so much so that the inspector almost didn't bother looking through the exercise books. Nothing she said or did during her 'inspection' peeled back the thin veneer of a faked home-school set-up. We sat no exams; we studied no curriculum, yet the inspector didn't seem at all perturbed by any of that. Instead, she and Mummy would chat away, nineteen to the dozen. You could almost see the strings on the puppet the inspector became as Mummy manipulated her this way and that. It was an utter failure. This wasn't an inspection, it was a masterclass in the magician's art of misdirection, and Mummy was full of special stagecraft and razzamatazz – year after year after year. I would be looking at the floor, acting the part of the autistic child that I had played for so long. I had this voice inside me and I wanted to talk, but I couldn't.

The inspector would nod and smile and 'ooh' and 'ah' and wave us all goodbye, and we, perfect children – those of us not pretending to be autistic, at least – would wave back with grins pasted tightly on our faces, straining to smile as hard as we could, so that Mother didn't beat us later. We were always unnaturally well behaved in public; people would remark on how we were good as gold, and Mother would smile, a prim, prideful smile, as if she knew our excellent manners were entirely down to her.

That's something I can't take away from her: we certainly had good manners. We were too terrified not to.

Only if our hungry bellies forced us to would we show her up in public. I remember she would sometimes take Judith and Charlotte to dancing lessons at Eckington village hall, and the three of us demon children would be exiled to the kitchen, not permitted to join in the fun. There was a big box of biscuits in that kitchen, and temptation proved too much for us starving kids. We took some of them – only a few at a time, to avoid arousing suspicion – and we thought we'd got away with it, week after week.

We hadn't. One of the staff took Mother aside one evening: they had noticed the biscuits were going missing, and they had identified the culprits as her kids. You can imagine how that went down.

No one wondered why we might have stolen the biscuits in the first place – but just in case anyone did, in a clever twist all of my mother's own making, she took only Christopher and Alloma to apologise to the caretaker of the hall. Taking all three of us, she said, would make it look like something was wrong at home, as if we might have a reason for stealing. Taking just two looked like greedy, guilty foster kids, leading each other astray. It would lead any restless suspicions astray, too.

Life went on; an endless, chaotic life of shifting between George Dowty and the farmhouse. Mummy would spend the evenings watching her soaps in her high-backed green wing chair in the living room at home. She would sit back and put her feet up and watch the video recordings of her programmes – videos we children would have to tape for her, and God forbid if we missed the first five minutes, or included the adverts, or the machine packed up …

As she'd watch, us three would often have to sit on the 'invisible chair' inside the living room, our legs burning with mind-numbing pain. Mummy had a wooden ruler with a bit of leather or string on it, like a strap, and she'd swing it round and round on her index finger as she watched TV. If our feet slipped, which they often did, soaked in sweat from the torturous effort of maintaining the position, she would lash out with the ruler and hit us hard. And then she'd start swinging it again, round and round and round. I could never take my eyes off that ruler, even as my legs were on fire and my eyes watered with the pain.

That green chair was the setting for another scene from our childhoods, too – a peaceful one, strangely at odds with the rest of our interaction with our mother. She would lie back and put her feet out on a low stool, and we'd gather round like a SWAT team of miniature beauticians. We'd have to pick the dead skin off her feet, or brush out her long, greasy hair.

I enjoyed those quiet, peaceable evenings, my small fingers grooming my mother. For if she was off her feet, if we were hard at work picking the calloused, dead skin from her heels, and cleaning neatly between her toes, that meant she couldn't get up and hurt us. If I was standing behind her, brushing out her hair, I felt safe. There was no chance of her sneaking up on me and lashing out when she was lying back with her eyes closed, enjoying the attentions of her little slaves. So I wouldn't grimace at the feel of her dirty hair on my fingers. Instead, I counted myself lucky.

And that was our life: trying to please this woman, who could never, ever be pleased. We thought that life was pretty bad already. We had no idea that it was about to get much, much worse.

CHAPTER TEN

'Here you go, children. Sweeties for you all!'

Nanny held out her hands full of treasures and all of us children selected some penny sweets from her palms. I smiled up at her and she tousled my blonde hair.

'Right, let me get on with this washing-up. You run off and play, now.'

Nanny had popped round to see us, on her way to the Co-op. Mummy was out, away on the farm somewhere, or perhaps at Morrisons, where she often went to meet a Jehovah's Witness friend for long lunches. Sometimes she would take us with her, and leave us in the parked car outside for hours as she went in to natter, the van positioned so she could watch it from her table in the supermarket café. But today she had left us at home.

It was lovely when Nanny came round. The washing-up was, of course, our job, but Nanny would bustle in and tidy up if she was going past. I don't know what she thought of her daughter's home, riddled as it was with animal droppings and towering stacks of useless stuff, but, whenever she got the chance, she would pop round and try to make things clean and tidy for us all. It was so nice to have a grown-up come in and take the hard work off us kids for a bit.

Her generosity with the sweets, however, presented us demon children with a dilemma: to eat or not to eat? That was the question. It was a gamble that had painful consequences if we got it wrong. If Nanny didn't mention the treats to Mummy, we were home free. But if she happened to say, off the cuff, 'Oh, I gave them all some sweets,' there would be a raging row if we'd eaten them and couldn't produce them on demand. Mummy would go doolally.

'You sly, thieving liars!' she would yell. We'd be kicked downstairs, or made to drink washing-up liquid and then eat our sick, or sit on the invisible chair – because we knew we weren't allowed sweets, they were only for Adam and Charlotte, so it was the height of naughtiness to have scoffed them down with wanton abandon, knowing full well we didn't deserve them.

Next, she would interrogate us about Nanny's visit. What she'd said, what we'd said, what happened when, what happened next: each second of the visit had to be accounted for; not a single line of conversation missed. Mummy wanted to know everything that had gone on. She was a complete control freak.

And that desire to control extended to all areas of our lives – and I mean *all*. Mummy and I had long fought battles over my toilet habits, and her training technique from when I was small, of tying me to my potty until I 'performed', was one she was keen to reuse. Every morning, we had toilet inspections. We had to do a poo every day, on demand. Try pooing when you've been starved for three weeks, it's quite a challenge.

We had to sit there all day, straining, until we did it. Over time, I learned how to fake a poo, to make it look like I'd been. I might be able to squeeze a little bit out, with a couple of dark wees, and then I'd put some tissue and shampoo down there, mix it round until it looked half-convincing. I tried all sorts of things to get round it – because if you couldn't go, if you really couldn't go, Mummy had a trick up her sleeve to *make* you go.

She'd drag me off the loo by my hair, and tut crossly at the lack of performance in the bowl.

'Take your clothes off,' she'd spit out. 'Lie down on the floor.'

She'd throw me into the kitchen, and the tiled floor was always cold against my naked, goose-pimpled skin. I'd lie on my back, waiting patiently while Mummy finished her preparations at the sink. When she turned round, she'd be holding a big, thick, plastic syringe, filled to the brim with washing-up liquid. She would give it a test squeeze – her nurse's training coming to the fore – and a jet of gelatinous liquid would spurt out the top of the enormous teat. Always she used to remind us that she had been a nurse as she did it: 'I know what I'm doing.'

Mummy would then walk swiftly over to where I lay on the ground. She'd seize me by the ankles and yank my legs firmly up into the air. Then she'd stick the huge syringe up my backside and push the whole measure of washing-up liquid deep inside me. She would concentrate on the motion, her eyes clinical, not a trace of anything other than cool professionalism on her face.

My belly would ache after that. Oh, it hurt so much. And she'd say, 'You're not to go to the toilet, you've got to wait.'

I told you: it was all about control.

I'd have to wait, and wait, and wait. My belly would be cramping hard, and I'd be squeezing my butt cheeks together, desperately trying not to let anything out until she said. I was punished if I did; I could only go once she'd said.

After a while, she would let me on the toilet. I'd be in agony and sit there gingerly, my stomach fiercely cramping, until the release finally came. When it did, it was painful and messy and it hurt like hell.

Our punishments were relentless, daily. Even on a 'good' day, when Mummy might be in high spirits and seemingly happy, I knew it would never last. And sure enough, sometime before the sun went down, the spell of her buoyant mood would be broken, and our real mummy would be revealed.

Then one day came when she showed us a new trick; when she performed a 'big reveal' that left us all reeling. Five stars for the magician with the dyed black hair and the cold, cold eyes: none of us saw this one coming.

We were at George Dowty. I can't remember what had happened, now, what thing I had done wrong. I was about nine years old. And Mummy just snapped.

'Get in the car,' she said quietly. Mummy would still sometimes rant and rage at us, but more and more often these days she would be cool, and calm, and calculated. She was getting more confident, and it showed.

I scurried out to the car and slid inside, as fast as I could. Mummy started up the car, and she drove off. I didn't know where we were going. From my seat in the back, I could see her hands clenched around the steering wheel, her knuckles white and tense. We drove in deadly silence.

That silence was terrifying. It felt like I was waiting for an explosion – an explosion that never came. Instead, the tension kept on festering; Mummy's anger simmering, the dynamite getting drier and drier as we drove.

We kept on driving. We drove out of Tewkesbury, heading north. We passed the waterpark. We drove through Bredon. We drove for nine miles, until we entered Eckington. We went past the post office and the village shop and the graveyard where they'd buried John Drake. And then, right at the end of the village, we swung swiftly off the main road and Mummy parked on the driveway of the farm, close by the gate so no one else could get in.

Mummy turned off the engine, and there was silence, not even the thrum of the car's motor to fill it.

'Get out.'

We all got out. Charlotte and Adam ran off to play.

'Inside.'

I walked through the back door, an old-fashioned white door with a metal handle. The cold hit me immediately. It was always cold at the farm, and John Drake's fusty, old-man smell still lingered. Through the washer room, through the kitchen with its red stone floor, and then we turned right. Mummy led the way, and I followed. I knew I had to follow.

Mummy stopped outside the living room.

'Get in.'

I went too slowly for her, and she kicked me in the small of my back, forcing me inside. She followed me in and went straight to the thick green curtains that hung at the sash windows, pulling them round. The daylight vanished, and the room went very dark – but not before I'd seen her collection of sticks, lined up against the big Welsh dresser that dominated the room.

'Take your shoes and socks off.'

I bent down to obey, leaning on the sofa.

'Get off the sofa, get off it!'

She pushed me, and I fell.

'Faster.'

I couldn't drag out the removal of my shoes and socks any longer than I did. All too soon, I was standing before her with my little feet bare and vulnerable.

'Lie down.'

I lay on my back, as Mummy looked up and down her collection of sticks, selecting her weapon. Because of the renovations, she had an array to choose from – there were bits of wood all over the house: some narrow and reedy; others thick, like a cricket bat.

When she was ready, she turned back with her chosen stick in her hand: a thin spindle. She patted it into her own palm, sizing it up, feeling its weight and girth.

'I'm going to beat you on your feet one hundred times. If you scream, I'll start over. Remember, feet don't bruise. Nobody will be able to tell what I've been doing.'

She lifted my legs up without further ado, and held my trouser legs around the ankle, keeping my feet exposed and still. Then she brought the stick down violently on the soles of my feet.

I tried not to scream, I really did. But the pain was so intense, the thin stick like a solid whip against my tender flesh, that a scream tore through my throat and out into the darkened room, again and again as she beat me harder.

Abruptly, Mummy stopped her steady counting and stared down at me.

I had screamed before during punishments, especially the feet beatings. I would cry, beg her to stop, shriek because I was in so much pain. Because, of all the punishments, this was the one I tried desperately to fight against. I hated it; it was so, *so* painful. Mummy always saw my screams and wriggles as trying to get one over on her; she took it personally. She was beating me with the best of intentions, and for me to fight back only emphasised what a naughty child I was. Sometimes she would get Judith to stand on my windpipe to shut me up.

Now, she had a different idea.

Mummy went calmly back to the collection of sticks. She picked out a second one and came back to me. I looked up at her warily.

And then she tried to jam the stick down my throat.

My lips and teeth automatically gritted together, trying to keep her out. She stabbed at my mouth, over and over, as I desperately tried to keep it closed. But just as she had when she'd force-fed me as a baby, her metal spoon making my months-old gums bleed, Mummy always got what she wanted. Her angry thrusts with the stick pounded at my mouth, smashing my teeth out, just breaking through any barriers my body tried to erect. I choked and spluttered, but she didn't stop pushing until the stick was all the way down the back of my throat. Now I was quiet.

I couldn't swallow; I could barely breathe. I could feel the stick's sharp edge all the way down, and I could taste it on my tongue. It tasted like wood, and there was a gushing taste of blood, too: a raw, metallic, iron tang. My mouth kept filling with saliva and I wanted it to stop because it just kept coming and I'd have to swallow, but the more I tried to swallow the more it hurt, hurt, hurt. Tears streamed down my cheeks, but I had no means to cry aloud. I was so distressed, but not a whisper of sound passed my lips. It was deathly quiet in the living room at the farm.

Mummy nodded, satisfied. And then she went back to the beating.

'One, two, three …'

If I moved, in any way, she would start again. So, in the end, I lay there and took it. In a way, it was better with the stick down my throat – because it forced me not to scream, which meant the beating was over faster. Without it, I know she would have gone on and on and on; but with the stick, there was a kind of freedom. The way I describe it is that I kind of gave up at that point. There was nothing else I could do. I couldn't breathe; I couldn't do anything.

But I could still feel. The pain was so overwhelming that I couldn't function. I don't remember staring at the ceiling, or her, or at my demon siblings lined up, watching the beating from the sidelines as she had commanded them to. I was in so much pain that my eyes rolled loosely in my head, crying tears without me making a sound, my body in silent agony, willing it to stop.

Eventually, as with all things, it did. She slung my ruined feet to the floor, grabbed hold of the stick down my throat and roughly yanked it out. It tore at the soft tissue in my throat as she did so, and blood and saliva came out in long wet strings attached to the stick. It came out solidly, a thick wooden rope in my throat, and I gagged on it as she pulled. She flung it carelessly in the corner, ready for the next time.

'Get up!'

I dragged myself up, and put the weight on my feet, walking gingerly on the edges of them to try to lessen the pain. My feet might not have bruised, but they were bloody sore to stand on.

'Walk *properly*, you autistic twit.'

Then she made me watch, as she performed the same punishment on my brother and sister. She could only beat one of us at a time. Like they had done before me, I just stood there and watched, my throat raw with pain as I tried to swallow down saliva, and guilt.

Somehow, it was even worse seeing somebody else get beaten than being hurt myself. I wanted to save them – but I couldn't.

There was nothing I could do to save them. As an adult, that's the worst thing I have to live with. For I never even tried to pull her off them. It seemed impossible, somehow: she seemed too strong and untouchable, her power too great.

'Get out of my sight.'

We were dismissed. I limped out of the living room and back to the kitchen, trying to walk normally. As I reached the stone floor, its cool surface was like a balm on my battered soles. But we weren't allowed to stay in the kitchen; as usual, we were banished to the outdoors, with no shoes on. The gravel pierced my tender feet, making me wince and cry again.

'Little Mummy!'

Adam came running up but he stopped short, looking at my wet face, my bloodied mouth; my shattered teeth. He burst into tears.

I bent down and picked him up. 'There, there,' I murmured. 'It's OK.' I smiled at him – keeping my ravaged lips closed so my broken teeth didn't scare him. And then I held him close in my arms, each of his sobbing cries catching at my heart and making it even harder for me than it already was. But, with great effort, I stopped my tears and I whispered to him, 'It's all OK. Little Mummy is *just* fine.'

Well, what else could I say?

CHAPTER ELEVEN

The beatings at the farm were a regular occurrence after that. Sometimes they were daily, sometimes twice a week. Sometimes they were twice a day – she might yank you back in if you didn't walk out the room properly after the first one. The tally of strokes at each beating would add up, especially if we weren't at the farm when some misdemeanour occurred. 'That's a hundred and fifty strokes now,' she'd say. 'That's two hundred.' She'd make a mental note, and the punishment would hang over us like a guillotine.

I always hoped she might forget about it, but she never did. If she said we were to be punished later, it was only a matter of time before those green curtains would be pulled round and the sticks jammed down our throats. It was only a matter of time before she'd tell us to get in the car, and we'd drive the nine miles to hell. We used to long for there to be mail at the farm, because she'd check the post when we pulled up: anything to delay her, to hold back the unbearable pain for a few minutes more.

We became connoisseurs of torture. Mummy had a favourite stick to beat us with and, by chance, it happened to be my favourite, too. It was a broad one she used. It was a horror if she shoved it down your throat, as its width would leave splinters studded down your gullet, but if she used it to beat your feet, its broad flat surface was less painful, less intense, than some of the thinner sticks. I was always, shall I say, happier when she beat me with that stick.

Meanwhile, her other punishments hadn't stopped. We were still starved for weeks on end, and disciplined for stealing food.

Our mouths were still washed out with washing-up liquid or bleach, or whatever cleaning product was to hand. We still had to stay awake all night, running up and down the stairs. We were still drowned in the bath.

Adam wasn't immune to what was going on; of course he wasn't. Mummy kept him and Charlotte sheltered from the worst of the beatings, but she so regularly punched me in the face or pinched my windpipe or kicked me in the shins that he couldn't help but see some of the violence. And, bless him, he, of all of us, would stand up to her. He would stand behind her as she hit me, screaming his little blond head off, begging her to stop, almost hysterical as he yelled at her not to hurt me. 'Mother, leave her alone, leave her *alone*!' he'd cry.

She would pause in the beating for a moment to call Charlotte in and get her to take Adam out of the room ... and then she'd continue, harder than before. I think it infuriated her that Adam loved me, when she wanted everyone to hate me, but, as I was the person he spent the most time with, it was almost inevitable that, as a young child at least, he would care for me a bit.

I couldn't believe my eyes when he first stood up for me, brave as anything. Other than my nan, he was the first person who had ever defended me, and Nan never saw the physical violence, so he really was the only one who'd had the courage to stand up to her when she was throwing her fists and using me as a punchbag. I loved him all the more for it. He had a good heart, little Adam, and I will never forget that.

He was also a very boisterous little boy, however; a complete handful. Like all small children, he learned from the world around him, and our world was a violent, physically aggressive one. He was forever throwing his toys, or whatever came to hand, including food tins – all of which would cut our heads open, because he'd throw them at us. And because Mummy never said no to him, he became impossible to deal with, hyper and demanding and spoilt. I knew it wasn't his fault, but it was still difficult. I can remember having to play with him in the dark at the farmhouse – because Adam had absolutely demanded that the lights be turned off. And all of us would be sitting there in the dark, just because he had decreed it. It was madness.

Mummy decided to take medical action to address the issue. She'd heard of Attention Deficit Hyperactivity Disorder (ADHD) and its accompanying drug, Ritalin, and she had it in her head that maybe this would sort out both Adam and Christopher, whom she thought played up very badly, though to my mind he was nothing like the bright spark who'd first arrived at George Dowty all those years ago, and certainly nowhere near as badly behaved as Adam. She brooded, too, on my 'autism', and on how she had never quite managed to get that magic diagnosis.

And so one day, one hot summer day in July 1997, when I was eleven, I found myself getting on a train with Mummy and heading east of Tewkesbury – heading to the dazzling lights of London, and the hallowed road of Great Portland Street, where private doctors were ten a penny, albeit with rather more expensive fees.

Mummy marched me from the Tube to our scheduled appointment with the private doctor. I felt scared being out of Tewkesbury. Everything was so unfamiliar, so noisy and loud. The train and the Tube seemed so complicated. Having only attended school for a very short while, my world revolved around the red-brick walls of the house at George Dowty, the rural setting of the farmhouse, the occasional homeliness of my nanny's house, and the interior of my mum's parked car. To get on a train and travel across the country, to a place where the buildings were packed tightly together and towered over my head, where people pushed and shoved and car horns beeped in irritation, was to be transported to a different world. Mummy had already threatened me and told me that I had to keep my head down and not make eye contact, and I had no trouble at all obeying her.

When we got to the doctor's, it was a serene oasis in the raging storm of the city. Mummy registered our presence with the receptionist and handed over a sheet of paper, to be passed to the doctor. It was an account of my 'medical history' that she had written herself, and it was on this – together with the forthcoming personal examination – that the doctor would base her diagnosis.

In time, we were called in to our appointment. Mummy rose and kept her hand on my arm as we walked in, a 'reassuring' presence. She stayed to watch as the doctor put me through my paces.

I kept my eyes firmly fixed on the carpet. All the while I could hear Mummy's words in my mind: 'If you don't look at the floor, you will get your head knocked off. If you look up so much as half an inch, you know what's coming as soon as we get home.'

The doctor tried to engage me. She ran some tests, she tried to talk to me, she carried out her high-brow assessment. I kept my eyes on the floor, and I thought, *I've only got to lift my head and I'm dead when I get back.*

For once in my life, I performed to Mother's satisfaction. A letter was issued from Great Portland Street on 15 July: 'Victoria has a complex clutch of disorders which include a possible autistic spectrum disorder and/or a possible developmental dyspraxia as well as her attention deficit disorder.' The letter went to my local doctor, who had long said he didn't think I was on the spectrum, and who had not referred me to the specialist unit in London, despite Mummy's many requests. Instead, she had 'self-referred' us – and not just me, but all my siblings. Successful to the last, she got each and every one of us diagnosed with something: Asperger's, ADHD, autism. Each of us received a prescription for various drugs and, from what I understand, Mummy received a boost to her benefits for looking after five disabled children. That would help to pay for the farmhouse renovations, and Adam's growing toy collection.

It was mine and Alloma's job to make sure the boys took their pills. We sometimes had to pinch their noses to get them to take them, which I felt awful about. But Mummy was right about one thing: the pills did calm down the boys; they became docile, and Adam wouldn't throw his cars at your head quite so much.

We noticed that one of the pills had the opposite effect on us: they made us stay awake, very alert. For a child who was always being beaten for being lazy if I fell asleep, they were a godsend.

And I was still as tired as ever. I was frequently sick with throat infections and tonsillitis, no doubt caused by those awful sticks, but whether I was poorly or not, it was my job to look after Adam all day, and I would be completely exhausted by the time I had tucked him into Mummy's bed and then came downstairs to start the rest of my chores. We all had chores: Alloma was in charge of the cooking and looking after the animals; Christopher did the chickens and lots of outside work, slaving away on a farm that was swiftly sliding into rack and ruin. I was on Adam duty most of the day, and then I'd have to sort his toys out – not just tidy them away but spend hours separating out tiny bits of Lego and Kinder Surprise egg toys, and alphabetising his books. So, bedtime didn't happen for us demon kids; we'd stay awake all night.

I'd have to help my siblings with their chores, too. I can remember one mammoth task when the chicken feed, which we kept outside in the outbuildings, got everywhere because the chickens had pecked a hole in the sacks. Mummy made Alloma and me sit on the floor out in the barn all night, and divide the pellets from the corn. We couldn't just sweep it up, we had to separate it. And if we didn't get it done in time, by the time the sun came up, we would get another beating.

It was quite useful having a pill that kept you awake at times like those. I ended up taking them every night. They made me feel horrible – skittish and overly nervous, with a pounding heart and restless legs that would twitch, all along my calves – but when I weighed up the alternative, I thought the horrible feelings were more than worth it.

Alloma, though cowed by my mother's torture, somehow retained a feistiness about her, the fiery nature she'd always had. Perhaps she'd managed to keep it because she'd gone to school for longer, or had had more time in her loving parents' care as a child, but she seemed to know, more than the rest of us, that what Mummy was doing was wrong. For my part, I thought she was doing it with the best of intentions, and that *we* were the ones who were stopping her best intentions, her ideal of the perfect family, from happening. Alloma would rarely give in like I did, succumbing to my fate. She would still speak up, and speak out, even though it meant a beating. And one day, she didn't just speak out – she *broke* out. She ran away. She was so very, very brave.

Her crime had been to contradict Adam. He'd been watching *Budgie the Little Helicopter* all day at the farmhouse, and Alloma had suggested we watch the film *Free Willy* for a change. My mum was listening in, and when Adam kicked off and yelled that Alloma was making him watch something he didn't want to – 'She's making me do it and I *don't* want to!' – Mummy had shouted at Alloma to get in the living room and wait to be beaten. And, for once, Alloma didn't do as she was told. She ran straight out of the farmhouse into the night. It was freezing cold outside but she didn't stop to get a jumper or anything, she just ran away in whatever she had on, which wasn't much.

When Mummy found out she'd gone, she took us all back to George Dowty. Despite the hoarding, it looked more habitable than the half-renovated farmhouse. She and Judith went out looking for Alloma. When they couldn't find her, they came back to the house and, in a strangely subdued voice, Mummy gave us all a speech on the topic of 'What do you say if anyone asks how I discipline you?'

Once – and only once – she was assured that we were all on message about 'protect Mum' mode, she phoned the police, played the part of the concerned mother, and the authorities went looking for the missing little girl.

I was worried. So worried. Worried the cat was out of the bag for my mum – was she going to be OK? And worried for Alloma, concerned she was going to get run over, or killed. It was freezing cold and I was in a panic that she would become ill and die. My mind played the same message over and over: *She's got no money, she's got nowhere to go; what's going to happen to her?* And, worst of all: *She is going to be in so much trouble when she gets back …*

I never had a flicker of hope in my heart that she would make it, that she would get away. Too many times in my life I had seen my mother charm doctors, and social workers, and teachers, and wrap them round her little finger: a whole host of professionals, all across the board, in so many different areas. The police would find Alloma eventually, I thought, and they'd bring her back, and Mummy would wrap her in her arms and thank the policemen, and they'd dip their caps and turn right round and walk straight out of our lives. And even though I was concerned for Mummy that Alloma might tell, I also knew what Mummy always told us: 'Who would believe you if you told? You're naughty foster kids, from broken homes. I'm an upstanding, religious woman. No one will ever believe you.'

As usual, Mummy was right: Alloma caught hypothermia that night, but she was returned to the fold, safe and sound. And I'm sure, I'm absolutely certain, that the ice in her soul as she crossed back over the threshold was far more chilling than the numbing cold in her fingers and toes.

CHAPTER TWELVE

That wasn't the last time Alloma tried to run away. What did I tell you? She was feisty. Each time she returned, brought back by the police, the beatings continued, for all of us, and the sticks down the throat. Those sticks, those sticks …

Those sticks were what prompted me to say something, at long last, to the only person in the world I trusted.

I loved my nan with all my heart. I was a very sensitive little girl, so cowed and quiet. I rarely spoke, but that didn't mean I didn't have a brain inside my head, that I wasn't watchful, taking everything in, making assessments of the world around me. I had to be very, very careful what I said and did, at all times, so I got into the habit of never saying anything. Something for which Mother beat me, too: 'You don't speak! You don't say anything!' she would roar, as she pummelled me around the head.

I was a deep thinker, instead. I would watch, and observe, and consider, and decide. And I could see clearly, very clearly, that Nan saw good in me, and that she loved me. I could see she was a simple soul, innocent and kind and thoughtful. So I considered it, and I decided: I trusted her.

Things at the farm were very, very bad. Imagine being beaten as we were, on a daily basis, walloped with hard sticks on our feet, more wood choking us and cutting up our throats as it pressed against our tongues, silencing our screams. The invisible chair, the strangulation, Mother's fingers pinching our windpipes closed as she yelled in our faces, 'You're the scum of the earth!'

But it was those sticks that really got me because, with them, it wasn't just the moment of the beating that was agony. For weeks afterwards, the simple act of swallowing was its own special kind of torture. Our throats were literally shredded. I couldn't eat or swallow; I got throat infections over and over. And this was a time when it was happening a lot. It was relentless. We had a routine at last, and it involved almost constant abuse. It was very scary, and it never let up. I was in a very, very bad place.

One afternoon, we were round at Nanny's. Alloma and I were there; I'm not sure where the others were. Nanny was bustling about the place as usual, making sure we were both OK, rustling up a plate of jam sandwiches for us that we devoured hungrily as soon as she slid them across the table to us, with a wink and a message: 'Don't tell your mum.'

I watched her carefully as I ate my sandwich. She smiled at me, and her eyes twinkled as they always did when she smiled in my direction. From a very young age, I knew Nan was on my side. I felt very safe when I was in her presence and that day, with my mum not around and my deep-thinking brain having weighed it all up, over so many years, I probably felt the most secure I ever had.

I think she asked us something. It would have been some innocent concern, nothing serious, but with things so bad at the farm, and me feeling so safe on that particular afternoon, the world turned on its axis, and I opened my mouth to speak. I remember feeling that I was about to take a leap into the unknown. I was very scared, but I loved Nan and I trusted her.

And so I told her about the sticks. Alloma, confident soul that she was, chipped in, too. As we told her, we didn't cry. We had become so used to it that it was just what happened – there was no drama or emotion to it; not for us, not anymore.

Nan was upset, though. I don't remember her hugging us, but she looked us in the eye and she said, 'Are you telling the truth?'

We both nodded, multiple nods, yes, yes, yes, and we told her we were.

'Don't worry,' she said, 'I'll sort it out.'

My little eyes drank it all in, and I began to fret. Even as she said those words, I didn't believe her. My mind started to play back all the years of my mum manipulating my nan, of Nan leaping to my defence but my mum beating me for it, and I suddenly thought, *What have I done?*

The sky didn't fall down at first. My mum and my nan didn't happen to speak to each other for a few days. But then, a couple of days later, Mum walked up George Dowty Drive and went to see her mother. I saw her coming back to the house through an upstairs window, in such a temper as I'd never, ever seen her before.

Bang!

The front door flew open, nearly coming off its hinges; its handle left a big dent in the wall. And I knew, oh I knew: Nan had said something.

'Victoria! Harriet!'

I ran down the stairs at her shout. She lined us both up in the hallway.

'What have you said to Nan?'

I don't know why, but we both said: 'Nothing.' We were so petrified of her, I guess we didn't want to confess openly to having betrayed her, even though it was clear that Nan had told her what we'd said.

She fixed me with a glare. 'You're a liar. You are a sly, horrible child, and you have evil eyes. And do you know what you have done? You have probably made my mother and me fall out for life. That's my *mother*! To do that to a mother and daughter is the cruellest thing you can do in the world. And I am going to punish you.'

And she did. Oh, she did. The full repertoire was thrown at us: washing-up liquid down our throats; night after night of running up and down the stairs until our little bodies were exhausted. We were drowned in the bathtub, just enough not to kill us outright. I'd gradually learned, as I grew older, to lie still when she drowned me, because she'd think you were dying and she'd bring you back up for air. And I'd learned how to keep still so she would bring me back up again. By this time, though, I think she'd cottoned on to what I was doing, so she'd plunge my head into the water again and again and again, holding me beneath the surface for longer and longer periods at a time. We were put on starvation for three whole months, too. We were beaten with crowbars; we were choked with the sticks. We were not to be trusted.

We were banned from seeing Nan.

When we did eventually see her again, probably months later, she never said anything at all to me about it, as though our conversation over the jam sandwiches had never happened. It was odd. Mum, of course, had told her we were lying. She had told her time and time again that I was a very, very naughty child, and years of bad propaganda worked against me. Even though Nan had a soft spot for me, and never saw that naughty child herself, she couldn't help but believe her own daughter.

I remember my mum telling me, laughing at me, really, saying, 'When I was a little girl, I could get right round my mother.' She used to say how Nan would try to smack her on the bottom for doing something naughty – usually something manipulative – and little Eunice would run round and round the sofa, chased by Nan like something out of a Benny Hill sketch. They'd go round and round and round until they both landed in a heap on the sofa, giggling their heads off. And my mum told me: 'I always got away with it.'

And so I tucked my new knowledge of what telling someone led to away in my heart. I didn't blame Nan for doing nothing; my mother could be very persuasive. In my nan's mind, she had checked it out, and my mum had reassured her. And if experts could be dazzled by Mum, I reasoned, then my simple nan didn't stand a chance. I think I sensed, too, that what we had told her was so horrifying to her that, really, she didn't *want* to believe we were telling the truth.

Yet she had been my only hope. I didn't trust anyone else; I didn't *know* anyone else. From that moment on, I never spoke out again.

CHAPTER THIRTEEN

The best lounge at the farmhouse had been transformed into a Disney princess's kingdom. Mother and Judith had built an entire castle by hand, filled it with presents and strung it with twinkling fairy lights. It looked beautiful; it looked perfect.

It was all more make-believe than Disney itself.

I stood at the sidelines, watching quietly as the other children played: children of Jehovah's Witnesses who had been invited round to this party held in Charlotte's honour. I was dressed in a princess outfit; we were all dressed up: Charlotte, Alloma and me in colourful, shiny princess gowns; Christopher and Adam clothed as little princes. The theme of the party was in fact *Beauty and the Beast*, my favourite, but I took no pleasure in any of it – I knew it was all for show. A princess dress wasn't suddenly going to make me happy, not when I was almost certainly going to be beaten as soon as the guests had gone. I looked at the floor, as I'd been instructed beforehand.

Mummy clapped her hands. 'Presents, children!' she cried. And we all had to enter the castle, which was swimming with presents, and pick out a gift; there were presents for us all. With not a hint of joy I unwrapped mine. I knew from experience that she was just showing off to the Witnesses – look at me, what a generous and giving mother I am – and that as soon as the heavy farmhouse door shut tight, the gifts would be confiscated, apparently for us to 'earn back' by being on our best behaviour, but inevitably we would never, ever be good enough.

Charlotte had no such worries, though. She sat like the princess she was in the middle of the sea of presents, her long, dark hair flowing prettily down her plump back, giggling with her new friend, Wanda. She was now thirteen years old, but she was dressed as if she was three.

Wanda was a new figure in our lives. She and her mother, Scarlet, were just coming into the Truth, and they were struggling with the idea of not having Christmases and birthdays. This whole extravaganza had been staged to show them that joining the Church didn't mean you couldn't have magical celebrations. And I think now, looking back, that my mother possibly had another motive, too.

She had become very pally with Scarlet of late. Scarlet was a single mother, and Mummy seemed to gravitate towards people who were vulnerable, and in her eyes incapable. She had another friend whose granddaughter had had a teenage pregnancy – she'd had a little girl at a very young age – and Mummy was always saying how she was trying to get that child off her to give her a better life. As Mother darted about the living room now, gently touching Wanda's ginger curls as she giggled together with Charlotte, she looked the perfect parent, caring and considerate: perhaps just the person to turn to if you were struggling to look after your little girl.

The centrepiece of this elaborate ruse was the cake that towered upon the trestle table that had been laid out in the best lounge. Mummy had made it all herself. It was an ostentatious castle cake, with all these tiers and turrets – it must have taken her hours to make. But it was all done to impress the guests with how wonderful she was, how she was so skilled in all these

107

different things. A rich fruit cake, it was covered in marzipan and bright white icing, and positively shone in the glow of the fairy lights. To us kids on starvation, it seemed like a mirage, too good to be true.

As always happened, the good times didn't last. Very shortly after the party – it might even have been the next day – a chicken nugget went missing from the freezer. Food was always going missing because one or other of us demon kids was always on starvation. Mother counted each and every slice of bread, every nugget and fish finger in the freezer, every single can of beans. She knew instantly whenever we had stolen food, but we did it anyway out of a desperate need to survive.

I think it was probably my brother Christopher who took the nugget on this occasion, but I don't know for sure. For as soon as the crime was discovered, just as I had done with the chocolates a few years before, we all denied taking it. As if that would help; as if that would spare us.

The moment the missing nugget was noted, Alloma, Christopher and I were summoned to the farmhouse kitchen to be interrogated. We all lined up and Mother walked up and down, asking each of us: 'Who's taken the nugget?'

'Not me, Mother,' we all said, sweetly.

And because Mother liked to keep us on our toes, sometimes she would believe one of us at moments like these, to the detriment of the others. Keeping us divided, that was what it was all about. It was Alloma's turn to be in her good books, so she chose to believe her and she let her run off. My brother and I were not so lucky.

'Get upstairs, filthy thieves!' she screamed.

We ran to obey her as she pushed us up the half-renovated stairs, hitting us as we went. We were thrown into one of the bedrooms, a room with bare wooden floorboards. There was barely anything in it, only an empty, white metal bedframe and a huge Victorian wardrobe with great big handles. Like most of the house, the room was falling apart; copper pipes showing through the plaster on the walls. Its sash windows rattled when the wind gusted outside, which sent a cold breeze blowing icily all through the room.

She flung us in and stripped our clothes off. We both stood there, naked, shivering in the wind. Then she began kicking us round the floor. She kicked me over and over, right in my face, until my lips were hugely swollen and dripping blood. Blood was pouring from my ears, too, and from my nose. I put my hands up to try to protect myself, wrapping my arms around my head as her feet pounded my skull, but of course she pulled them down and kicked me even harder.

When she'd had enough of kicking us, she ordered us into separate corners of the room. Christopher went in the corner on the right, while I was in the corner on the left, near the wardrobe. For a moment she disappeared, and when she returned she was carrying something. She marched over to me and roughly tied a scarf around my eyes, so my world went black. It was a blue scarf, and it stank of rats – I think it came from the barn. She blindfolded Christopher, too.

'You're on starvation, and I'm locking you in here,' she informed us coldly. 'If you put a rotten piece of fruit in a fruit bowl, it turns the rest rotten. You're rotten, the pair of you. You need to be kept away from everyone else.'

And with that, she slammed the door behind her, and we heard the clank of the heavy Victorian key as it turned in the lock, and then the scraping sound as she took it out. We heard her footsteps walking away, leaving us there.

I sat naked on the hard floorboards, the blood dripping from my face. I listened out for Christopher – but I couldn't hear a thing. Like me, he was accepting of our fate.

We were too far gone to cry.

My tongue felt like sandpaper in my mouth. I was so thirsty. My mouth was dry, and it hurt to swallow.

I didn't know how long we'd been in the room – time had taken on a strange quality as we sat quietly in the dark, our blindfolds so effective that we couldn't even tell if it was day or night. From time to time, Mummy would come in with a tiny cup of water for us; her visits were very regimented, and she'd say: 'This is all you're having.'

Sometimes, when we thought Mother wasn't around or likely to come in, Christopher and I would sneak out of our corners and try to comfort each other. We'd crawl into the middle of the room and find each other with fumbling fingers stretched out before us, like some kind of cruel game of pin the tail on the donkey. We'd try to have a cuddle, more for warmth than love. We were so cold. The wind would gust through the room and our naked bodies would shudder – but huddling together, like penguins in Antarctica, seemed to ward it off a little. One of us would sit with their back to the other and we'd wrap our arms around each other. We used to argue about who would have their back exposed.

110

Mother only really came in to give us the water, just enough to keep us alive, but occasionally she would pop in to tell us things, like she was taking our sisters to see *Carmen*. Just so we'd know what we were missing. She loved her mind games – and one of these was to leave the big Victorian key in the door from time to time, and the door unlocked. We'd have to weigh up whether or not we could sneak out for some food, or whether it was a trap.

One day, we decided to risk it. Christopher and I slipped off our blindfolds and crept out of the room and downstairs. No one was around – they might have been out in the grounds, or at the supermarket, or even at George Dowty. We had no clue, but our food raid had a green light.

Down the stairs we went, our bare feet scampering on the floorboards. We passed by the best lounge, where the *Beauty and the Beast* party was still set up, the over-the-top decorations at odds with the chaos in the rest of the house – and we paused. In we went, drawn by the glitter and the princess theme. I shuddered as I stepped over the threshold, though, because this was the room John Drake had died in, and that freaked me out. I hated the idea of death and dead bodies. Perhaps I'd come too close to being one myself, or maybe it's just an ordinary fear.

There, laid out on the table still, was the perfect princess castle cake. Christopher and I shared a look. Perhaps we were devil children after all, or maybe he was just perched on our naked shoulders that day, whispering in our bloody ears, because, with a greedy glint in our eyes, we snuck up to the table, and seized one of the tiers to carry upstairs. We might even have giggled a bit in glee: this really was getting one over on Mother.

Back up to the room we went, where we devoured the piece we'd stolen. We were starving hungry – we hadn't eaten in days – and our hands were like paws as we crammed the moist cake into our mouths, our taste buds in jubilation at the sweet thickness of the icing and the almond goodness of the marzipan. We devoured that cake, chunks of it dropping onto the floor as we ate, getting crumbs in our hair and on our cheeks as we munched it as fast as we could, conscious Mummy might come home at any moment. Together, we ate as much as our tummies would allow, and then I hid the rest under the floorboards, saving it for later, for a time when she hadn't left the keys in the door and we couldn't sneak out to scavenge.

Perhaps the starvation, and the isolation, had driven us mad. Perhaps the gnawing hunger was just so intense we didn't think. I have no clue what we thought was going to happen; how we thought we were going to get away with having destroyed the perfect castle cake. Of course it wasn't long before Mummy came home, and she was straight up those stairs and into our prison.

'Did you take the cake?' she roared. She was so angry, that cake had been her pride and joy.

As we always did, deceitful children that we were, we lied. 'No, Mother,' we said, eyes down on the floorboards. But it was obvious we were lying this time: we had fruit cake stuck in our teeth, for goodness' sake; our guilt was as plain as day.

'Out!' Mother commanded. She took us out of the farmhouse and into one of the freezing outbuildings. Since Charlotte had inherited the farm she had so many places to beat us; really, she was spoiled for choice. In the outbuilding she beat us and beat us and beat us, until we begged her to stop – but our torment wasn't over yet. Mummy's endlessly inventive mind had devised the perfect punishment for the thieving, lying, greedy little pigs we were.

She sent us into a garage and told us to wait. We did so obediently, bodies bloody and bruised, snot and tears running down our faces, simply from the pain. We waited in the dark for her to return.

When she did, to our surprise she was carrying the rest of the enormous cake. She placed it before us, almost ceremonially.

'You want to eat it, do you?' she said, as sweetly as the yellow marzipan that curled on the plate. 'Well, you eat it. You eat it *all*.'

Christopher and I had already eaten almost a whole tier of this gigantic cake. We were stuffed full; our bellies, shrunk from starvation, smaller than most children's. But no child could have eaten the monstrosity before us; no adult, either. We looked up at Mother, aghast, certain she didn't mean it.

But she did. 'Eat,' she said, her eyes narrow slits as she stared back at us.

We had no choice and so we reached out our hands and began to feed ourselves the cake, the cloying sweetness that had seemed such a joy only a short time before now nauseating. I pushed fat ropes of marzipan into my mouth, forcing my teeth to chew and my throat to swallow. In went the thick white icing, inches deep, sticking to my tongue as I tried to eat it. She gave us no water. There was just endless cake.

It didn't take long before it became too much for us. Our bellies ached to the brim and our noses twitched at the sickly sweet smell of the huge cake. It seemed to overwhelm our senses: the touch of it in our sticky hands, the sickening taste of it in our mouths, the sight of so much more cake still to go, the sound of our mouths as they masticated reflexively on the cake that never seemed to get any smaller.

Inevitably, we threw up. We were crying and retching and vomiting, and the vomit was pure cake: icing sugar and marzipan and red cherries and black currants mixed in with our stomach acid. She made us eat, eat, eat, and she told us proudly, 'You may win the battle, but I will *always* win the war.' That still haunts me to this day: 'Whatever you do, I will find out, and I *will* get you. You may win the battle, but I will win the war.'

We ate and ate and ate: the cake, and the vomit, and the vomit, and the cake. We were locked in the garage all night, and the next day she made us keep going. We had to eat that cake day after day after day. Day after day after day, until it was all gone, and we were properly cowed.

Then she threw us back in the room.

'Three months' starvation,' she ordered.

And the door slammed shut.

CHAPTER FOURTEEN

I was shivering hard, and my arms ached. They were pulled taut behind me – Mummy had tied me with a belt to the copper pipes in the wall. I guess she didn't trust us not to get out again. I couldn't see anything, for the blue scarf was once again wrapped painfully tight around my eyes. Every time I shifted my weight in my black world, my body protested, pain shooting through me from yet another beating. I could feel dried blood stuck to my face, trickles that had run from my nose and my ears, and eventually stopped. My blindness meant I couldn't see my body, or the changes it had gone through, but I could feel them. I was now just skin and bone. The knobby bone in my bare bum was really, really sore from sitting for weeks on the hard floorboards. I tried to get up onto my knees, just for something different, but the bones in them protested, too.

My mouth was so dry. It had been hours since Mummy had last come in with water, and I now had a pressing sensation in my bladder.

Of course, Mummy wouldn't let us out to pee. Chained against the wall, I had no choice but to wee in my corner, right onto the floorboards where I was sitting, like an animal.

The stench of ammonia filled my nose. I knew Christopher, chained up across the room from me, would be able to smell it. I could smell it when he'd had to go. Mummy had left us nothing to go in, so we had to do it on the floor.

Understandably, Mummy was disgusted when she came in and the reek of it hit her, the damp stains showing her exactly what I'd done.

'Revolting child!' she hissed at me. She grabbed my bony shoulder and forced my face to the floor, right into the wet patch. 'Lap it up.'

I stuck out my dry tongue and pressed it to the wooden boards. The taste of it made me want to vomit, but there was nothing in my tummy to throw up. The only benefit of the starvation was that it meant we didn't have to poo. She'd have shoved our faces in that too if we had.

But I wasn't lapping fast enough, or something. I felt her fist seize me by the hair and my face smashed into the floor, right into the wee. She rubbed my face in it. I could barely breathe; the stink of the ammonia went straight up my nose. Eventually, after what seemed like a long while, she threw me back down on the floor, my arms twisting awkwardly as the belt held them tight behind me. I could feel my wet fringe on my face, damp with wee, dirty and smelly.

'Nanny's come round,' she told us. 'It's Sunday. She's made us all a Sunday roast.'

My stomach lurched with hunger.

I heard my mother leave the room, and the disappointment settled on my shoulders, a heavy cloak upon my nakedness. But then I heard her footsteps returning, and as she came through the door, an incredible smell came with her. My stomach lurched again and my dry mouth was suddenly slick with saliva. I could smell my nanny's roast dinner. Oh my, oh my! Mummy had brought us up a dinner. All my senses were suddenly alive.

I felt her fingers loosening the blindfold. Light spilled in, and I squinted against the sudden glare. And there, set down upon the floorboards, were two plates of the most exquisite food I'd ever seen. My nanny made a mean roast dinner, and she had gone to town on this Sunday. There was the meat – chicken, my favourite – swimming in gravy. Roast potatoes, golden yellow and crisped at the edges, just the way I liked them. Green peas, bright and beautiful, were nestling amidst the rest of the dinner and coated in meaty juices from the gravy. Fragrant steam rose from the plates: the piping hot food would help both our hunger and our frozen bodies. Mummy loosened the belt and my arms fell numbly to my sides. I wiggled them, getting the feeling back into them, excited I was going to use them to eat this delicious meal. I loved my nanny's roast dinners. My sunken eyes were out on stalks, drinking in every item of food on the plate, anticipating each mouthful to come.

Mummy stood in the doorway, and she turned to look at us both, crouched down on the dirty floor, physically leaning towards the plates; hunger writ clear on our faces.

'I've counted up every single pea on that plate,' she told us, in a low voice, 'and if you touch so much as one of them, or any of it, I will beat you to a pulp.'

Calmly, she turned away and shut the door gently. The key turned in the lock. She headed back downstairs, where presumably she told Nan that we'd been sent to our bedroom for misbehaving, and would have to eat in our room. She brought the food up so Nan would think we were being fed – and then she used it to make us suffer.

We had to sit and watch the food until she came back up. Watch as the gravy congealed on the plate, a skin forming on its surface. Watch as the hot steam gradually subsided, and the food became stone cold. Watch with our stomachs hurting so bad, yearning for the forbidden dinner. But we were so weak now, Christopher and me, that we obeyed our mother, and we didn't touch a single pea, just as she had said.

The punishment continued. As time went on, there came another day when the keys were left in the door, and the skeletal children in the bedroom came out to play. We'd been in there for so long that Mummy had to give us some food now and again. She would bring three crusts of bread for the two of us; that was all we had to eat. So, when the opportunity to scavenge was laid out before us, I knew I had to take advantage of it.

I crawled to the door, feeling blessed not to be tied up, not thinking maybe that had happened for a reason. My little hand reached up and turned the knob, and the door swung open.

Alloma was standing outside the door. We nodded at each other, but we didn't say anything. I went downstairs, walking stiffly on my cold, bony legs, and I stole some cornflakes from the kitchen. I took them back upstairs, and Christopher and I shared them out and hungrily ate the dry flakes, before hiding the rest under the floorboards. And we thought we'd got away with it.

What we didn't know was that Mummy had made a deal with Alloma. 'You watch them,' she had said, 'and if they come out for food, you tell me, and you'll have a meal tonight.'

When I'd seen Alloma outside the room, I didn't know. She didn't say anything to us. Sometimes we'd all be united and other times not, so it was always hard to know if we could trust each other. I don't blame her; I'd probably have done the same in her shoes. We all did the same when we were in the good books, trying desperately to keep Mummy on side, and food in our own tummies. We all knew what it felt like to starve, and the human survival instinct is a strong one.

When Mother came home, Alloma told her all about the cornflakes, and Mummy came and washed our mouths out with a bottle of bleach. Bleach was so much worse than washing-up liquid. I couldn't breathe as she forced it down my throat: my whole head felt as if it was on fire, even the inside of my nostrils burned, my nose and eyes running as I choked on the caustic flow being poured down my searing throat. It burned all the way down: lips, gums, tongue, throat, gullet, stomach. It was so scary. I was sick for days on end, chronic stomach pains doubling me over with pain, as I lay naked on the hard, wooden floorboards, spasms wracking my body. She did the same to Christopher, but to be honest my own pain was so intense I don't have a clear memory of him then. My brain was set on fire by the bleach and it burned out everything else.

Still, the punishment continued. In time, my brother left our little prison. I don't know why he left first. Perhaps Mother thought I should have been more responsible, as the older sibling, and shouldn't have let him steal the cake. Perhaps Christopher was weaker than me, being younger, and she was worried she'd pushed him too far. Perhaps she just hated me more than all the others, the devil child who had turned her bad, who never, ever learned her lesson, whom she'd tormented since I was ten months old.

It was even lonelier in the room after Christopher left. I was lonely, and bored, and cold. Most of all cold. I'd sit on my bony bottom and shiver non-stop, my arms tied behind my back, fixed to the copper pipes, and my eyes blinded with the blue scarf. I was very, very quiet; I had no energy to do anything else. Starving hungry, dry-mouthed, I sat in my dark, wintry world, and still the days passed by.

One afternoon, I heard the key turn in the lock. I braced myself: I'd weed on the floor, in this pit of a prison, and I was worried Mummy was going to make me lap it up again.

But it wasn't Mummy who turned the handle and walked into the stinking room. There was a beat, a shocked beat, and then I heard: 'Torrie, are you OK?'

It wasn't a voice I knew. Yet it was unfamiliar for another reason, too. It was a kind voice, a voice so caring I could almost see the care in it, as it reached me through the dark, through my tight blue blindfold.

It was Becky: the prodigal daughter had returned.

CHAPTER FIFTEEN

My prison was above the kitchen, which meant I could hear the almighty row that kicked off as Becky stormed downstairs to have it out with Mum. She had only come by to get some of her stuff – she wasn't expecting to find a skeletal child chained up in a bedroom. All hell broke loose, and I could hear screaming and arguing. Becky was threatening to go to social services.

At that, I thought, *Oh, crap, I've got Mummy in trouble! I've got her into trouble and she's going to go off on one. And I've made her and Becky fight and she's going to punish me for that too ...* I felt sick to the very pit of my stomach.

The sash windows in the bedroom rattled as Becky stormed out of the house and slammed the door. Moments later, I heard Mummy at the doorway of the bedroom. She quickly came in and untied me and took the blindfold off. I was waiting for the punch, for the slap across the head, the poke in the eye ... but it never came. It never came. It was the first argument anyone had ever had with her about me where my mum didn't take it out on me afterwards.

It was the only time she didn't take it out on me.

Within half an hour of Becky storming out of the house, I was downstairs in the kitchen. Mummy gave me a new outfit to wear. A multi-coloured tracksuit, it hung off my skinny frame, baggy and big. It felt strange to be wearing clothes again, after so many months in the nude; it took me a long time to warm up.

I was wary as Mummy sat me down at the kitchen table. She made me some scrambled eggs on toast, my first proper

121

food in months. I looked at her steadily for a long time when she encouraged me to eat it, wondering what the trick was. Eventually, the smell was too tempting to resist, and I wolfed it down.

Of course, I threw it straight back up again; my body in shock. Yet Mummy didn't get angry at me; she didn't have a go at me; she didn't force me to eat my own vomit, which was really odd.

After that, she sat down next to me. She looked me in the eye, very seriously, and pronounced, as though from a pulpit: 'You're forgiven now. You can turn over a new leaf and we'll forget everything that happened.'

Then she went through with me what I was to say if anybody asked me what she did to me. She made me say it over and over until she was happy. I knew exactly the way it went; I'd long been an expert in 'protect Mum' mode. Punishments included no pudding, no magazine, no penny sweets or pocket money. No mention was to be made of the blindfold, or the starvation, or my face in the wee.

And for a short while after that she was nice to me, *very* nice. Social services never came; later, I learned that Becky had thought long and hard about going to them, but in the end she'd decided there was no point in telling, because Mum always managed to persuade the authorities that she was God's gift to parenting. So she'd be in the clear – and we'd all be in the doghouse with her, for bringing shame on the family.

So she didn't tell, and Mum was nice; so nice that it was all very novel for a bit.

But I knew, all along, that it would never last. I always knew – and I was right.

*

'*Woof, woof, woof, woof!*'

The sound of yapping puppies filled the air, and I thought I might just have died and gone to heaven. Mum had decided Charlotte was to be given a brand-new puppy, all her own, and the whole gang of us had been shepherded along for the ride, so Mother could show off her picture-perfect family at this scene of great generosity.

The puppies were black Labradors, and they were the most beautiful creatures I had ever seen. I had long loved dogs, but the dog we had at home, the terrier Meggie, I found grumpy and miserable. She never used to show much character, and we never bonded. But these pups … oh my! They tumbled over each other in the pen, little black balls of fur. I just wanted to go and cuddle them.

Naturally, I wasn't allowed to. Mum made me stand at the gate while Charlotte went into the pen to choose one. This was Charlotte's treat, not mine.

On the way back, Mum, Adam and Charlotte discussed the issue of the name.

'What shall we call him?' Mum asked her two favourites with a sickly smile, delighted to be spoiling them, her long black ponytail flicking over her shoulder as she turned to gaze at her much-adored children.

Adam, sitting next to me in his car seat, where I was tasked as usual with looking after him, pointed at the sky and shouted, 'Aeroplane!' with all the enthusiasm a five-year-old can muster for a type of transport.

Mum considered his suggestion, and then she said, 'We can't call him aeroplane – but what about Jet? Because he's jet black, and it's like jumbo jet, which is an aeroplane.'

So that's what was agreed.

Of course, Charlotte didn't house-train the puppy, or do any of the work that Jet brought into the house. All that fell to Alloma, and sometimes to me. Alloma would sleep under the kitchen table with him, and I was a bit jealous of how close they were. Because I loved that dog from the moment I saw him. He was like a magnet for me; I was just drawn to him. When I looked at Jet, somehow all my troubles seemed to fade. There wasn't much that took my pain away, but he did. He was so gentle around us and so soft and sweet, a very loving dog. For us demon children, he was a blessing in so many ways.

As he got older, he used to bark when Mum hit us – I can remember him barking in the hallway of George Dowty. She'd lash out and hit him for protecting us, and he'd yelp and cower against the stairs. He ended up with a big bump on his nose.

Of course, this being my mother's household, Jet's arrival wasn't an entirely joyful experience. As Alloma house-trained him, Mother would frequently rub her face in the dog's faeces until he learned not to defecate in the house; she did the same to me if ever I was supposed to be looking after him, smearing stinky poo all over my skin and up my nose. Once, when he was in my care, he chewed the back door, as puppies will. He chewed it so much there was a chunk of wood hanging off. And she picked up that length of wood and she beat me with it; she kept shoving it in my mouth, saying, 'You want to chew it? You want to chew it? Go on then, *you* chew it!' She was scraping it in my mouth, smacking me in the mouth, and then she just kicked me, flung the wood at me and walked off, the brief, intense storm over – for now.

On the whole, though, it was amazing to have someone else in the family, especially someone who would give his love so freely, coming across to you as you sat, broken, on the kitchen floor, nudging his black furry head under your arm and giving your hand a lick with a wet pink tongue. I loved having Jet around – he was the best family I'd ever known.

My birth family was on my mind, too, as it happened, as my siblings and I had discovered something very unexpected in the stash of stuff at George Dowty Drive. Mum had piles of stuff everywhere at George Dowty: money, paperwork, photographs. We once found a provocative photograph of her in a bikini, which was very unexpected, given how against anything 'worldly' she was. She was much skinnier in the picture than the size-fourteen Mum we knew: we could see her ribs. Mum was always on fad diets, trying to control her weight – perhaps she was trying to recapture this lost body. We also found wedding pictures, and discovered for the first time that she'd been married twice. Any time we came across something that we considered a jackpot of information, we put it back exactly as we'd found it, and never let on that we'd seen it.

For me, the most powerful discovery was a pile of letters and photographs that were addressed to me. They were letters from my real big brother, Tom; letters I'd never been shown. Every year, it turned out, he'd sent me a card and a picture of himself – or, at least, he did until they petered out, which was understandable as he never received a reply. Mum had never let me see them, but she'd squirrelled them away in the ironing cupboard – a cupboard full of ironing that never got done – and we found them there.

In the photographs my brother had piercing blue eyes and very blond hair. He looked handsome, I thought; nothing like me, who was such an ugly girl. He looked happy. He seemed like an impossible dream, and the fact that he was taboo, and that I could never, ever speak about him, only emphasised that slightly unreal quality I felt when I looked at the snapshots: my big brother. He was no more accessible to me than the soap stars Mum watched on the telly every night.

Our strange life went on, a constant stream of chores and punishments. When I was twelve, Mum took us all to Disneyland. I think it was another staging of the perfect family life, and Alloma and I were punished for not smiling hard enough in the pictures of us standing next to Mickey Mouse. Our trip coincided with Hurricane Georges, and Mother revelled in the Armageddon-like atmosphere as we evacuated our holiday home. She grilled us on who to call if something happened to us in the imminent emergency, and we all had to recite Becky's telephone number back at her. As usual, I couldn't get it, and she beat me for that; so much for a holiday. Then we came back to George Dowty and the farmhouse: to the incessant medication, the beatings and the sticks, the never-ending violence.

Of course, those acts of violence did have consequences. She might hit my brother with a piece of lead piping so hard that his gaping head wound wouldn't stop bleeding, and she'd have to take him to hospital, with a story of how he came off his bike. I went to the doctor's several times with blood streaming from my ears, a result of my 'brother' kicking me in the head. Then there were my teeth. She was so fond of jamming sticks into my mouth, forcing them through the slim resistance I put up, so fond of hitting me in the face with a baked-bean can or her boot, that my teeth were always breaking, shattering in the face of her unremitting strength. So, she had to take me to the dentist every now and again, and get them fixed.

My medical notes say that I went to the dentist at least four times with lost or broken teeth. I remember having them replaced at least double that, fake caps covering the stumps along my gums: all that was left after my mother had smashed out my natural teeth.

And what a mother she seemed as she escorted me into the dentist's room, her hand gripping my arm, her mouth doing all the talking, while my eyes were glued firmly to the floor as her threats rang through my head: *look down, look down, or else …*

'Yes, she's autistic,' she'd sigh, her voice heavy with the burden, yet her world-weary half-smile somehow lifted her above the trauma, like a beatific saint, 'very, *very* autistic. And it makes her clumsy, you know? She is always falling over, falling over drainpipes and whatnot. I've got to really look after her. It's so hard to keep your eye on them all the time, though, isn't it?'

The dentist would suck it up, cap my teeth for the dozenth time, and then we'd go home.

On one of our visits, my mum was, as usual, doing all the talking for me. And perhaps because I was now a bit older, or perhaps because the penny had finally dropped that my frequent visits were somewhat suspicious, the dentist sensed something was up. He contrived to get me on my own.

'Mrs Spry, if you could just step out of the room, I need to take an X-ray of Victoria's mouth.'

My mum's eyes narrowed; her senses were always on high alert for anyone suspicious of our set-up. Her mouth pinched into a tight, disapproving pucker and she said sharply, 'You've taken an X-ray with me in here before.'

There was a beat as she and the dentist looked at each other, and then my mum kicked off. 'How *dare* you ask me to leave my child!' she raved, every inch the indignant mother, perhaps even a protective one, saving me from the clutches of a professional predator. We stormed out of his office and we never went back again – and that was how it worked with everything. If anybody ever came to the point where they were questioning anything, which only rarely happened, she moved us on, she got us out, so nobody could dig any deeper. She switched our address from George Dowty to the farmhouse and back again, so nobody kept track of us. She changed doctors and dentists, over and over; that was her tactic.

We went home after the dentist's that day, and she was in a foul mood. That was my fault, of course. It was my fault because she was only doing all this because I was such a bad child, and now I was getting her into trouble. That was how I lived my life, getting Mum into trouble, even though I never meant to.

The saddest thing of all was that, even if the dentist had succeeded in his plan, even if he had got me on my own, if Mother had somehow allowed him five minutes alone with me, time enough for him to sit me down and look me in the eye, and to ask me, in all seriousness and with a caring voice, if everything was OK, and did I need any help – even if all that had happened, I still wouldn't have said anything.

I was even better trained than Jet when it came to protecting my mother.

CHAPTER SIXTEEN

'Here's one I made earlier.'

The voice of the *Blue Peter* presenter rang out in the house at George Dowty. I ducked my head, trying to see the TV screen from my vantage point at the top of the stairs, peering through the bannisters at the elaborate construction covered all over in brightly coloured sticky-back plastic.

I wasn't supposed to be watching TV, of course; I was meant to be folding Adam's clothes, but Mum was out, she'd nipped down the road to my nan's, and I was taking advantage. She was usually a couple of hours at least when she went to see Nan. Nearer the time she was due home we'd taken to posting someone on lookout, so we all had warning as she sauntered up the street, her black ponytail flicking back and forth, and time to get into position. Jet, cheeky thing, would have gotten up into her green wing chair while she was gone, and we'd all yell, 'Quick, Jet, get off the chair!' And Oakie the parrot would squawk the same phrase back at us, and there'd be thirty seconds of panic and noise, but, by the time her key turned in the lock, order would have been restored and we'd all be in whatever position she'd commanded when she left.

Charlotte and Adam were the ones watching TV – watching it properly, I mean, not just squinting through the bannisters. Charlotte would have put it on for Adam, because her tastes in popular culture, these days, had changed: she was now into boy bands like 911 and Boyzone. She hid her interest from Mum, of course – pop music was worldly, and Mum would have hated the idea of her little princess growing up. But Charlotte and Alloma both liked boys and music these days, even if it wasn't allowed. They were proper teenagers, sixteen and fifteen years of age, and it had finally started to show.

As usual, I was behind the times, slow to change and slow at picking anything up, even my burgeoning adolescence. I was fourteen, but I was still a complete innocent, into my dollies and my dogs, and more interested in caring for Adam than in catching the eye of any romantic love interest. I didn't even really know what love was. The only man paying me any attention was Uncle Phil, his dry alcoholic's hands still taking any opportunity to touch me, when he could get me alone. He loved asking me about my boob size, too, not that I had anything to write home about yet, and he'd quiz me on whether I'd started my period. I hadn't; I didn't even know what he meant.

Mum's beady eyes, missing nothing, had started to notice Alloma's curiosity in boys, however – and how her foster daughter had begun to appreciate the skinniness the starvation punishments caused, as her young woman's body emerged and her tiny waist only served to emphasise her bust. Mum took to forcing her to eat huge blocks of white lard – sometimes raw, sometimes melted in a pan in a coagulant mess – and to hacking off her striking gypsy curls in an attempt to make her ugly. It didn't work as far as I was concerned. I always thought Alloma was beautiful, just like Princess Jasmine from *Aladdin*.

I heard a funny noise, but my brain failed to compute what it was. Too late, I saw the front door swing wide and Mum enter the hallway, in a black mood. *She must have had a row with Nan,*

I thought, *and she's come back early!* Quick as a flash, I stood up and ran into Charlotte's bedroom, still with its Paddington wallpaper on the wall, and started folding Adam's clothes.

They were silly clothes. Honestly, they really were. Mum dressed him like an eccentric Georgian page boy or something, with puffed cropped trousers, dickie bow-ties, knee-high socks and waistcoats. She ordered him ridiculous outfits from posh French catalogues, get-ups that came with coordinating accoutrements like epaulettes and elongated ties. And she kept Adam's hair long, curling over his shoulders; its baby blondness, now he was seven, long since turned to the traditional family black. He looked very girlish, and over-groomed, his fat bottom wiggling about in these smart, old-fashioned breeches. His bottom was always fat, because Adam was still in nappies. Mother wanted to keep him a baby, untouched by any worldliness, not even knowing how to use the loo.

I frantically sorted and folded, sorted and folded. And then my heart dipped: I came across an outfit that had a matching tie, but the tie was nowhere to be seen. Mum would go absolutely doolally if I couldn't find that tie, but George Dowty was such a mess I knew I didn't stand a chance – not in the half a minute I had before she came to check on my 'work'.

As expected, I failed the inspection. Mum told me to strip naked and lie on the bed, where I'd just folded up all the clothes. She went downstairs while I followed her orders; went downstairs and out into the garden, where she selected a branch to beat me with, a spiky stick full of jagged edges. And then she beat me black and blue, reminding me in a forced whisper to be quiet. 'Shut up, the neighbours are going to hear!' I knew already, of course, from the fourteen years I'd spent in this place, that you weren't to scream at George Dowty. So I pressed my face down into the pillow on the bed, and made only muffled whimpers as the stick cut and whipped and bruised me, all over my body.

It was better that way. My theory was: if I made a noise, I'd get it twice as bad. Far better just to suck it up and stay silent.

When she was done, she went downstairs and chucked the stick outside. I crawled along the landing to the brown room and collapsed on the floor. The brown room wasn't really any kind of bedroom anymore: my mother's hoarding had touched here, too, and our old bunk bed was full of junk, overflowing with it. We generally slept on the hallway floor now, when we were at that house, covered over with a filthy duvet if we were lucky.

Because Mum rarely went into the brown room, though, it had become a bit of a sanctuary, so I dragged my beaten body in there and lay down, trying to let my muscles relax, trying to avoid putting pressure on anywhere that hurt – which was everywhere. I heard a strange noise in the doorway, and turned round, twisting my sore neck. My heart was beating fast in case it was Mum come to teach me another lesson.

But it was Charlotte.

She was crying. She came into the room and looked at my bruises with absolute horror. Charlotte was protected from so much of the violence, you see. She didn't really see it, not the beatings themselves, and certainly not how regimented it was, day in and day out. Mum protected her from it; she wasn't allowed to see. Yet those bruises were impossible to hide.

A chest of drawers had been dumped in the brown room. An old-fashioned piece of furniture, with one of those three-sided mirrors on top, it gave me pretty much a 360-degree view of the bruises all over my body. I was in such a state.

Truth be told, even I was shocked by the damage this time. Because usually Mum was careful not to let the bruises show, or she'd beat us on the feet so there'd be no visible evidence. This time, the spiky stick had desecrated my naked body. Everywhere I looked there was a bloody cut, or a sharp splinter studded in me, or blooms of purple and red: bruises already blossoming on my skin, dark roses for an innocent teen.

Charlotte was very, very distressed. I felt terrible because she looked so sad. She came over to me and she crouched down and spoke to me in a whisper.

'Right, that's it. We're going to tell someone what she's been doing.'

Charlotte left me for a second, and when she returned she had a red plastic camera in her hand. It was a Virgin Airways one, and I think she might have got it from when we went to Disneyland. She took photos of my battered body, as evidence, and then hid the camera back in her room.

Charlotte's reaction was in stark contrast to that of Judith. She couldn't have cared less about any of us – apart from Charlotte and Adam, who, like Mum, she loved as favourites. Very, very occasionally, I had heard a row between her and Mum, when Judith threatened to go to social services. Every time, Mum would give us a beating as a result; one time she made me stand in the shed all night, where there was barely room to stand but plenty of rats to scare me witless. And she'd say it was my fault she was beating me, my fault she was falling out with her precious children; it was all because of me. I always seemed to be causing trouble, all of the time; I was such a naughty girl.

More often, though, Judith was complicit in the abuse. She would happily come and stand on our necks while Mother beat us, practically reading the paper while Mum raised her stick again and again, and brought it down as she counted: 'Eighty-one, eighty-two, eighty-three ...'

Then one day, not long after the horror of the branch beating, Judith took matters into her own hands. I was sitting with Adam on the bunk bed in Charlotte's room, just playing, keeping him occupied, and something irritated her about the situation – I don't even know what it was, anymore.

She dragged me down off the bunk bed by my hair and along the landing. Judith was thirty-seven now, and my skinny, starved fourteen-year-old self was no match for her adult strength. I wouldn't have fought back, though, even if I could; I knew my place.

She'd just had a bath, and she pulled me into the steamy bathroom and shoved my head under the dirty water, just as Mum had done a thousand times before in her presence. As I thrashed and flailed she held me down. Once my body had wilted limply in her hands, she pulled me out, waiting until that very last, tipping-point moment – just as Mother had shown her. Then she threw me down the stairs. I tumbled all the way to the bottom, and landed in a breathless, gasping, but deathly quiet heap. Well trained as ever, you see.

It was all done in anger, not calculating, like Mum's violence so often was, but I thought it was a sign of things to come.

Mummy's little helper was now all grown up.

CHAPTER SEVENTEEN

'That's so pretty, Charlotte!'

It was a few days later, and Charlotte was packing, showing us her clothes as she put them away in her little tweed case with ponies on it. She had been bought some new shoes and a dress and a sparkly handbag; its shiny sequins had caught my eye as they twinkled in the living room light. Alloma and I were watching as she packed her treasures away. We weren't jealous or resentful, though; it was just the way life was. It was normal. She was our sister and we loved her, simple as that.

We were all going on holiday: a trip to Pontins, for a long weekend. Mum and Judith, us five kids, Nan and Granddad, and Uncle Phil. A couple of Mum's Jehovah's Witness friends were coming, too.

Things didn't start off too well, though: it was raining when we arrived. I took Adam off to a playbarn and watched him run about like he owned the place in his Little Lord Fauntleroy outfit, laughing his head off wildly. Adam had a very loud, raucous, dominating laugh, with a slight edge of hysteria to it. Growing up in our household, I guess that's none too surprising.

He didn't play well with other children; he didn't know how to share. In our home, he was a mini-king, with us three demon kids slaves catering to his every whim. And so, in Adam's eyes, through no fault of his own, every toy belonged to him alone.

By the time he'd finished playing, we were able to check into our chalets. It was heavenly being away. I was on a pull-out bed, and the smell of the nice, crisp, clean bedding was like aromatherapy for my soul. So comfy and cosy in our tidy, neat chalet, I never wanted to go home.

Having the others around meant that there were no beatings on holiday: a blessed relief. Charlotte and Adam were given money to go on go-karts and other activities on the Pontins site, but we weren't – well, apart from one 'treat'. Uncle Phil paid for me and Alloma to go on a special bike with him: it had a big bench seat that all three of us could squeeze on together. We couldn't say no, thank you very much, we'd rather not – that would have been showing disrespect to Mother's family.

Uncle Phil lifted us up onto the seat with his big, dry hands. He positioned himself between us, and then he draped his stinking arms casually around his two best girls. I remember looking at his face beside me on the bike, and that alone was enough to put the fear of God into me: he looked pleased as punch. He pulled us close to him with his grimy paws, rubbing his fingers up and down our arms, and grinning widely at the camera as someone took a snapshot.

Weston-super-Mare has a sandy beach that we traipsed along on that long weekend, and we were allowed to go on it. But it wasn't complete freedom: salt-rippled wind in our hair and all our troubles blown away. I was on high alert in case I said something wrong, or walked the wrong way. Always, I was on my guard. Mother liked to tally up beatings to carry out when we got home, so you had to be on your best behaviour constantly. Yet we were away from the filth of George Dowty and the horror of the farmhouse, and we knew we weren't to be beaten for at least seventy-two hours. Good times all round.

Too soon, the Monday morning dawned, and it was time to head on home. Typically, it was a blazing hot September day now that the vacation was coming to an end, and sunshine warmed our skin as we milled in the car park, sorting out the travel arrangements. It was decided that Charlotte, Adam and I would travel home in Judith's blue Rascal van: the three favourites all together, plus Adam's 'nanny' along for the ride.

'Torrie, come and have a look in the gift shop before you go,' Nan said. She swept us inside, determined to spoil us. Adam was bought every character toy there was going, and my lovely nanny bought me two dollies. *Two* dollies! They had red coats and I thought they were wonderful. I may have been fourteen, but I was still so young. To my mind, dollies were the best thing in the world.

Nan treated me to a bag of sweeties, too. Even better than that, Mother saw *and* said I could have them for the journey. Guilt-free sweeties! Had I died and gone to heaven?

We all got into the blue van. I looked at Adam, bouncing manically on the seat beside me, and I realised we were missing something. I looked quietly around at all the adults, wondering if they would spot it, but no one spoke up. It had to be me.

'Where's Adam's car seat?' I chirruped from the back. I rarely said anything at all, so it took a lot of courage for me to speak up, especially given how wary I now was of Judith. I didn't want to say the wrong thing. Judith replied, 'It doesn't really matter,' but, with Mother's permission, I hefted it out of her car and put it in Judith's, and got on with the laborious task of untangling the straps, which were all twisted up.

The car park was full of hollered goodbyes and the noise of car doors slamming. Mother leaned her head out of her car window, the muted faces of Christopher and Alloma visible behind her on the back seat, their expressions grim. We all knew what awaited us when we got home.

'Don't be late,' she warned Judith, eyes flashing. 'We'll all have dinner at Nan's house. See you later – see you at home!'

And she rolled up the window and set off, leaving us behind.

Freedom. Judith drove to the seafront, and we stopped. It was a gloriously sunny day, and the heat of it beat down on the blue Rascal van. I was hot in my Donald Duck jumper and navy trousers. The jumper was too small for me, but at least the fact that the sleeves stopped halfway down my arms meant my bare skin was free to breathe in the summer air. It must have been worse for Judith: she was wearing a navy jumper and navy leggings, her long black hair down around her shoulders, and I remember thinking she must have been roasting.

As we pulled up at the seafront, Judith asked if anyone needed the loo. I didn't, but she and Adam got out and went for a walk along the promenade and to change his nappy.

Charlotte and I stayed behind in the van; Charlotte in the front passenger seat and me in the back. We had the radio playing worldly pop music, and the sun was shining, and we weren't to see Mother again for a couple of hours, and I had two new dollies *and* some sweeties … and I was happy.

As the music played, I fiddled with Adam's car-seat straps, still all tangled up. It was a lion car seat: the straps had 'paws' on to protect his chest, and there was a cushion under his head. I kept plugging away at untangling the straps, even as Adam hopped back in the car and settled in his seat, swinging his little legs, which were clad in a pair of vivid yellow dungarees as bright as the sun.

Judith pulled out into the traffic. It was about 11.30 a.m., and if we were going to make it back in time to meet Mother, we had to get on with our journey sharpish. Charlotte turned the radio off and slipped in a tape that Judith had lying in the van. It was The Corrs, and I remember her singing along with their Irish accents in her high-pitched voice. She was wearing her favourite jumper, a lime-green sweater with 'Papaya' written across the front, her hair was up in a ponytail, and she looked so young and joyful: sweet sixteen.

We came down the slip road onto the motorway, just as I had finally untangled Adam's straps. I flattened the cushions behind his head, making him comfortable.

The traffic was at a standstill. *Uh, oh.* We were going to be in trouble with Mother if we were late. We craned our necks, but we couldn't see what had caused the problem. Judith pulled up neatly behind a red car, sandwiching it between ourselves and an enormous Lidl lorry, and joined the stationary traffic.

I clicked Adam's straps together, safe and sound, and then settled back into my own seat, my new dollies and Katie sitting by my side. I looked out the window at the green fir trees bordering the road, enjoying the sunshine and the music and the unfamiliar liberty.

Then there was this almighty screech and a bang – and my world turned upside-down.

Forever.

PART TWO

SOMETHING'S GOT TO GIVE

CHAPTER EIGHTEEN

No one was making any noise. There was just a *whoosh, whoosh* sound, over and over again. Every breath I took hurt. It burned the inside of my nose: raw, raw. Overpowering petrol fumes dirtied each atom of air that entered into my aching lungs, so strong I could taste them.

I opened my eyes.

Judith was right in front of me, inches away from my face. *How…?* I had been sitting behind her in the car, yet now I was lying above her, suspended from the ceiling: hanging from the seatbelt that had saved my life. My leg stretched awkwardly behind me, jammed into the radiator of the 24-tonne truck that had just smashed into the back of us.

I could see a mass of flesh, my sister's dark hair all mangled in it. Her body was imprinted with glass, all over, little blue flecks of paint mixed in with it. Her face was studded with so much it looked like a mosaic, a mosaic of glass. I could see her eyes, staring wide in front of her, frozen.

There was blood running from her nose, from her ears, from her head, from … everywhere. Blood was pouring everywhere. She was in all these dark clothes and yet there was this bright red blood coming out, unstoppable, glowing neon against her navy sweater. Her body was completely distorted, bones sticking out of her arms and legs, the steering wheel embedded in her chest, her guts everywhere. Her clothes had ripped and she had no dignity; you could see her breasts hanging out. And there, in the footwell, were her feet, still solidly encased in her shoes: severed from the rest of what was left of her.

I couldn't look away. I couldn't move my neck; I couldn't turn it.

I didn't realise it was because I had broken it.

Whoosh, whoosh. That sound was the cars on the other side of the motorway, I realised. I moved my eyes, trying to see outside the car, flicking them nervously to the side.

Then I saw Charlotte. Still in her lime-green sweater, worn so many times in that sweet-sixteen summer, she had blood coming out of her ears and her nose. And her eyes.

What I did next was instinctive. 'Wake up!' I yelled at them, my throat rasping hoarsely against the burn of the petrol fumes, which seemed to be getting stronger. 'Wake up, wake up, wake up!'

I screamed at Judith, over and over … but she didn't wake up. My brain wouldn't absorb what my eyes were telling me. It was starting to hit me that they were poorly, but I didn't think they were dead. I began to panic. I screamed at Judith to wake up, and then I screamed at Charlotte to do the same, but neither of them did; neither of them did. And then I screamed for Adam.

Silence. Nothing but the *whoosh, whoosh* of the cars on the other carriageway, and in the far distance the sound of sirens. I called him again, but there was no answer.

Nothing.

And then, as I hollered his name, my baby brother's name, there came the most bloodcurdling scream I had ever heard, in all my years of hearing children cry out in abject pain, in horror. Adam sounded so desperate and frightened, I just wanted to go and save him.

'I'm coming to get you,' I told him firmly, in my best reassuring 'little mummy' voice. 'You're being so brave. I'm coming to get you, Adam.'

I thought he was behind me, still on the back seat, but his world had turned upside-down, too. His car seat had been shunted right up into the ceiling of the vehicle by the impact of the crash. The seatbelt had snapped, but that lion bucket chair had protected him nonetheless. He'd flown right over the top of Charlotte and had landed by her feet. He was ahead of me, but I didn't know that. I started struggling to get back to him, pulling at my leg, but it wouldn't budge; stuck fast in the radiator of the lorry behind. Yet nothing else mattered to me but to get to him. I fought even harder to free my leg.

'You've got to keep still; you really must be still,' said a voice to the side of me.

I tried to look in its direction, but I couldn't move my neck. I became aware that a big man was holding my little hand in his large palms. He was standing outside the van, reaching in to me. On the other side of the vehicle, I heard a sweet female voice talking to Adam, telling him to stay awake and that he was being really brave.

I started to lose consciousness again. The man who was holding my hand was saying, 'I promise you're going to be absolutely fine.' I tried to focus on his words, but it was too hard. 'You're being really brave, sweetheart,' he told me kindly, as my brain ebbed out into blackness.

My last, dying thought was: *That is the nicest anyone has ever spoken to me in my whole entire life.*

*

It was later, but I was still trapped in the car. Green blankets had been placed over Judith and Charlotte. From my fixed position, suspended above them, watching through my eyes that I couldn't avert, I could see dark ruby blood seeping through the green. I wanted to look away, but the paramedics who had taken over from the kind man kept telling me to keep my eyes open. I tried to focus on the Lidl van in front instead, the back of it marked by those horizontal lines that kept going wobbly as my vision blurred.

The red car that had been in front of us when we pulled up wasn't there anymore. Its driver had happened to stop on a slight angle, so when the blue Rascal van rammed into him, his car had shot out to the side, out of danger. The driver, I later discovered, broke only his elbow.

With the red car gone, there was nothing to stop our blue van: nothing but the vast wall of the massive Lidl lorry, all 38 tonnes of it. We went right into it, under it, and it crushed the van. Crushed it to a third of its original length.

'Adam, it's going to be OK,' I slurred. I was losing a lot of blood; it was pumping out of me with every heartbeat. I could hear the doctors debating whether or not they should amputate my trapped leg at the roadside, but my brain didn't really register it. My focus was on Adam; he was my little boy and nobody loved him like I did. I kept on talking to him, trying to reassure him, as a screeching noise rent the air and firemen began cutting into the metal of the van. They were trying to get us out.

Well, to get *me* out – because Adam was long gone, airlifted to hospital. They had told me that, but my brain wasn't taking anything in, so I kept on talking to him, trying to chat to him above the sound of tearing metal and the constant, jolly ringtone of Judith's mobile phone. Someone was calling – *I know who* – but Judith wasn't picking up.

The paramedic took my arm, and I felt the prick of a needle on my skin.

'*No!*' I yelled, snatching my arm away.

'It's just some morphine, to help you with the pain.'

'No, no – no blood, no blood, Mummy says I can't have blood,' I shrieked hysterically. I thought he was attempting to give me a blood transfusion, and even in my delirious, life-threatening state, I knew better than to go against Jehovah; or, rather, to go against my mother. From when I was a tiny girl I had been punished for breaking the word of God – '*You. Are. Evil. You have just gone and coloured. In. A. Bauble.*' – and I was desperate to avoid another beating. My throat was already burning from the petrol fumes; I didn't want the additional pain of those unforgiving wooden sticks shoved down it by my unforgiving mum.

The paramedic desisted in the end; he could see it was getting me more and more upset, and they needed me to stay calm. Eventually the firemen lifted me from the van, my skinny body no challenge to them as they rushed me to the emergency helicopter; my life in such jeopardy that its blades never stopped spinning as they spirited me inside. I was flown to Frenchay Hospital in Bristol, where I fought another battle – a losing one this time – as the nurses cut my blood-sodden, too-small Donald Duck jumper from my body, so the surgeons could operate on me.

'Don't do that, *please* don't do that!' I cried, as their silver scissors sliced into the sweater. 'Mum's going to be so angry with me, *please* don't do that!'

They ignored me. I was rushed down the corridors, the overhead lights flashing *bright, dark, bright, dark* as they wheeled me into emergency theatre. There were voices all around me, pressing me for information. 'What's your name? Who was in the car with you? What's your address? Where's your mum? How do we contact your mum?' I remember a big round light above my head … and then my world went black once more.

CHAPTER NINETEEN

I was in the bedroom of the farmhouse. My hands were plunged into a bowl of warm soapy water and I rubbed at the navy sweater between my hands in increasing desperation.

The bloodstains wouldn't come out. It was Judith's jumper, with flesh all down it, and I couldn't get the blood out, no matter how hard I tried. It was still as I had last seen it, covered in blood and mangled skin, and matted with Judith's long dark hair.

Mummy was going to be so angry with me.

Then I was in a depot, a big wide-open depot like the ones that Parcelforce use. There were red velvet bags all over the place, and red conveyor belts that carted items around the warehouse. I was sat in the middle of the depot, sat on this chair, my eyes wide as I looked at the body parts being carried along the conveyor belts. I looked down at the red velvet bag that my feet were being pushed into, and I fought so hard against it.

Because I knew what was inside the bags: a liquid soup of flesh. The Parcelforce staff kept forcing my legs into this white flesh and blood, and it was gritty in between my bare toes, a thick, gritty, fleshy soup that threatened to submerge me.

I screamed and screamed … and woke up.

Beep, beep, beep. As I opened my eyes, I could see a light-grey, tiled ceiling; institutional-looking. Machines pulsed and bleated at my sides, and tubes snaked all around me. There were wires down my nose feeding me; catheters, cannulas and blood transfusions – *oh no, oh no*; drips stuffed full of cocktails of drugs, intended to stabilise me and keep my pain at bay. So many wires, all drowning out my teenage body, as my chest was pumped up and down mechanically by a ventilator; the machine breathing for me, keeping oxygen flowing through my lungs.

I tried to move my head, but I couldn't. I was pinned into place by a metal halo, its screws pressing against my skull and pelvis and all down my back, stopping me from moving one inch. It was like a massive cage that was screwed tightly into my skin. One leg was raised above me, in traction with a weight on the end, and I could feel a firm, unyielding brace around my neck. The tears from my nightmare coursed down my cheeks, but I couldn't even lift a hand to wipe them away.

I was in hospital. I didn't really know it, but I had been close to death; the closest you can get without crossing over to the other side. Unbeknown to me, the doctors had had to resuscitate me and bring me back; thanks to their care my body had clung onto life. It had kept on fighting, through multiple operations, through a coma, but perhaps never more so than on the very first night they'd brought me in, after the crash. The night they told my mum I would die unless I had a blood transfusion, and she'd said doggedly and repeatedly that I was not to have it, no matter what.

I'd heard the nurses talking about it, in my haze of waking-dreaming-sleeping-hurting, while I lay motionless, my brain neither here nor there nor anywhere. The doctors had had to go to court to overrule her, I'd heard, in order to save my life. And that was why the rich red blood now hung beside my bed, dripping slowly into my veins, every drop a bright red mark against Jehovah.

Even after I'd had the transfusion, it had been touch and go whether I would make it. They'd told Mum that – they said I was probably going to die – and they suggested she might want to sit with me for my final hours on earth.

Of course she didn't. She went to be with her golden boy, her Adam. It was a stranger who held my hand that night, some random nurse, and was there to see in with me that first morning-after; who was the first to know that – against the odds – I had made it through the night. I was fourteen years old, and my mother hated me so much that she couldn't even bring herself to encourage me to live. Nevertheless, I'd hung on, my body fighting alone, week after week.

I'd been in a coma, but now it was time to wake up. I listened dully to the machines that told me I had survived, feeling shocked and traumatised.

Before too long, two nurses came in to move me. It turned out this was a regular thing; they came in every half hour to move me about so I didn't get bed sores and eventually removed the neck brace, though the cage stayed in place. They bustled around me, grunting with the effort of shifting my weight. The steroid drugs I was on, combined with the physical trauma of the multiple operations I'd had while I'd been unconscious, meant my body had ballooned to twice its usual size. I didn't look skinny and starved anymore.

They were gentle as they moved me; had I been able to look down, I would have seen that my stomach gaped open: a surgical wound that was covered over with medical wrap, but not sutured, as the surgeons still needed to do much, much more work on my mangled insides.

Perhaps it was just as well I was pinned in place. I don't think my brain could have coped with seeing my own insides spread open before me.

'You sleep again now,' the nurses said kindly as they finished adjusting my position. 'You concentrate on getting well. We'll just go and let your mummy know you've woken up …'

When I came round from the next nightmare, or the one after that, or the one after that, she was standing there, watching me scream.

'Shut up!' she shouted at me.

My terrified shriek cut off in my throat. There was silence.

'How's Adam?' I asked, after a long pause, wanting to know that more than anything, more even than how I was.

'Fine,' she said crossly. And he was: he'd broken both his legs badly and injured his elbow, but he was otherwise A-OK. She wouldn't have told me herself, but the nurses had let slip that he'd been asking for me. She'd have been angry about that; him asking for me over her, over Judith, over Charlotte. My sisters …

'How are Judith and Charlotte?' I asked, innocently. I didn't know they were dead. Even though I'd seen what I'd seen, no one had told me they had died in the crash. Whenever I'd asked after them, the nurses had shushed and soothed me, under doctor's orders to keep their fate a secret, lest the shock made my already precarious condition weaker still.

I guess I didn't want to believe what my own eyes had told me, either. In fact, I was regularly hallucinating that I could see them both, alive and unharmed, going swimming by the nurses' desk in the high-dependency unit, where I'd been moved after being discharged from intensive care.

Mum's eyes narrowed at my question and she rushed to my bed and stared down into my own eyes, her anger seeming red hot. I stared back at her in confusion, pinned to the bed by my metal cage.

'They're dead, you stupid cow!' she spat out viciously.

'But how can they be dead? Where have they gone?' Slow as usual, the autistic twit had failed to grasp the situation, strung out on drugs and shock and blind denial.

Mum gripped the bars on the side of my bed with white knuckles. 'Don't be so *stupid*,' she told me, 'you saw them die. You were there, you saw it all.

'In fact, you probably made it happen.'

Usually, her blameful words would have cut me as deep as a surgeon's scalpel – yet her tongue seemed to have lost its power to unsettle me; for the moment, at least. I was more concerned about what she was saying. My sisters were *dead*? It didn't seem real.

'I-I can't believe they're dead,' I ventured.

'You should know better than anyone they're dead – you've killed them,' my mother spat at me. Her eyes were cold. 'You see the devil looks after his own.'

She told me bluntly the funerals had already happened, that their bodies were buried in the ground. That somehow made their fate even harder to adjust to. I might have seen them die … but I never had a chance to say goodbye. It was as if I'd been in a time capsule, and the whole world had changed while I'd been sleeping.

'Did you wrap them in quilts?' I asked her, urgently. I was thinking, *If they've been buried, they're going to be cold*. I went on and on about it. 'I'm worried they'll be cold.'

Mum pinched my windpipe hard between her thumb and forefinger, until my breath failed and the machines around me beeped faster in time with my speeding heart rate.

'They're not cold, they're *dead*,' she told me again. 'You've killed them.'

Her words finally sank into my dazzled brain, and I thought: *She didn't need to do that*. Because as soon as I started to accept that they had gone, my first thought was: *What could I have done to stop my sisters dying?*

You should have done something, I told myself, over and over. *You should have jumped out of the car and you could have ended up dead but they'd still be alive. You should have sat in the front instead of Charlotte* – even though demon children were banned from the front seats. *You should have gone to the toilet at the seafront, then none of this would ever have happened.*

I didn't need my mother to tell me I was guilty for wrecking everybody's lives. Hadn't I been doing that from the very beginning?

All that had changed was that I could now add murder to my long list of crimes. I had blood on my hands, and my mother was never, ever going to forget it.

CHAPTER TWENTY

'I'm afraid it's time, Victoria. Let's take a look at Colin.'

That was Bev, one of the nurses. She was lovely; all the nurses were. Colin, however, was not: he was my colostomy bag.

Because I was not quite so lucky as Adam in the crash: I had suffered severe internal injuries that couldn't just be patched up with a quick fix. I had to have so many operations on my internal organs that still the surgeons didn't close the gaping wound in my torso: they kept my stomach open, covered over with its bit of medical wrap, so they could go in again and again to make adjustments to my insides.

Among my injuries was a ruptured rectum, which meant I couldn't go to the loo in the normal way. One morning, I had woken up to find the nurses cleaning out a smelly, brown-smeared plastic bag that, I saw to my horror, was attached to my stomach. It was just horrible, lying there on my tummy like something from a terror movie Mum had made us watch. Bev had tried to make up a funny name for it – thus, Colin – to help me come to terms with it. Best of all, she told me that the doctors were confident that, when I was a bit better, the colostomy could be reversed, and I could live without the stoma bag in the future.

It was something to cling onto, as I tried to adjust to my other injuries: my broken neck, which they had had to operate on through my voicebox; my broken leg, now missing most of its cartilage. I caught MRSA in hospital, and then pneumonia, from lying on my back day in and day out inside my metal cage, and they put me on a ventilator to breathe for me again.

I was in hospital for months. Months and months. Eventually they moved me to the children's ward, to a room right opposite the nurses' station. They called my room 'the goldfish bowl' because its walls were made of glass, so the nurses could be alert to any sudden change in my condition. My mother loved that room. She used to say, 'They can see everything you're doing … and so can I.' But when had she ever not been watching my every move?

The truth was, however, that I wasn't doing much of anything at all. Ridden with guilt about killing my sisters, I stared at the ceiling day after day, imprisoned in my metal cage and in the torture of my thoughts, and I wished I could die, too. My thoughts were impossible to escape. I would see my sisters' bloody bodies in my mind's eye constantly, and I would feel repulsed that I'd been hanging above them, two lifeless corpses, for almost an hour while the firemen tried to cut me out of the van. And then I'd cry because I'd think, *They were your sisters, you shouldn't feel repulsed by them*, and I'd feel so guilty. I couldn't talk to the nurses, I didn't have any friends, and my siblings were infrequent visitors under Mother's thumb; in fact, Alloma and Christopher were staying with some other, kind Witnesses at that time, while Mother kept her daily vigil at Adam's bedside. Nan and Granddad visited just once – Granddad was in a wheelchair now, and suffering from Parkinson's, so it was very difficult for them to make the journey – but Nan wasn't the woman I remembered when she came. She was distressed, stricken by grief, and she didn't know what to say to me.

I couldn't even talk to a counsellor – Mum put paid to that. 'My family don't get depressed,' she told my consultant, brooking no argument. 'We're strong.'

My body didn't seem to listen to my mental anguish, though. Slowly, though it took many months, I began to recover. That made Mum very, very angry. She would rant and rave at me: 'My two beautiful daughters have died while scum like you still grace this earth!' She would tell me I should have died in the crash. One day she flung two pretty hair clips at me, yellow and pink flowers adorning their sides, and she told me I could keep them. I accepted them meekly, with shock, as an unexpected get-well gift – perhaps staged for the nurses' benefit – but then she leaned in close to me. 'Becky bought these for your funeral,' she said. 'They were bought for you for when you died. You were supposed to be buried in them.'

I couldn't look at them after that; I put them in a drawer by the bed, and I kept the drawer shut tight.

The nurses, with whom I tried to be happy and chatty, the good-as-gold child always trying to please, noticed that I fell silent whenever my mother was in the room, fear of her overriding everything else. It was in complete contrast to how I was the rest of the time, as I tried to reassure them as they cared for me. The nurses had the tough job of washing saline solution around the pins that held my cage in place; metal pins that had rubbed my skin raw. It was an excruciating process, but I had learned a long, long time ago not to cry when I was being hurt, so I put up with the pain as the salt went into my wounds. I would paste a smile on my face and even joke with them, trying not to make them feel so bad about hurting me: 'Don't worry, Bev,' I'd say, from the inside of my metal cage, 'I'm a bit like the Millennium Dome.'

Eventually, though, the difference in my behaviour was so marked that, as so many other professionals had done before them, they raised it innocently with my mother. 'Victoria doesn't ever talk when you're in the room, Eunice – she's really chatty when you're not around.'

Then Mum would pull the blinds around my bed and she'd tell me, with an ever-present threat in her voice and her fingers round my windpipe, 'You autistic twit! You're supposed to be autistic. Autistic people don't communicate.' She would remind me, at every opportunity: 'You've done this. You do realise your beloved grandparents will never get to see their first-born granddaughter ever again.'

And my burden of guilt would grow heavier still, as I added Nan and Granddad's grief to my own.

The only bright thing about the many painful months of my recuperation was that I saw very little of my mother. She was never by my bedside; she was always with Adam. But it wasn't any kind of freedom. I was dealing with life-threatening, life-changing injuries, shock and grief, and a depression that was sucking at my soul. I'd had no confidence or character anyway – that had been beaten out of me long ago – and the depression seemed to fill me up like a shadow creature eating away at my empty insides. I looked out on the world through the same two blue eyes I'd always had, but if anyone looked through them at me, they would have seen there was nothing left inside. Nothing but guilt, and fear of Mother's terrifying threats, which I knew she would carry out as soon as she had me back at home. The sticks down the throat, the beatings …

People sometimes ask me why I never spoke up in hospital, but it never crossed my mind. It wasn't even to do with being scared of Mum, not really. The truth was, I thought I was doing all this to her: I was an evil child. The biggest and most important job in my childhood was to protect her and stop her from getting into trouble, and yet I'd done all this; I'd killed her precious daughters. That was all I could see.

It was while I was in hospital that I experienced a rite of passage that, in most young girls' lives, is a source of some pride and happiness, or at least a milestone that they will remember as the moment they grew up. Lying within my metal cage one day, as the nurses came in to move me, they paused as they drew the covers back and then said, 'Oh, you must have got your period. We'll clean that up.'

It was my first ever one, but I didn't tell them that. I just lay there as they sorted me out. They must have mentioned it to my mum, because I remember her being spitting angry about it. I tried to reason with myself that it was because it was a sign of me growing up – something her beloved Charlotte would never do now. But it was something else entirely that had got Mother's goat.

'Damn,' she hissed at me, looking down at me with unconcealed resentment, 'we could have got more money if you couldn't have had children.'

For Mum had wasted no time in getting onto the compensation people after the crash. Even while I was still in hospital, she was planning how to spend the thousands of pounds she would receive because of my injuries: she had her eye on a nice Italian fireplace for the farmhouse. Claiming the crash had made me infertile would have netted her another lump sum, but sadly for Mother this was not to be.

Still, she didn't waste too much time in worrying about it. She'd had another idea as to how she could maximise her income from my beleaguered body, while at the same time keeping me right where she wanted me.

And what Mother wanted, Mother always got.

CHAPTER TWENTY-ONE

'Come on, Victoria, I *know* you can do this!'

I was in the basement of the hospital, having physiotherapy with Caroline. My metal cage had gone now, leaving only a couple of pins in my hips. I had been prostrate for months, however, so freedom didn't come as easily as the removal of my aluminium architecture. Caroline was trying to help me learn to walk again, on my weakened legs that hadn't been used in so long.

She grabbed my hands and pulled me out of my wheelchair, lifting me onto the parallel bars so they could support me.

From the corner, Mother watched. Her eyes were like laser beams, invisibly fixed on me, yet weighted with invincible power. She had given me a firm talking to before Caroline came to collect me for my session, whispering to me behind the curtains drawn around my hospital bed, 'You're not to get out of that chair, do you understand me? You're not to get up. You're not to cooperate.'

Dutifully, down in the basement, terrified by the ice in her constant stare, I let my legs bend beneath me and I collapsed to the floor.

Caroline gave an exasperated sigh, and hefted me back into my chair. She fixed me with a look that lidded her eyes with disappointment – and confusion. There was no medical reason why I shouldn't be able to walk; she couldn't understand why I didn't seem to want to learn how to do it, why I wasn't desperate to build up my strength so that, when the time came for me to be discharged, which wasn't too far away now, I could walk out of the hospital and into the rest of my life. She looked at me like I was a naughty, nasty child who was wilfully ignoring her, and I could have cried.

From the corner, Mum spoke up. 'She's always been a lazy child, I'm afraid, Caroline. The trouble I had with her when she was a toddler … you wouldn't believe it. I'm so sorry she's being so very lazy again today.'

Caroline ran a hand through her short hair. 'Come *on*, Victoria,' she said firmly, if not a little harshly, trying to encourage me with stern words to try my best.

I wanted to try my best – oh, how I wanted to. I didn't want to be in a wheelchair for the rest of my days. Still only a teenager, I was just weeks away from my fifteenth birthday, and I had a pair of working, if weakened, legs. I wanted to say to her, 'It's not me, it's *her*.' It was head-banging. But of course I couldn't show any of that. I was so, *so* scared of Mum.

She hadn't ever threatened me, in those whispered conversations behind the closed curtains, but she didn't need to: we both knew what she was capable of. Instead, she would tell me about how she could get money for my incapacity, and she would say, 'It's the least you can do. Your granddad's getting on now, he's getting poorly. He's in a wheelchair and he's got Parkinson's, and he's going to need an outhouse built, and all that costs money. The least you can do is get that built for him by not cooperating. Do you realise your granddad is going to die knowing that his first-born granddaughter has died – and you've killed her? It's the *very* least you can do.'

And so I tumbled to the floor again, her words ringing in my ears and my eyes locking onto hers as she stood in the corner, assessing my every move, judging me and finding me wanting.

Caroline sighed again, for the final time. 'I think we've done all we can today, Victoria,' she said tightly. 'Perhaps you'll feel in the mood to try a bit harder next time.'

She settled me back into my wheelchair, and went to take me back to the lift – but Mum interrupted her, settling her strong hands onto the bars of the chair, usurping Caroline's place behind me.

'I'll take it from here, Caroline,' she said smoothly. 'Thanks so much for your help. I'm sorry Victoria didn't see fit to repay your dedication.'

And she pushed me off and then back upstairs, where a lecture awaited me: 'You looked like you could walk there,' she hissed at me, once the coast was clear. 'You did too well. I told you not to try, you autistic twit. Don't you love your granddad? Don't you want to atone for murdering your sisters?'

Those sessions were torture. I could see that Caroline cared and wanted to get me walking, but I just couldn't cooperate; I didn't dare to, not in the face of my mother's wrath. And so, on the day when the nurses gathered round to wave me off with a homemade goodbye card, which they'd inscribed with messages about what a lovely, smiley girl I was, it was in a wheelchair I left, with Mother at the helm of it, my colostomy bag tucked under my shirt.

The nurses had given me another gift to take with me, too: a handmade pinky, peachy towel, with a dolly picture printed on it and the name 'Katie' sewn at the top. I'd been in tears when I realised that my beloved dolly, friend for life, had been ruined beyond repair in the crash. Even if someone had managed to salvage her from the wreckage, she would have stunk of the petrol fumes that had burned my nose so badly. And anything from the accident scene would have reeked of death; I did so myself, for a long time afterwards. Katie couldn't be saved. The nurses had made me this replacement, though, and I'd slept with that towel every night from the moment they gave it to me. I took it with me as Mum and I headed back to George Dowty Drive on that cold winter's day in December 2000. The nurses waved us off, but I kept my head down, conscious of Mum's eyes on me, and of the knowledge that, once again, I was back in her 'care' for good.

To begin with, we moved in with my nan. All of us: me in my chair, Alloma, Christopher, Adam, Mum and Jet. We slept on blow-up beds in the living room. I believe social services may have had a hand in ensuring I was being discharged into suitable accommodation, so Mum had opted for Nan's rather than the filthy hoarder's hovel that was number twenty-four. As Nan and Granddad lived in a bungalow, Mum argued, it would be easy for me to use the bathroom and the shower. Since Granddad was also in a wheelchair, it would help me to adjust to my new, crippled life.

It wasn't so bad, being home again, at first. Being reunited with Jet was an unadulterated joy: he would come up to me in my chair and rest his silken black head on my lap, as I fondled his floppy ears. He became very protective over me, now I was in the wheelchair – I think he sensed I wasn't well. And I felt safe with my nan around, living in her home with its lovely Nanny smell, clean and human. Mum would still scream and shout at me, spit in my face and yank on my hair, but she hid the really violent stuff from Nan, which meant there was a period of respite.

Nan used to stand up to her about even the screaming, but, as she grew older, it was as if she had learned to be quiet – because by now she knew we were going to get it in the neck if she said anything. Or maybe the grief at losing her granddaughters took some of the fight out of her. Nevertheless, though she spoke up less, her presence alone was enough to stop Mum being really bad.

No, being at Nanny's was fine. It was when we went back to number twenty-four that things got hard. Very hard.

I can still remember opening the front door for the first time after the crash, and wheeling myself inside. My chair barely fitted into the narrow hallway. And all of my senses were assailed: assailed by Charlotte.

Nothing had been touched since she had died.

Her things were all over the house. Her clothes, her bits and pieces – even the items she'd decided to leave behind on that final night of packing for Pontins. The things she hadn't placed in her tweed, pony-covered case still lay strewn across the living room. Her smell was everywhere, overpowering.

I felt like I'd killed her all over again.

In the hallway, by my feet, were a series of black bin-liners. They reeked of the petrol fumes that I knew so well. The police had given Mum back what they had recovered from the crash site, and she had slung the bags in the hallway, not sorting or clearing or tidying, nor allowing anyone else to touch them, and there they remained, a constant reminder of the crash, a sensory overload that gave me nightmares for months on end.

Worse still for nightmares, though, was a little day trip Mum had planned. One day, she announced we were going to Somerset: 'You need to come down and see the crash, you need to see what you've done,' she told me.

When we arrived at our destination, I saw there was a tarpaulin laid out over a crushing truck. It was thrown back to reveal the blue Rascal van – or, rather, what was left of it.

Vomit threatened at the back of my throat as my eyes sucked in the sight. It didn't much resemble a van anymore. Not only was it far too small, crushed impossibly in on itself, the roof had been pulled apart in long fingers of jagged metal, where the firemen had cut me out. It stank of petrol, too. Looking at it, I couldn't believe I'd got out alive.

Yet all I could really see, when I looked at that van, were the two dead bodies forever imprinted on my mind. It was like I was looking at the inside of my sisters' coffin.

The Corrs' tape had unspooled in the smash and there was brown shiny ribbon flowing from the tape deck. Mum hopped up and picked it up, and then she removed the hubcaps to take home: more grisly souvenirs to add to the mausoleum.

Even that day, however, was as nothing compared to the day we saw the driver of the 24-tonne truck sentenced for the crash. The whole family went to Bristol for the court case, in September 2001; all of us under strict instructions to behave as Mum had said. I wanted to see the face of the person who had driven into the back of us, who had put me in this chair and who had made Colin such an unavoidable part of my life. But when I did, when I looked down at him, standing in the dock at the trial, it was so surreal. He had longish greasy hair and he just looked so normal.

It came out in the case that he hadn't taken the rests he was supposed to, and that he'd been fiddling with his radio just before the crash happened. He hadn't seen that the traffic wasn't moving and he hadn't slowed down. He was found guilty of two counts of causing death by dangerous driving and sentenced to eighteen months in jail. I felt no joy at the sentence. Nothing could bring my sisters back. If anything, I felt that I should have been the one standing in the dock.

Afterwards, the media gathered outside the courtroom to get a reaction from our family. It had been a reasonably big news story: two people killed, an autistic teenager crippled and another little boy also put in a wheelchair, albeit temporarily, while his broken bones healed. We must have looked quite a picture, Adam and me, both in our wheelchairs as we posed outside, my eyes burning holes in the pavement as I followed Mum's instructions to look down, look *down*.

She stood alongside us, her face drawn in a perfect etching of grief. 'I don't want to sound a vindictive woman,' she commented to the media. 'I'm grieving very much for my daughters. We are not going to be able to put the pieces back together – because there are two pieces missing. I would have liked more than nine months, which realistically is what he's going to get for having devastated my family. I'm glad he had a custodial sentence.'

The media cooed all over us: that poor, grief-stricken mother, everyone thought. The public perception of her turned even more in her favour. What a noble, noble mum she was.

She had, of course, lost her daughters; her grief on that count was truly genuine. But as we stood outside the courtroom, lined up obediently alongside our preaching mother, not one of those high-tech cameras recorded what was really happening.

Not one of them saw the truth.

CHAPTER TWENTY-TWO

Absolutely nothing changed after the crash. Nothing – except that my mother now hated me even more than she already had done, and I was now completely at her mercy. Living back at number twenty-four, free from the constraining influence of Nan's twinkling eyes, Mum was free to pick up where she had left off before the crash.

She had been a bit subdued when I'd first come out of the coma but the better I got, the angrier she became. It was as if she somehow saw me getting better as me screwing her over, as me getting one over on her – something my mother resented more than anything else in the world. *You may win the battle, but I will win the war.* By the time we were back at home, me stuck fast in my wheelchair, and no longer any nurses or doctors or Nan around to interrupt her rants at me, she had free rein to treat me any way she wanted.

'Get out of the way!' she'd yell at me, as I sat awkwardly in my wheelchair, always blocking her path in the small suburban house. Her hand would fly out and swipe the back of my head. In the chair, I could no longer squeeze myself down the side of the cooker, in that sweet spot by the breezeblocks. I was out in the open, with nowhere to shelter, and always in her way. It was incredibly stressful.

She'd lash out at me as I sat quietly in the chair, whenever she walked past. With her hand, or her fist, or – a new favourite – with a long length of beading that was hung up in one of the doorways. She'd whip me with it as I cowered in my seat, the sharp shapes slicing into my skin, like tiny, thin pointed nails, leaving my hands raw and bloody. She'd seize a piece of sandpaper and rub my face with it fiercely, as though she was trying to rub me out of existence, get me out of her sight. She'd position my hands in the living room door and then slam it shut on my fingers. If I recoiled, or snatched my fingers away in anticipation of the crushing slam, she'd say, 'Right, I'll do it again and I'm going to do it twice now.'

Very occasionally, when my injuries merited it, especially from the sandpaper, she might be forced to take me to the doctors. Medical notes from that time say the doctors considered my wounds to be 'self-inflicted' – if it wasn't so sad, it would be funny. When I'd been in hospital after the crash, I later learned from my medical notes, concerns had again been raised about our care – the change in my demeanour had been noted, from happy to the 'dull affect' of my 'autism' – but once again Mum had made sure no one got too close; and that any out-patient appointments were conducted in her presence, if at all. She asked the doctors not to test me further for my ability to walk, citing her worry that further tests meant further trauma for me. In reality, she was applying for Disability Living Allowance. Further tests might mean further confirmation that there was nothing medically wrong with me. Someone might ask why I wasn't walking; they might discover it was because I was petrified of her.

I never showered. I never washed. I never brushed my teeth. I couldn't, not at George Dowty, there was no downstairs loo. I had to change Colin in the kitchen, throwing the detritus into a black bin bag. Unbeknown to me, the doctors had told Mum that I was now ready for reconstructive surgery to remove Colin, and return to normal, but – a bit like my tests for walking – Mum 'was not keen to pursue this', according to my medical notes. So it didn't happen. Colin stayed where he was, in the emergency position the surgeons had selected, thinking he was only going to be a temporary guest; an emergency position that meant he used to leak all the time.

After the crash I was badly incontinent with wee for a long time, too. I would wet myself in the wheelchair, but I couldn't ever say anything to Mum. She wouldn't have taken me to the hospital to get it sorted. I just had to clean myself up as best I could, as I did when my periods came, too. Mum had gotten so angry about them, every month, that I didn't ever mention them to her anymore, nor complain about the dull ache of my period pains; it wasn't like she was going to be sympathetic about them. I'd just shove some loo roll in my knickers and continue with my chores.

Oh yes, I still had chores: looking after Adam, looking after the animals. At least the first job had become somewhat easier in one respect because, while my eight-year-old brother had been in hospital, he'd finally been toilet-trained and so he was out of nappies at last.

But in another way, it had become even harder. I couldn't chase around after him anymore – I couldn't even get upstairs, because Mum had banned me, in case shuffling up on my bum strengthened my legs in any way. I was supposed to keep Adam downstairs, but that was a rule he would constantly break.

More even than my crippled state, though, the hardest thing of all when it came to looking after Adam was that he and I were no longer quite as close as we had once been. Perhaps it was because he was growing up. Or perhaps the time apart while I'd recuperated in hospital had meant my mother's influence became that much stronger. Maybe the years of being told he was king, and seeing the way Mum treated me, just took over. At any rate, Adam's naughtiness now seemed to know no bounds, and he even became a little spiteful. He'd walk past me and tilt me out of my wheelchair onto the floor, laughing his head off. I felt very insecure, very vulnerable. It seemed I could do nothing right.

And then the day arrived that I'd been dreading ever since I returned home from hospital. I'd committed some misdemeanour, and Mother fixed me with a glare and told me to wheel myself out to the car. It was time for a nine-mile drive. Time to return to the farmhouse for a beating, and those horrid, horrid sticks down the back of my red-raw throat.

I obediently followed her instructions and endured that sickening journey, watching the rural countryside flash by outside the window, while my brain saw only the green-curtained sitting room; the collection of sticks; my mother's sweaty face, red with the effort of beating us.

All too soon we arrived at the farmhouse. We piled out and I wheeled myself into the kitchen, my heart thudding in my chest, my throat already tightening in anticipation of the terror to come.

Just before the crash, Mum had replaced the floor with a kind of marble granite. I wheeled myself across it, following her lead … and heard a dreadful screech, like nails down a blackboard. My wheels had scratched the posh new floor, badly, and – oh, my – my mum was spitting angry; she was very materialistic in that way, despite her religious passion. In a rage, she told me I was banned from coming inside; I was *never* to come inside again.

Which meant I never, ever had to go into that room again.

I burst into tears and I cried and cried and cried, saltwater pooling on my lap as the realisation hit me. I cried tears of pure relief, of thankfulness, of grim salt-tanged happiness.

It was the one time I was grateful she had forced me to stay in the chair.

CHAPTER TWENTY-THREE

'All aboard!'

Our family was heading off on a months-long cruise; a cruise aboard the canal boat Mum had recently bought; either with compensation money or funds from John Drake – I'm not sure which. There were no two guesses as to what had inspired the purchase, though: the boat was called *Charlotte*.

They were weird months aboard the boat. Nan and Granddad came with us, so to a degree there was freedom from pain. But Uncle Phil came too, and my new crippled state made me an even easier target, just at the time when my ripening body made him ask me more and more intrusive questions, about my periods and my increasing bra size.

The others would get off the boat and he and I would be left behind. I'd be sitting in the wheelchair and he'd just come up behind me and wheel me into the bathroom and slide the door shut, locked, and that was it. He'd tell me to take my top off, and his eyes would drink in my adolescent boobs while his hand fisted at his cock urgently until he came all over the toilet, or the floor, and then he'd make me clean it up. Or he might grab at my chest with his big, dry, dirty paws while I looked down, looked down, not wanting to see his bloodshot eyes leering at me.

I used to beg my mum to let me get off the boat with the others. But then, one time in Wales, Uncle Phil volunteered to take me. He wheeled me off, his large hands gripping the chair in excitement, and took me into a pub toilet. Once there he touched me, touched my bits all over, and then we came out and he gave me a little address book with pictures of dogs on it, as if to say sorry.

After that, I didn't want to get off the boat again. Mum would slap me and roar, 'You're so bloody ungrateful! He'll get you off the boat and now you don't want to know!' But taking her wrath was better than being molested by Uncle Phil.

Even though we all slept on the boat, it didn't stop the abuse. If anything, he became ever more confident: he'd even sleep with his willy hanging out, pig that he was, loud, whisky-ridden snores shaking his big belly. Alloma and I shared a bed, and neither of us wanted to sleep in the outside spot, away from the wall, because then we were more accessible to Uncle Phil.

Things hadn't really changed between Alloma and me since the crash. Mum's years of using 'divide and conquer', together with our very different personalities, meant we were never close. Mum keeping me in the wheelchair, even though I should have been able to walk, added another layer of secrecy that I couldn't break; it was a secret that kept me bound to her and even more isolated from my siblings. Nevertheless, Alloma was my sister and I loved her, with all my heart. No matter what Mum did, or made us do to each other, all three of us demon siblings tried to remain a unit; we tried to cover each other's backs when we thought we could get away with something; we wanted to protect each other. So I was on Alloma's side one morning when, sometime after the canal trip, when I was sixteen and Alloma seventeen, Mum called us both to the van and bundled us inside for a trip to Bristol.

Alloma and Mum had been rowing a lot lately. They had always rowed, of course, because Alloma was feisty, but things had been very bad in recent times. I didn't see a lot of it because of being banned from the farmhouse: I was always outside in my wheelchair, or in one of the unheated outbuildings. Now, from my perspective as an adult, I think maybe Alloma was finally getting too much for Mum to handle. Perhaps Mum was finding it harder to control her now she was growing up, and that feisty spirit was no longer encased in a little girl's body, but in a very nearly fully grown one – albeit one that had been weakened by years of beatings and starvation. Whatever the catalyst, the trip to Bristol wasn't just a random day out.

Mum was planning to abandon Alloma – and she was making me her accomplice.

I never thought she would go through with it. For a start, wouldn't Alloma tell? Wouldn't she rush straight to the nearest police station and spill the beans about the beatings, and the sticks, and everything else we had gone through? My mother was a woman who loved control, and to orchestrate an unpredictable situation like this seemed very out of character. But I think Mother reckoned she had done her work well in the ten or so years Alloma had been with us. I think she was convinced Alloma wouldn't dare tell; she wouldn't know how.

Arriving at a youth hostel in the middle of the noisy city sometime in 2002, we all got out to have a look around, and Mum paid for just a couple of nights in advance. She didn't leave Alloma any other money. In fact, she patted her down before we left, just to check she hadn't stolen anything from the farmhouse.

Then she made me search her, too. And that was just the most awful thing: I was so frightened for Alloma, so scared she was being left behind. I was scared for me, too, if I'm being completely honest – I didn't want to be without her. She was the only girl besides me now, my only sister, and she was one of the 'grown-ups' in our strange sibling set-up. What would it be like without her there?

I couldn't look at her as my hands patted down her orange anorak, double-checking she hadn't secreted anything away to help her in her life on the 'outside'. She was clean; she'd taken nothing. And I felt like I should protect her, help her, but I didn't know how – and so I did nothing. Nothing but run my hands down her sides, and rifle my fingers through her pockets. It makes me feel sick to say that.

Mum watched with satisfaction as I searched her, as though she was trying to destroy any relationship between us and was proud of her years of handiwork. I didn't cry as I did it, even though my heart was breaking. I'd learned not to show any emotion: it just gave oxygen to what my mother was doing, and she needed no encouragement.

Once it was clear Alloma had only the clothes she was standing up in, Mum put me in the van and then jumped into the driver's seat. She drove off without a backwards glance, leaving her teenage daughter alone on the doorstep of the hostel. I tried to watch my sister for as long as possible, until she faded from my sight, and I sent a silent prayer towards her.

I hope you say something, Alloma, I thought, *I hope you can get us out of here.*

I was sick with worry for my sister, day and night. Her leaving didn't make me want to leave; I found my mum's abandonment of her frightening. My mind ran wild with all the different varieties of trouble she could get herself into, as a vulnerable young woman alone in a big city. It was just terrifying. And of course I couldn't ask Mum about her, or how she was doing. Alloma was now an outcast to the family; her name was mud – it couldn't even be mentioned.

Time passed. With it, so too did my hopes that we might be rescued. It took me a long while to come to terms with the fact that Alloma was out but nobody had come to save us: it made me feel sad, like she didn't care about us. It didn't mean I didn't still love her, and of course I had no comprehension of the battles she herself was fighting. In fact, I thought in the end maybe one of the awful scenarios I'd imagined in my head had happened, and that was why she hadn't said anything. Ultimately, though, I think 'protect Mum' mode kicked in, that and 'protect Alloma' mode: she did what she had to do in order to survive. She said nothing.

But she and Mum remained in touch, unbeknown to me, and one day Mum mentioned her name again, for the first time in a year or so, with a very odd smile on her face. She told me Alloma was going to have a baby. And she said to me with glee, 'Your sister's not going to be able to feed the baby and look after her properly. I'm going to buy her some new baby clothes, and I'll give them to her when I see her. And then we'll see where we are.' She went off to the posh baby shop in Tewkesbury, the Orange Pig, to get some presents – presents that were intended to communicate to Alloma, just as Mum had told Alloma's own mother all those years ago, that she was better able to look after the child, that she could give her all these lovely clothes and many more opportunities besides, and wouldn't it make things easier if Mum just helped her out here and there…?

I'm sure Alloma wouldn't have fallen for it in a million years, but it still chilled me to the bone to hear Mum talking about my sister's baby in that way. In the end, something awful happened, which distracted Mum's attention from her potential new recruit.

I remember her coming home from Nanny's house one day. She pushed my wheelchair up against the wall, my head slamming back into it, and then held me in place, her fingers round my neck. Without ceremony, she said bluntly, 'Nanny's got cancer. And it's probably your fault because you made me fight with her, and you've made her ill. Ever since you walked into this house, you've been nothing but trouble. We used to be such a happy house. You've come into it and destroyed our lives.'

I believed every word she said, my guilt growing tenfold as I realised I had poisoned the one person I had ever truly loved.

It was horrible going round to see Nanny; she looked so frightened. I was so worried about her; I wanted to help but I didn't know what I could do, because Mum controlled everything. I couldn't even try to show her my support in my eyes because Mum would pick up on that and beat me later.

Nanny was very sick; she had chemo- and radiotherapy and was in Gloucester Hospital a lot. My granddad was still struggling along in his own wheelchair, struggling even more with my nan being so ill, and so in the end my brother Christopher was sent to stay with them, to care for them both.

In truth, I think Mum was pleased to be rid of him. Like his sister before him, he was getting a bit out of control now, this fifteen-year-old boy who was just starting to stand up for himself. If she said, 'Don't do x, y or z' to Chris, these days he would do it, regardless of the consequences. It was best for him to be out of the way.

Best for him and her, maybe – but definitely not for me: for with both my siblings gone, all my mother's rage fell on me. For more than a decade she'd had three demon children to vent her anger on. Now, there was only a so-called cripple girl in a wheelchair, and I took the full brunt of her fury – as well as having responsibility for all the chores, and thus even more opportunity to mess up and incur her wrath. Cooking, caring for the animals, looking after Adam: I had to do it all, and on impossible schedules, too. We had seven cages at George Dowty; rabbits and hamsters and guinea pigs, dogs and cats, the snake and the parrot, a goose and a duck, and rat infestations everywhere you looked. I had to do everything, in my wheelchair, without using my thin, spindly legs to walk a single step.

My legs were the only thin things about me these days. For some reason, Mother had stopped the starvation punishments. And so, stuck in my wheelchair all day, every day, with no hope of exercise and not a whisper of physiotherapy, relying on a cocktail of pills that made my weight balloon, I grew fatter and fatter – until the charity-shop clothes I pulled over my greasy head and used to cover up Colin were a size eighteen. I was a fat cripple girl, but my larger size was no deterrent to my mother, who would still fling me to the floor as though I was a rag doll when she was displeased. She'd kick me out of the chair and I literally just became her punchbag because she had nobody else. I was taking it all on my own; it was a very lonely place to be.

Adam was no help either. Sometimes, out of desperation or hope, I'm not sure which, I would bravely try to walk in the kitchen when she wasn't looking, or I'd slip the metal feet pieces off my chair, so I could put my feet flat on the ground and pad them up and down. But Adam had found a little spyhole spot on the stairs, from where he could see into the kitchen, and sometimes, depending on what mood he was in, he would tell on me.

Mum would go absolutely mad. 'You're building up the muscles in your legs!' she'd cry in a rage. She knew there was no medical reason why I couldn't walk, so she wanted the muscles in my legs to waste away – so much so that there would eventually be proof as to why I could never walk again. She'd snatch up the heavy metal foot pieces and slam them into my shins, over and over. Oh God, that pain. Right on the bone. Bruises and cuts would blossom beneath my dirty tracksuit bottoms.

Even though the starvation punishments had stopped, and the stick beatings, and even the drownings because I never went upstairs, Mother still had plenty of tricks up her sleeve. She loved to strangle me in the chair. The wheelchair was about the same width as the hallway in George Dowty, and she'd grab me by the neck and push me, and me and the chair would roll back down the hall, the walls flashing past on either side of me, and she'd ram me into the wall and my head would smash with a loud *crack* against it. She'd put both her hands around my throat and choke me. If the hot food I'd cooked was not to her liking, she'd throw it in my face. She'd use the sandpaper, and the beaded whip, and the living room door, and her hands and feet and fists. She liked to stab her car keys into my skull and twist them into my scalp. I was just the right height for that, seated in my chair.

She still loved to play with my mind, too. One day she asked me, as though proffering a gift on a silver platter, 'Would you like to see your real mum and dad?'

I made the mistake of being honest. 'Yeah,' I said.

She slapped me hard across the head. 'That's the wrong answer,' she said coldly. 'I'm your mother. *I'm* your mother!'

I just ducked my head and took it. Unlike my brother and sister, I never once stood up to her. Over the years, I had become a chameleon, adapting to survive, and so, to try to avoid being hit – even though it rarely worked – I went along with whatever she said, scared out of my wits. By now, I couldn't even stand up on my own two feet without her striking me, so I hadn't a hope in hell of finding any other kind of strength.

At night, she and Adam would go upstairs to their room. Adam was twelve now, but they still shared a bed. His voice might have been breaking, but Mother tried desperately not to break the spell of his childhood. He couldn't tie his own shoelaces; he didn't know how to read. She kept him as young as she possibly could – it was all about control.

They'd go upstairs, and I'd be left downstairs in the dark, in my chair. She'd call Jet up to her and he'd obediently lollop up the stairs and lie down beside her bed. But then, once her snores reverberated around the house, he'd sneak back downstairs to me, to where I'd be lying on the hallway floor, covered over with a stinky, filthy old duvet. He'd come and lie by me and I'd hug him for warmth, but inside my heart would still be cold.

For the depression I'd felt in the hospital had never lifted, not in all these years. Why would it? I was still a murderer; still the scum of the earth. And now I was a demon child with not even any other demon children to be beaten alongside. I missed Alloma and Christopher; I missed them desperately.

Night after night I lay in the dark, hugging Jet, and I thought about his leads hanging up by the back door in the kitchen, next to the coats. And I thought how easy it would be to slip one of those leads around my fat neck, throw the other end up to the light fitting in the kitchen … and end all this. How very, very easy.

And it was so very, very tempting.

CHAPTER TWENTY-FOUR

'Please can we go, Mother, please, please, please, please, *please*!'

Adam's loud, whiny voice begged my mum to allow him to attend a Jehovah's Witness meeting on his own – well, with his nanny/chaperone too, of course. She would never have let him have complete independence.

What Adam wanted, Adam always got.

And so the two of us found ourselves out one afternoon – out without Mother – in the spring of 2004, with Adam pushing my wheelchair to the bus stop for our first taste of freedom. We had to get a bus to the Kingdom Hall. It was only a short journey – maybe ten to fifteen minutes – but it was a hugely daunting prospect for two teenagers who had never been schooled. I had just turned eighteen, but I had no clue how to read the bus timetable, or sort out our money for the fare. Mum was no help at all; she'd just say, 'You're eighteen, you're an adult, you should know how.' But I'd never been shown, I'd never had any money of my own, and it was tough to figure it out. I felt a real sense of achievement when we got on the right blue, orange and white bus, and the driver gave me the tickets and my change, and we arrived safe and sound at the hall, having navigated the confusing maze of streets with signs that I could barely read.

Adam and I went to the meetings every week. When we got home, Mum would have returned from her renovations at the farmhouse to grill us as usual. 'What did you say? What did they say? Who did you see? How long were you there? Tell me *exactly* what happened.'

To begin with, I never said a word at the meetings. I rarely spoke anyway, and there seemed no point; not when Adam was there to do the talking for both of us. People would ask me a question, and he would answer for me. It was so normal to the pair of us that Adam's opinion would be the only one worth hearing, and I was just to shut up and sit there.

But then a strange thing happened: people said they wanted to know what *I* thought. Some of the Witnesses would even tell Adam off for talking for me. They would say, 'Will you let your sister talk now, please?' Or, 'No, I asked your sister first.' And they spoke to me with respect.

It was the oddest thing I had ever experienced.

Over time, I started to get to know some of the Witnesses a bit better. There were some young girls my age at the meeting, and also some older women to whom I was drawn, including one of the elders' wives, Jackie. The girls and the women would talk to me and, eventually, I started to talk to them too, very hesitantly. Without Mother around to remind me constantly, 'Look down, look down,' I dared to meet their eyes, and even venture a phrase here and there.

There was one girl I really liked: she was a pretty blonde called Amy, who was training to be a nursery nurse and loved children as much as I had always loved my dollies. When, a few months after our first meeting, Adam got permission from Mum for us to go on ministry, knocking on doors, I plucked up the courage to ask Amy if I could go with her.

As it turned out, she already had something else on, so she apologised and said she couldn't make it. I looked at her mum, Judy, and said, 'Can't you make her go?'

Judy looked back at me with a surprised and even horrified expression on her face. 'No, Victoria,' she said, almost wonderingly, 'of course I can't make her go. She's a young woman, it's her choice, she can choose. I can't make her do anything.'

I didn't realise at the time the impact that exchange had on me, but I went away and it bugged me a lot: *She's a young woman, it's her choice, I can't make her do anything.*

I was a young woman, too. But I never had a choice, never ever. Or did I?

I was sitting at the back of the Kingdom Hall, my wheelchair parked in the shadows, with Adam sitting by my side. Mum had beaten me the day before, her fingers wrapped tight around my throat as she had screamed and spat in my face, and purple bruises shaded my fat white neck, one for each of her fingers. Red pockmarks studded the skin where her dirty fingernails had dug into me; already the bloody holes swelled with pus and infection, painful and sore.

Whenever my bruises showed, I made Adam park the wheelchair out of the way in a room at the back of the hall, where we were less likely to attract attention. Usually I could cover up the marks with a jumper, nice and easy, but Mum had really lost her temper yesterday and my bruises could be clearly seen.

The visual evidence of the attack didn't bother her in the slightest, though. She'd looked me up and down just before we left the house that day, and told me with sly cunning, 'If anybody asks, just say it's your brother, Christopher, who did it. He's naughty. We'll all say it was his fault.' Christopher was still living with Nan and Granddad; Nan had now been given the all-clear from cancer, but with Granddad's health in continual decline, Christopher had stayed there to care for them and so we barely saw him. I'd just nodded meekly as my mother gave me my instructions, wheeling myself out of the house and down the road.

The meeting finished, and I saw Jackie watching me from the side of the room. She caught my eye and left her husband, Duncan, to come over to me. As she reached my chair and bent down, I saw her eyes flickering over the marks on my neck.

'Are you OK, Victoria?' she asked, concern heavy in her voice.

My eyes dropped automatically to the floor, and 'protect Mum' mode kicked in. The instructed lie was ready on my tongue, plump as a poisoned plum, but I hated blaming my brother; it was the worst thing in the world. I didn't mind saying I'd fallen out of my chair or that something had fallen on me – those kinds of untruths I'd grown up with; they came to me as naturally as breathing – but when I had to blame another human being, an innocent, that felt very wrong. Naughtily, I swallowed down the lie and said instead, 'I fell out of my chair.'

'Again?' Jackie asked, her eyes looking closely at the bruises, though I didn't see that: my gaze was fixed firmly on the floor, dishonesty like a thick cloak around me, keeping Jackie's warmth and kindness out.

'I'm very clumsy.'

Jackie nodded slowly, and then stood as another Witness came over to us.

'Can I offer you a lift home again, Victoria? Adam?' he said. That was Daniel – he'd taken to giving us a lift home regularly, saying it must be so difficult for us to catch the bus when I was in my wheelchair.

'Thank you, Daniel,' I murmured, glad to get away from Jackie's questioning eyes.

He pulled up as usual at the top of George Dowty Drive. Mum wouldn't allow him to stop outside the house; it was too close – perhaps close enough to notice the curtains were always drawn, that the house stood too silent, sheltering its secrets. He had to park at the top of the road instead, and Adam and I would walk from there.

Mother wasn't keen on our new friends – not keen at all. Amy had asked me along to a girls' get-together but Mum wouldn't allow me to go. Even though the people we were spending time with at the meetings were devout Witnesses, Mum would purse her lips together tightly if Adam or I brought them up at home: she didn't want us getting close to anyone. Mum wouldn't let us spend time with other people if she could help it, certainly nothing beyond the strictly religious weekly meeting. She did everything in her power to make sure I looked as unappealing as possible, too, so no one would want to be my friend. She'd taken to hacking my hair off, chopping it off in mad blonde clumps at the back, just for discipline, as a way of controlling me in public.

In public now, I beamed at Daniel as he helped me into my wheelchair by the side of the road. I was very self-conscious about my smile – my two front teeth had been knocked out long ago by Mum, and, since the incident with the X-ray and the dentist, she didn't bother taking me to get them replaced anymore, so I had gaping holes in the line-up of my teeth – but I wanted to show him I was grateful.

'See you next week,' he said, tooting his car horn jollily as he drove off.

Adam and I made slow progress down the road, knowing Mum's interrogation awaited us when we got home. We got through it, with neither of us saying much. I think the meetings were a bit of a refuge for Adam, too, and even he wouldn't say a lot about it all when she asked him. That was fine by me. *The less she knows*, I reasoned, *the less I'm going to get hurt*. I didn't like being beaten.

It was when I came to lock up that night that the first sick sensation hit me: I couldn't find my keys anywhere. I looked and looked, but they had gone; I wouldn't be able to lock up. When Mum did her nightly inspection check, the door would be unlocked and my duties unfulfilled.

Sure enough, she fired a question at me as soon as she tried the handle on her way up to bed – and the door opened wide. 'Where are the keys, Victoria?'

'I dropped them in Daniel's car, I think,' I mumbled. 'I think they must be in the footwell of his car.'

'Well, you text him and tell him to get them back here right now.'

She held out her mobile phone to me, and I laboriously plugged in an apology and the request to Daniel. The phone beeped with an incoming message.

Got the keys. I can't come back right now, though. I'll drop them in tomorrow for you, is that all right?

'No, you tell him that is *not* all right! And you tell him he's not to come to the front door.' Mum wanted no one at the front door: she had to control everything.

But Daniel must have thought it ridiculous – and time-consuming – to wait for us down the road when he could drive straight up to the house. The letterbox flapped, an unfamiliar noise, as he posted the keys through it, and Mum went absolutely ballistic that he'd come to the door. You could smell the stench of the house from there, you see, and the smell betrayed the fact that she wasn't the perfect home-keeper and mother she presented to the world.

'Adam,' she said, in such a measured tone. 'Go down to Nanny's house, now.'

There was a beat once Adam had pulled the door to behind him, and then she went for me. She pulled me out of my wheelchair in the hallway and kicked and kicked me round the floor.

There was a lot more of me for her to connect with these days. Her black shoes pounded every inch of my body. She was wearing purple jeans and I watched her violet legs kick and beat me until I was a mash of purple myself. Then she moved on – on to beating me with a bit of wood; on to strangling me; on to poking me in the eye, and pulling my lips out so she could press them into what was left of my teeth. She hit me round the face and that's when I knew she'd really lost it: she punched me in the face until it was cut all over and my eyes were bloodshot orbs, streaming with tears from the pain, until I could barely see her raging face, her dyed black hair up in her ponytail, grey wispy bits falling out of the band as she beat me as hard as she could. She might have been getting older, but she was still as strong as ever, and no match for a cripple girl like me.

There was no hiding these bruises. When we went to the meeting the following week, even though I hid out in the room at the back, I could feel the watchful eyes not only of Jackie, but also Ruth, another elder's wife, searching over my face. They came and spoke to me with kindness, and I stuttered out my usual excuse about falling out of the wheelchair. I'm not sure they even tried to conceal their disbelief anymore.

Their kindness was the most confusing thing. Back home at George Dowty, while Mum and Adam watched TV in the living room and I sat alone in the hallway in my chair, I tried to work through the bewildering puzzle. *What the heck is going on here?* I wondered. *Mum has told me time and again, for eighteen years, that I'm the devil's child, that I'm evil. But if that's true, then why are Jackie and Ruth being nice to me?*

I was confused, and depressed, and so lonely. That night, lying on the floor beneath my dirty duvet, I turned to the person I'd been hearing so much about at the meetings. I turned to God.

'Dear God, please help me,' I whispered under my breath, hot tears pricking at my swollen, black eyes as I prayed. 'Am I good? Am I bad? Please help me. *Please* help me. Please help me understand.'

Because – for the first time in my life – I was seeing a difference: a difference that made no sense. A difference between the way I was being treated at home, and the way the Witnesses treated me.

But … I almost didn't want to see what I was seeing – because, if what was happening at home *was* wrong, then I had no idea how I was going to get out of it.

So many times Mum had read the rulebook to me: 'No one will believe you. You come from foster care, you're a troubled child

– who's going to believe you, especially over me? I'm a wonderful mother.' It was as if the cards were stacked against me and her authority was all-powerful. For eighteen years I had watched her manipulate and control every official she'd ever come across. I couldn't, for the life of me, see a way out.

Well, there was one way. I heard Jet stir above me and come padding down the stairs. There was his dog lead; there was a way out if I really wanted to take it.

I pictured looping the lead around my neck, my legs kicking out a chair, and then kicking of their own accord as the noose tightened around my throat. I pictured Mum finding me … or Adam. Oh, Adam. How could I leave him? Because without me here, would she turn on him? Would she? Anything was possible when it came to my mother. I couldn't bear that; I really couldn't bear it if she hurt yet another child, all because of me.

Jet flopped down beside me on my pillow with a heavy, doggy sigh and snuffled his black snout into my face.

Please God, I thought again, *please help me. Am I good after all? Can it possibly – possibly – be true?*

Jet licked the tears off my face with his wet pink tongue. And I thought to myself, as my mad, muddled thoughts swirled crazily round my head: *Something's got to give*.

CHAPTER TWENTY-FIVE

I squinted in the September sunshine, my back protesting as I leaned down in my chair to adjust the flowers on my sisters' graves. We made a pilgrimage every year on the anniversary of their deaths to leave floral tributes to them: yellow freesias for Judith and pink roses for Charlotte. Charlotte had loved pink roses, as pink as her cheeks and her array of pretty dresses – which were still hanging up in the closet in her locked room at home, never to be worn again. I was still so confused by my sisters' deaths, and by the new world I was experiencing each week at the Jehovah's Witness meetings.

Jumbled thoughts ticked over constantly in my head, fuelled by the humanity I saw in people's eyes at the Kingdom Hall, by the concern I heard in their voices, and the love I saw them show each other, even me; these husbands and wives who had families of their own and tickled their children rather than beat them, who chased their toddlers round the Kingdom Hall with delight, and not a desire to hurt them.

Each day I felt like I was getting stronger, that blinkers were falling from my eyes. I even found the courage to tell Mum about Uncle Phil, and what he had been doing to me. It was a brave thing to do because she didn't want any of us children knowing anything about sex; what I'd learned had been from Phil alone. But one day in the van, when it was just the two of us, I told her what had been happening.

She looked me up and down as I sat in my wheelchair. 'Well,' she said at long last. 'At least you're good for something.'

I don't know what I'd expected her to say, but that wasn't it. It was almost praise. Almost. And even though I knew what she was like, her words still cut me. What Uncle Phil did to me sickened me so much. Despite everything, I'd still thought that maybe my mother would help ... fat chance. I think she did shout at him, but that just made me feel guilty for causing tension in the family.

Of course I was good for laundry, too, as well as countless other jobs. I did all the washing at home, making sure Adam's princeling outfits were clean and ironed and came complete with all their fussy accoutrements. One cold winter's day in December 2004, as I went to hang the washing outside amid the bare-branched trees, my heart pounded in my chest when I saw that a rogue blue sock had dyed the entire wash a sapphire shade: I would be in for it now.

I thought quickly, then wheeled myself up the garden and put all of Adam's posh French thermal pants in a bucket of bleach. Perhaps I could dye them back. You could smell bleach everywhere – the scent of it made my throat contract in memory of all the times Mum had forced it into my mouth to be swallowed down – but I hoped it would do the trick.

I left the clothes for a day and then rewashed the whole lot. That distinctive odour still emanated from the washing, though, and Mum was no fool.

'Have you used bleach?' she asked me crossly, when I brought the washing in.

'No,' I fibbed.

'Don't lie to me! I'm not stupid. You have, haven't you?' She dragged me out of my wheelchair and kicked me hard. She pulled me up the stairs by my short, hacked-off hair and then threw me back down. 'You're such a lying bitch. You're deceitful. You're sly.' Kick. Kick. Kick.

By the time she'd finished, my face was a kaleidoscope of contusions and cuts. It would be another backroom setting at the meeting that week; something I could really have done without. I felt like the pressure was mounting at the Kingdom Hall. More and more people were asking me if I was OK. I'd seen Jackie whispering to her husband Duncan, and Ruth chatting to her husband Mark, both casting worried glances in my direction. Jackie had even come round one day, to ask Mum about the bruises.

'We're all concerned,' she'd said on the doorstep, as Mum narrowed the door opening to a slim slit, so Jackie couldn't see the chaos inside. 'Where are all these bruises coming from? Why are there strangulation marks around her neck? Adam and Victoria have said it's Christopher doing it. Is it Christopher?'

Mum had smiled thinly and she'd concurred obliquely, 'Yes, mainly.'

'What do you mean, "mainly"?' Jackie had asked, shocked.

'Oh well, you know, Victoria's autistic. She's a very clumsy girl, she's always falling over.'

The door had practically been slammed in Jackie's face after that, and she'd had to leave. Nevertheless, each week I could see she was still thinking about it – and that made me very nervous indeed.

The final song and prayer faded out in the Kingdom Hall, and the main room started buzzing with the noise of chatter as the congregants milled and gossiped together. Now that the Bible study part of the meeting was over, I let Adam run off from our shared position in the back room to go and meet with the other Witnesses. I sat quietly on my own, keeping my head down, lest anyone should pop their head round the doorway and see me sitting there, bruises all over my face.

My mind ground over the same topic as always, these days. Something had to give.

You're going to have to kill yourself, or you have to say something.

But I can't leave Adam.

But you can't keep on living like this.

I looked up as I heard a smart tap on the door. It was Mark, Ruth's husband. One of the elders of the church, he was a tall, well-respected man in his early thirties, with a parting right in the middle of his neat, dark hair. He smiled at me as he walked over to my wheelchair.

'Hello, Torrie,' he said.

'Hi, Mark,' I replied, dipping my eyes out of habit.

There was a pause, a long pause, as though the world had stopped turning. I could hear the chatter out in the main hall. When I looked up again, Mark had his eyes fixed on me. My beaten face was reflected in the shiny brown of his irises, and he looked so pained; he looked so pained for me. He let the pause linger as we stared at each other, two still statues motionless in the hall, as the other Witnesses chatted and bustled about, some popping into the back room every now and again, but none of them disturbing us. I held Mark's gaze for a long time as he watched me silently.

'What's going on?' he said at last.

My brain disengaged. It wasn't a conscious thing, what happened next, but my mouth opened and I heard myself saying, 'She's been hitting me.'

Disbelief. Utter disbelief at myself.

I saw the same emotion in Mark's eyes: disbelief – just as Mother had said.

And I thought: *He doesn't believe me. He doesn't believe me.*

I opened my mouth to speak again. It was so important that I made him believe. 'You know, it's been going on for a while.'

Still, those shining eyes looked shocked.

'You know, I'm not making this up. It's been going on for a long, long while.'

Shit, shit, shit, shit, shit. My brain caught up with my mouth – but it was too late. *I'm going to get in trouble*, I thought. *I've betrayed her. Oh my God. I've betrayed my own mother. Guiltguiltguiltguiltguilt* pounded through my veins, pulsing harder with every heartbeat. *Traitortraitortraitor. You're sly. You're deceitful. You're the scum of the earth.*

I could have cried.

Mark found his voice. 'Stay here,' he instructed me. 'I'm going to speak to the other elders, I will be right back.'

I sat there, terrified. Absolutely terrified. I didn't know what was going to happen next.

Before too long, Mark returned. He was with Duncan. I was glad it was those two. Out of all of the Witnesses, I trusted them most. Both elders of the Kingdom Hall, they always took time to speak to Adam and me. Duncan was a wise man – older than Mark, in his forties – and what I liked about him was that, like me, he never spoke unnecessarily. When he did talk, there was a purpose behind it, and wisdom: he was a genuine, kind person. He had a gruff voice, but it was very gentle.

He spoke to me gently now. 'Mark's told me what you've said, Torrie. Why don't we go somewhere a little quieter and you can tell us all about it?'

Duncan and Mark took me into a smaller room, away from everybody else. They kept Adam out, busy with cups of squash and biscuits in the main hall. And I talked. Once I'd said it, that first time, I thought, *Well, there's no going back now.*

It was terrifying, so terrifying, and surreal. For so long, I had had to pretend not only that everything was A-OK at home, but that I couldn't properly communicate, autistic twit that I was. Now, I found my voice. I stared straight ahead and I told them in a plain, straightforward way exactly what was going on.

I told them about Christopher and Alloma, too.

I told them about the sticks.

And as I spoke, I listened to my mother's voice ranting in my head: 'They're not going to believe you! They're not going to believe you!'

I listened to that shriek, to that voice I'd heard for eighteen years ... and I kept on telling. I was completely numb. Emotionally detached. It was almost as if I was reciting a shopping list, or telling them a mundane anecdote over a cooling cup of tea. I shed no tears. I was almost not quite with it, as my mother's voice ranted and raved inside my head, and my eyes stayed fixed on Mark and Duncan, on their kind eyes, on their horrified faces.

I remember Mark kept saying, '*If* you're telling the truth ...'

I remember feeling quite indignant: *Well, why would I lie?* It felt unfair, that I had to convince them.

But most of all, I felt so very, very cowardly; so disloyal. I felt like the worst human being in the world. Because I was betraying my mum – and not just her, but the whole family, too. What about my nan, whom I loved? What would this do to my poorly nan? How could I do this to my nan, to Adam, to MumMumMum…?

I sat there thinking, *You've made her like this. You've just got her into whopping great trouble as well. You* are *the scum of the earth.*

But still I kept on telling.

CHAPTER TWENTY-SIX

I was in that room for about an hour, as it all came tumbling out. Afterwards, they hugged me, strong male arms around me, trying to communicate it was going to be OK.

'How do you want us to deal with this?' they asked me.

I didn't know what to say. It seemed inconceivable to leave her. I might have been a legal adult, eighteen years of age, but I didn't feel like one: more like a nine-year-old, a five-year-old, even. For so long I'd been stripped of personality that I had no confidence in myself or my decisions whatsoever. Not a grain.

'We will help you if you want us to,' they said.

And I thought: *I want your help*. I knew I had no other option – it was this way or no way. There was no other way. I nodded silently, not trusting myself to speak.

'You're not to go home and let her know we know this. OK? Can you do that, Victoria?'

I nodded again, a little more strongly. After all, I had kept Mother's secrets for eighteen years; I would keep this one for myself.

I went and found Adam, and the two of us went home. It was so surreal. I don't think it had sunk in even to me what had happened. I kept quiet as a mouse, but that wasn't hard, or unusual; Mum never wanted to hear what I had to say, anyway. When I saw her, I felt numb. I was almost waiting for the moment when her magic eye would swivel in her head and pin me with a look as if to say, 'I know what you did' … but the moment never came.

The house felt strange – and so did I: no triumphalism, no relief. I felt scared, anxious, depressed. I didn't trust anybody; I didn't trust that it was over.

The elders had reassured me that they wouldn't speak to Mum about it. In the room at the hall I'd told them all about the time I'd told Nan, and what had happened, and they promised me they wouldn't confront Mum about it. My biggest fear was that Adam would pick up on something, but he seemed oblivious, noisily tearing about the house as usual, making demands in his imperious, little-king voice.

Adam and I kept going to the meetings, for a week or so afterwards. Every time, I went straight out the back to speak to the elders; Jackie and Ruth would be in the main hall, making sure Adam was kept out of the way. I told them more about what had been going on. It wasn't upsetting for me to describe what had happened – this was my life, after all, it was just normal to me – and so I was matter-of-fact about it as I recounted the torture of the past two decades, as off-hand as though I was outlining different types of cake on a coffee-shop menu. I could see they were horrified, though, and shocked. But I think they were also running over the facts in their heads, remembering all the times I'd appeared with bruises on my face, or even what I'd been like as a little girl at the Kingdom Hall – and my story was supported by those facts, by the plain, hard facts.

'When do you want to leave?' Duncan asked me, at the end of another session in the small room. 'When's a safe time for us to come and pick you up?'

There was only one time I could think of: when Mum took Adam to his horse-riding class (yet another outward symbol of her perfect motherly care). Though she left the two of us alone more often these days, supremely confident there was not a chance I'd make a break for it, I would never have walked out on Adam, leaving him in the house alone. It had to be when Mum was with him; that was the only possible time.

As it was coming up to Christmas, there was only one lesson left before the holidays. One chance to get away. Tuesday, 21 December 2004 was the only day I could leave my mum.

The day before, Adam and I were at George Dowty as usual. Mum was away at the farmhouse, spending my disability benefits on her renovations that never seemed to finish. Knowing she'd be out, Duncan rang me on the house phone and told me to pack my things up and put them out in the back alley for him to collect. All the while I could hear Adam running his toy cars up and down the wooden bit at the top of the stairs, where Mum used to like beating my bare feet with a crowbar, back when I could walk. I whispered to Duncan that I would do as he said, my heart thumping in case Adam overheard. But the toy cars kept on driving without him missing a beat.

What stuff I had was kept in black bin-liners in the kitchen. I threw some of my clothes into a black sack. Carefully, I packed the peach 'Katie' towel the nurses had given me at the hospital into another bag, thinking I could sleep one night without it: my last night in this house. Quietly, I opened up the ironing cupboard, where those long-ago photographs of my real brother were squirrelled away, and I put one photo of my blond-haired, blue-eyed sibling into one of the sacks. Then I crept outside and put the bags in the back alley, as instructed.

It was a strange, strange day. As Adam and I played together, his happy, unknowing face smiling up at me, I thought, *This is never going to happen again. I'm never going to be here with my little brother again.* I felt so sad; there was no happiness. It was as if I was leaving him. I was his anchor and his stability, because Mum had never cared for him like I did. Even I could see her mad way of bringing him up was doing more harm than good, so I tried as much as I could to counterbalance it. Without me around, who knew what she would do? I felt like I was abandoning him – just like all the adults I'd ever known in my life had abandoned me. That was the hardest thing to cope with.

'Where's my dinner?' Mum roared as she came through the front door, flinging a black sack onto the ground, where it joined all the other mess.

'It's ready, Mother,' I said, my eyes rooted to the bag. It was one of mine, I knew it; Duncan must have missed one. But I couldn't worry about that now.

After dinner and the clearing up, I prepared Mum's hot water bottle for her, ready for bed, as was our nightly routine. It was a more difficult task than you might think: the low height of my wheelchair made it hard for me to reach the kitchen surfaces, so pressing out the air from the scalding-hot bottle was tricky to do. I struggled with it, boiling water spitting in my face. And I didn't do it well enough. I posted the bottle through the slats of the stairs as she made her way up, so she could pick it up as she went, and then I heard her shout at me from her bedroom.

'You stupid, silly autistic twit!' she roared. 'My hot water bottle is full of too much air rather than hot water. You do realise, you stupid bitch, that I'm now going to wake up in the night, and I'm going to wake up cold. Well, you can sit up all night, can't you, so, when I need my hot water replacing, you can be awake.'

'Yes, Mother,' I replied obediently, as I had always done for eighteen years. She turned out the lights, and the house was plunged into darkness.

I sat in my wheelchair in the hallway, waiting for her to wake up. It was cold. My legs started tingling; I got pins and needles really badly in the backs of my legs if I sat still in the chair for too long, the blood supply cut off. Eventually, they went numb. And still I sat in the hallway, in the cold and in the dark, knowing this was my last night at George Dowty.

My brain wouldn't take it in. I knew only this place; this place, and the farmhouse. Everywhere I looked there was a memory. Mum pushing me in the wheelchair down the hallway, so my head would smack into the wall. The stairs I'd been thrown down so many times; the blank patch on the wall at the bottom where her favourite mirror used to be. The worn bit of carpet where, night after night, I'd sat on the invisible chair; the living room door where she trapped my fingers, over and over. This was my home.

In the end, Mum never woke up at all during that long, dark night. In the morning she came down to where I was still sitting in my chair, and kicked me hard in the shins. She had the hot water bottle in her hand, and she unscrewed the lid and poured the water all round me, as punishment. Then she clouted me round the head with the bottle, its stiff, hard neck a useful weapon, until my ears were all red and throbbing.

'Get out of my sight,' she told me with disgust.

And so I got on with the morning chores. First, I got Adam dressed, helping my twelve-year-old brother to pull on his skin-tight jodhpurs and his riding socks. I placed Mum's handbag by the door, ready for her. And then I paused. The other thing Duncan had said to me on the phone was that I should take some

ID with me. Well, I didn't have any ID, but I did know that my mother had a bank card in my name in her wallet. She'd set up an account for me at Barclays, into which my disability payments went; an account to which she had sole access. A bank card was a formal bit of ID; it was all I could think of to take. Quickly, before I changed my mind, I slipped it out of her wallet and tucked the purse back inside her bag. Then I parked my chair in the hallway, ready to wave them off to class.

It was hard not being able to say goodbye to Adam. I told him to have a nice time, lightly, trying not to let my emotions show, or cloud my judgement. Then my heart sank.

'Come on, Jet!' my mother cried.

I wasn't expecting that. She didn't always take the dog with her. I stroked him on his back as he went out the door. *Thank you, Jet*, I thought. I felt so sad that I didn't get to say goodbye, to give him one last cuddle, friend to friend.

And then they were gone. Duncan and Jackie weren't due to pick me up until mid-morning, at about 11 o'clock. I busied myself with my usual chores, looking after all the animals and cleaning out their cages, until I was interrupted by the ringing phone.

'Hello?' I said quietly.

'You silly bitch,' my mother said.

My heart started pounding.

'Where's the card? The card's not here,' she said. 'I'm at the petrol station in Pershore, and the card's not here. You stupid bitch! I told you to get everything ready for me.'

I couldn't even think fast enough to stutter out an excuse.

'You autistic twit,' she muttered with venom. And then: 'I'm coming back.'

CHAPTER TWENTY-SEVEN

I got straight on the phone to Duncan. 'She's coming back!' I cried. The petrol station was only a twenty-minute drive away.

'Stay right where you are, we're on our way,' he said, in his gruff voice.

I sat by the front door, my heartbeat loud in my ears. There was no time to think about leaving the house for the last time; all I could think was that I had to get out before she came home. As soon as I saw their navy-blue estate car come roaring down the hill, I opened the front door and sat waiting. Duncan and Jackie both leapt out to get me. They lifted my chair and me up and down the step, I slid quickly into the back seat and they folded up the wheelchair and slammed the car doors. Duncan drove off, foot floored against the accelerator, engine squealing. There was no sign of Mum.

We had done it.

They took me round the corner to Ruth and Mark's, where it had been agreed I would stay. Duncan pulled up at their apartment block, and we rode the lift together to their flat.

As soon as Ruth opened the door, she embraced me in a big hug, her thick, dark hair like a soft cloud around my nose. She was a very maternal woman, an Irish mummy of a little three-year-old girl called Megan, and she had plenty of love to go around. She'd been expecting me, of course, and there were tea and biscuits laid out on the coffee table in their living room.

What I wasn't expecting was to see my clothes everywhere. Duncan had dropped my black sacks off at Ruth's the day before and she'd gone through them all and washed my clothes and underpants, and they were all hanging up around the flat to dry, my knickers on the radiator where anyone could see them, and I felt mortified. I was very distressed to think she'd gone through my private things. She was only being kind, but it felt like an invasion of sorts, like nothing was sacred.

We all sat down and had a cup of tea, and ate sweet, sugar-coated Nice biscuits with the warm brew. Mark was at work, but Megan was dancing round us, happy as Larry. It was very surreal. We were all waiting for the aftermath, for the bomb to go off when Mum got home and pieced two and two together. They all wanted to protect me, but I was eighteen and there was only so much they could do. Ruth told me she had phoned the NSPCC about me, back when she'd first been worried about the bruises, but because I was legally an adult, they told her they couldn't step in. No one was sure what would happen next.

Duncan and Jackie left after their tea. Ruth said to me gently, 'Shall we get you in the bath?'

I must have been very dirty, though I wasn't aware of it at the time. After all, there was nowhere I could have a bath at home, so I never did. She gave me a black swimsuit to put on, and she sat with me as I lowered myself carefully into the steaming, fragrant water.

'I've got you these,' she said, and she showed me some shampoo and conditioner, and a new toothbrush and a flannel. I thought they were amazing – I'd never had anything like that of my own before.

Ruth offered to wash my hair, but I didn't want her to. I didn't mean to be rude; it was all just so overwhelming. I was eighteen, and I'd just left home, where my own mum didn't even bother with me, but now people were washing my things and wanting to wash me and I was very, very confused by their kindness and their interest in me. I didn't quite trust it.

Ruth was fine with my response, though. She told me to wash my hair at least twice, and then put on the conditioner, and she left me alone in the bathroom.

I rubbed the shampoo into my hair, its fruity smell so alien. My insides felt sick with worry and concern. For years and years my mum had got away with what she'd done, no one had ever stood up to her. From a tiny age, I had watched her walk all over people and get her way, but now, somehow, some crazy how, it was me who was sticking my head above the parapet, and saying it was wrong, and that I'd had enough. Me. This person who wasn't at all confident, who had no self-worth, no identity, who had not a single clue who the 'me' inside me was … this person was the one who'd actually done this. It was on my shoulders and that was absolutely terrifying. I was waiting for the earthquake to strike me dead, and it was so scary.

I was worried about Adam, too. I knew what it had been like for me when the others had gone: she had to have somebody to take her anger out on. He had always been a favourite, so he should be OK, but you never knew … All these thoughts were whirling round my head. It was killing me to know I'd walked out on him. *I should have been there to look after him*, I thought, *I was the only sane one there to care for him. He used to call me his little mummy, but I've abandoned him when I was supposed to protect him. I'm his big sister, and I've let him down. I've let him down.*

Not too long after my bath, the phone rang. It was Duncan, telling Ruth he'd just heard from Mum. When she realised I was missing she'd quizzed Adam and he had mentioned that I'd been speaking a lot to Duncan of late. She'd screamed down the phone at him, 'Where is she? Where *is* she?'

Duncan told Mum I was safe but I didn't want to come home. He didn't tell her where I was. I remember looking at Ruth and thinking she was so brave to have me in her home. Everyone was so scared of my mum, she was so intimidating, but Ruth had taken me in, here where her precious little girl also lived, and I thought that showed great courage. No one had ever done that for me before.

Ruth and Mark lived in a two-bed flat. Megan had had her own room, but Ruth had cleared it out in preparation for my arrival, so I could have my own space. She made it look lovely. I remember getting into bed that night, it being clean and warm, and the bedding smelled of fresh detergent and a mother's love.

Ruth came in and put a nightlight on for me, so I didn't have to sleep in the dark. She brought me a warm drink, a hot chocolate, but I found it hard to eat or drink anything. She bade me a good night's sleep, but I couldn't sleep that night, or the night after that, or even the one after that. The black sack Duncan had missed had been the one with the 'Katie' towel inside, my snug that I slept with every evening, and I felt bereft without it.

Yet what was really keeping me awake, more powerful even than missing my comfort blanket, was my overriding, all-encompassing, nauseating fear.

What would Mother do next?

CHAPTER TWENTY-EIGHT

Dear daughter,
I know I've not been perfect, but I'd love the chance to see you.
Can you meet me at Morrisons so we can talk about this?
    I love you,
    Mother

Dear daughter,
Your granddad's very poorly. Won't you come home? He and
your nan are so stressed out about you going. They've lost two
granddaughters and they've now lost you. You're going to kill
them, you're going to drive them to an early grave, you need
to come back home. They can't cope without you.

Dear daughter,
I realise now you've had a nervous breakdown. I shouldn't
have done what I did to you …

Dear daughter,
I'm sorry for everything I've done. I love you, Victoria. I
love you.

My mother's daily letters were messing with my head. Never, not
once, in eighteen years of living with her, had she ever told me she
loved me before. Was this the truth? Or was it the other her who
was real? I felt so confused.

I wouldn't agree to meet her in Morrisons, though, or anywhere else. I knew if I saw her … I knew the power she had. There was a place in my brain that she knew how to switch on and off at will, so I just couldn't see her – because if I saw her I'd go back, and I couldn't go back. I could never go back.

She didn't play the part of the caring mother consistently. Her daily letters – these hugely long, passive-aggressive missives stuffed full of emotional blackmail, written on both sides of pages and pages of A4 paper, and handed to me via Duncan – mixed nice and nasty: so the disorienting 'I love yous' were interspersed with more typical rants against my character, saying what a naughty child I was, how I'd always been a bad girl. Those letters were easier to read: more familiar; more like home.

She took to directing carefully crafted speeches at Duncan as she handed over her missives for me. 'She's only a child, Duncan,' she would say, utilising all her powers of persuasion. 'We want her at home – she's autistic, she needs to be here. I need to be looking after her; she can't look after herself.'

Duncan would tell her I was eighteen, and doing fine, and that they were looking after me. The Witnesses asked her to give me back my comfort blanket, saying I needed it because I couldn't sleep.

'I don't care, she's not having it,' said my loving mother. 'If she wants it that much, she can come and get it.'

She wanted me to come round because she wanted to get to me. For she knew that for me, quiet little me, to have left, this was something serious. Perhaps she'd been lulled into a false sense of security over the years, and thought her world would never come crashing down; she wanted me back so she could damn well make sure of it. But I was never going back there. I never wanted to wheel my chair up to that stinking doorstep ever again. And – though little did I know it – I was about to choose a path to make that wish of mine come true.

About a week after I left, I found myself sitting on the sofa at Ruth's, with her and Duncan there to give me moral support. I was eighteen, and a legal adult … but without the strength they gave me, I might not have been able to do what I did next. They had to be really strong for me because I was so brainwashed.

I picked up the phone and I dialled the local police station.

'Hello,' I said, and then I paused. How do you say it? 'My mother's been abusing me,' I said in the end. What else could I say?

A police officer, uniformed up with a stab vest on, came round almost at once. He was about to go tearing round to save Adam and Chris but I reassured him; I said she'd never once hit Adam, and that Christopher was safe at my nan's. Somehow, I knew we had to be careful about alerting my mum to me going to the police. It had to be handled so carefully. I had seen her walk all over the authorities before, including the cops. This time, we had to get it right.

The Witnesses moved me out to Hereford. It was as if I was under house arrest, living at Ruth's, because I couldn't go out in case Mum saw me. It was while I was staying with some other Witnesses there that I gave my first full police interview. Two female officers came to question me. Their names, funnily enough, were Victoria and Charlotte.

Victoria Martell was the lead officer on the case. A tall, broad woman with very dark hair, she was reserved and distant, but I could sense an inner strength to her. And I thought, *We're going to need every ounce of that strength, Detective Constable Martell, if we're going to bring my mother down.*

The officers spoke to me for a couple of hours at that first interview. At the end, they asked me if there was anybody else who might speak up about what had happened.

I hesitated. 'Well, there's my sister,' I said. 'You could try her. Her name's Alloma, she lives in Bristol.'

In the end, Alloma corroborated everything I'd said. I'd hoped she would, once the police approached her directly. It was easier for her that way, not having to make the call herself. It was incredible to know she backed me up because I could tell the officers had had the same initial reaction as Mark – disbelief. With Alloma now part of the case, too, I thought: *I told you what I said was right.*

The police started taking away Mum's letters to me. She was so confident she was actually making generalised admissions in them, strategically apologising for what she'd done. The police filed them all away, and they began to build a case against her. Although I still didn't trust them, not really, I had no other choice but to do as they said. I was under strict instructions to talk to no one, in case rumour of the case got back to Mum.

I didn't like being in Hereford, away from all my friends. It was so lonely. The only good thing was that every day I was away from Mum, I felt stronger. The more I didn't see her, and her cold, dark eyes, the more strength I gained. Every minute I wasn't in her company, and was with regular people, the safer I felt and the more confident I became – so much so that, in the end, I found the courage to discuss with Ruth if I might possibly move back to hers in Tewkesbury, where I thought I'd be happier. She agreed it was a good idea.

Once I moved back, Ruth tried to help me adjust to my new life. She kept telling me that I didn't need to watch Megan, or follow her around: 'I'm her mummy,' she said, 'that's my job.' I was so used to watching Adam – and being beaten if I did it wrong – that it was second nature for me to find myself a 'job'. She went through my clothes with me, and made me throw most of them out. 'That's mildewed, Torrie,' she'd say, or 'That's far too big for you,' or 'That's badly stretched.' Lots of my clothes were stretched in odd places, because of where Mum had grabbed me to pull me out of my wheelchair or drag me round the floor. Ruth gave me a pair of her old jeans to wear instead and that was quite a moment. I'd never worn jeans before. As I looked in the mirror at the trousers on my legs, I felt an unfamiliar pride in my appearance. I was barely eating, and the weight was dropping off me. I thought I looked … well, *good*.

Jackie helped me put my name down for a council flat. I'd have quite happily stayed at Ruth's forever because I was so over-whelmed by all the new experiences, but I knew that wasn't fair.

At the council offices, they asked me if I could walk at all, so they could determine the kind of accommodation I needed.

There was a beat, and then I said, 'Technically, I should be able to walk. Everybody says I can't but …' I swallowed hard at the treacherous words cresting over my lips, betraying the secret Mum and I had shared for so long, '… but I've just not been allowed to.'

'Well, shall we try to get you up, then?' said the lady brightly. 'We've got to try to get that going.'

Jackie and the lady stood on either side of me. I slipped the metal foot pieces of my chair to one side and put my feet onto the floor, the unfamiliar ground giving an odd resistance to my muscles. The women helped me stand, and I almost collapsed from the weight of the guilt that thundered onto my shoulders, as soon as I was up on my own two feet. I heard my mother's voice in my head: 'You stay in that chair, it's the least you can do! You caused that car crash, you killed your granddad's granddaughters, he's going to die an unhappy man now and the least you can do is get some money for him.'

Every single time they got me up, I felt like I was betraying her. Tears streamed down my face at my unforgivable disloyalty. Jackie kept telling me, 'You're allowed to, Torrie. You're allowed to now.' They had to really, really convince me that I wasn't being bad.

It took a good few physiotherapy sessions after that before I could leave the chair behind me. I had to build my muscles back up slowly, but also overcome the mental barriers, and my guilt. I thought I was so evil, just as Mum had said. Beginning to walk again threw up new physical problems, too. My hips were no longer aligned properly because of the crash. I had cartilage missing from one leg, and that caused grinding pain every time I walked. My right side would sometimes give way completely and I'd fall to the floor. But I was out of the chair; I was walking.

One afternoon, Mark came home from the Kingdom Hall with a gift for me. The Witnesses in our community were, on the whole, being very generous, leaving presents for me at the Kingdom Hall, or money for Ruth and Mark to help care for me. It was a very confusing time for most of them – one moment I'd been in a wheelchair, now I could walk; one moment I'd been living with my mother, now I wasn't, which was highly unusual for a young unmarried Witness woman, and yet it was a situation supported by the elders. Some Witnesses were nosy as anything, but only four were openly on Mother's side; most were generous and kind. So it wasn't a strange thing for Mark to hand me a gift upon his return. This one was in a big silver box, all taped up.

I unwound the reams and reams of tape and reached my hand inside. It was a big soft teddy, one of those grey bears, wearing a purple woolly jumper. I had always wanted a grey bear like this. When I'd been in the hospital, I'd wanted one of these more than anything. My heart skipped a beat.

I turned the bear over in my hand. It had a slogan on its jumper. The slogan said: 'To a very special daughter'.

I'd never heard Mum say that before. It was too much for me. Tears coursed down my cheeks. I felt so guilty for betraying her.

Perhaps I should see her, just once, I thought. *She is my mother. Doesn't she deserve better than this?*

I called Ruth over to talk it through with her. The pain and the confusion were tearing me apart.

Ruth listened quietly, but I noticed her hands were shaking in her lap. And then she said to me, 'Victoria, if you go back now, I will slap you, and I'm serious.'

And cruel as that may sound, if she hadn't said it, I might have gone back. *I might have gone back.* It stopped me because I didn't want to be hit, not again. I knew what that was like. But also, to see Ruth that angry, it made me realise: *This is wrong, what Mum has been doing. This is very wrong.*

No wonder the police were ready to arrest her.

CHAPTER TWENTY-NINE

I was lying in a hospital bed, my stomach aching. The surgeons had finally got me in to operate on Colin. He couldn't be reversed, not for the moment at least, but they'd refashioned him into a more manageable position, rather than the emergency one I'd had for the past four years. I had staples all down my stomach, and a morphine drip in my arm. Though the morphine made me nauseous and drowsy, I was glad it was there: it took the pain away.

My mobile phone vibrated on the hospital table in front of me, and I reached forward to answer it, my stomach protesting at the movement. It was Victoria Martell.

'Victoria,' she said, 'we've arrested your mother.'

I'll never forget those words. They were so frightening. I just thought, *She's going to know now. She's going to know what I've done to her.*

DC Martell wasn't finished yet. 'The police went in this morning and we've got both of your brothers out, but neither of them are saying anything about the abuse. If they don't say anything, they're going to be allowed back home. Our last option is to bring them to you.'

No pressure then.

A couple of hours later, my private room at the hospital, where I'd been placed for my own safety, was full to bursting with social workers and police officers, all waiting to write down the details of my meeting with my brothers. I heard Adam coming first, that loud, imperious voice carrying across the ward. Christopher didn't make a sound. Like me, he'd been conditioned to be quiet.

It was now early February 2005; I hadn't seen Adam in just over a month. I wanted him to know that I loved him and missed him; that I was there for him, no matter what. He was laughing as he came in, this really high-pitched, over-confident laugh. It was a nervous laugh, I could tell. I learned later that the police had stormed George Dowty in a dawn raid that morning. It must have been very frightening for him, seeing Mum arrested, and Adam looked as if he was still in shock. He was still wearing his pyjamas, these blue, grubby flannelette pyjamas, with dirt round the cuffs, and his dark hair was all greasy. I could see the filth now my blinkers had been lifted. Adam might have been a favourite, but he was never cared for by my mother.

Chris, in stark contrast to Adam's exuberance, was very quiet, anxious and unsure. I was desperate for him to admit what was going on. Not for me, because I knew now I was never going back. But for him – so he could see that life could be better, that we did, in fact, have options.

The first thing they said to me was, 'We hear you're walking.'

I nodded. 'Yeah, I am walking. It was Mum who was stopping me from walking.'

Dozens of pencils scribbled down the exchange. I found the official witnesses very intimidating. We were here to talk about these secrets, these things that Chris and I had never even really talked about together, they were intensely private – but here were all these strangers, writing down our every word.

Adam went off in the end, to play in the children's ward; he didn't want to know. But that was all right. It wasn't him we really needed to speak to. He'd never been hurt – not in that way, at least. It was Christopher I really needed to talk to.

He came over to my bed, and I looked him in the eye. I was his big sister, and I said quietly, 'I'm not going back.'

I let him absorb that. I knew I had to get my message across so quickly, that I somehow had to break down years of everything Mother had ever told us. That was no mean feat; when even I, who had been free for a month, was still hearing her words in my head, day and night. I spoke over the inner running commentary from my mum, who was busy telling me how worthless I was, and I said to my brother, 'Please, look at me. I've been out weeks, and I'm walking, and I've just had the surgery she wouldn't let me get. I'm happier than I've ever been, Chris.

'I'm not going back.'

We stared at each other across the bed. I knew those eyes so well. I'd seen them widen with shock; screw up with pain; be kind and helpful, solemn and sad. Those eyes had looked at Nanny's roast dinner with me, when we were both locked in that bedroom, naked and cold. Those eyes had watched me being beaten. I had watched those eyes be beaten back.

Christopher could tell that I was not messing about. Enough's enough. It took him a while, but gradually he … melted. That's what it looked like. He let out a breath and he said softly, 'I was in "protect Mum" mode.'

I nodded; I understood. And then he started to tell the gathered guests about the sticks down our throats. As soon as he said that, they took him out to another room and cross-examined him on his own.

I was glad he'd told the truth, but I resented having to be the one who made him do it, having to be the grown-up when I still felt such a child myself. It took its toll, that meeting.

As did the get-well-soon card my mother sent me. Oh yes, she was let out on bail, and she came straight to the hospital. Luckily she couldn't find my private room, though she wandered up and down the corridors searching, her distinctive black-and-grey hair tied up in a bandana. In the end, frustrated, she gave the card to another mother on the ward, and that mother gave it to a nurse, who gave it to me. I opened it up in innocence.

Love Mummy, it said.

I went cold. Because I knew what those words really meant. They meant: *I know where you are. I know what you've done. And I will get you.*

You may win the battle, but I will win the war.

The police continued to build their case while my mum was out on bail. They raided the two houses in their search for evidence to support our story. Our neighbours reported that Mum had tried to clear up after I'd left – and the police found traces of big bonfires of stuff that she'd attempted to burn – but she was a hoarder, and she'd been beating us for decades, and there was no way one old woman could get rid of it all, especially now she was missing her army of mini-slaves. So they found my teeth that she'd knocked out; she kept them in a container. They found chair legs and door wedges and those long, spiky sticks, all marked with the tell-tale semi-circles of children's teeth, with blood and saliva all the way down them, from where she'd shoved them in our throats. They found my notes with 'Will you be my new mummy?' written on them, from back when I was five.

They collected evidence from us, too. Us three demon children gave hours of interviews. I spoke almost begrudgingly in them, because telling the truth about what had happened went against every natural instinct I'd ever known. I'd spent my entire life trying to conceal it from people. I couldn't look Victoria Martell in the eye, though that was partly because I could see the hurt in her eyes, and that hurt made me feel sad, like I'd brought this horror to her door and was personally responsible for her pain. I told her about Uncle Phil, too, but we both agreed my mother was the priority and that the case against her had to be prosecuted first.

Victoria didn't write anything down. We gave the interviews in a special house where cameras were rigged in the walls, like on *Big Brother*; a special house where the police interviewed traumatised children in surroundings as normal as possible. I could tell which sections she found particularly relevant or important, though, and that was a strange thing about our story finally coming out. People paid attention to different bits; they placed greater or lesser importance on the various elements of our torture. For example, the officers and everyone else were particularly interested in the time when Christopher and I had been locked in the bedroom and starved. But for me that was just a very small thing, personally. I couldn't understand why people kept emphasising that. I mean, it was awful, but there were a lot worse things than that – the drownings, the sticks, the hundreds of beatings on my poor bare feet. The bedroom was only a couple of months out of nearly twenty years of torture.

They took evidence from our bodies as well as our mouths. I had to go to Cheltenham police station and take my clothes off while a female chaperone photographed my scars. It was all very cold and clinical, and I felt like a piece of meat in a factory. I remember thinking, *Why do I have to do this? Why do I keep having to go through horrible things all the time?*

The answer was, of course, because it would prove what I was saying was true. The only good thing about those photos was that I knew each scar, each missing tooth and each mangled bit of my body revealed the truth.

Another time I had to go back to Frenchay Hospital to have the back of my throat photographed, so they could collect evidence to support our claim about Mother putting the sticks in our mouths. I arrived to find Christopher and Alloma in the waiting room outside; there to have their own pictures taken. They were with their real parents, all happy families, reunited at last; after Mother had been arrested, social services had told their parents about their children's 'change in circumstances' and their parents had requested to see them; an initial meeting that had grown into regular visits and, eventually, a loving relationship. I told myself I was being selfish in feeling sad to see them together: *That's their mum and dad and you've got to be happy for them.* But I felt like I didn't know where I belonged, anymore. They had been my family, we'd been through so much together, but now they were moving on. I told myself I had to be positive for them. *Just because you haven't got parents doesn't mean you can't be pleased for them now that they're with theirs.*

I was called in for my photographs. It was a horrific experience: I had to sit in this dentist's chair and lie back, while they put a lollipop stick in my mouth to hold down my tongue and keep it out of the way of the camera. That lolly stick reminded me so much of the other sticks, pressing relentlessly on my tongue; I was so scared, I was hyperventilating. I tried to rationalise that no one was there to hurt me, and that I had to do it for the evidence. That's what they said to me: 'You've got to do this because there is so much evidence there. You need this.'

The whole way through I thought of Mum. I remember asking DC Martell afterwards, 'Did you see scars?'

And she said, 'Yes, we did. We did, Victoria, we did.'

They had got what they needed.

I moved out of Ruth's while the police investigation was going on. A council flat came up – coincidentally only a couple of doors down from Ruth's mum, Jill – so Jill and I went to look at it. It was like an empty shell when I first walked in, and I had no idea how I was going to make it a home, let alone work out how to pay my bills. But the Witnesses at the Kingdom Hall rallied round: they gave me rugs to lay out on the bare floorboards, and my new friends helped me to paint it.

One of my really good friends now was a Witness called Jo, who had had the party where her mum had passed me a present through the car window, and Mother had gone so mad. Jo and I had become close now that I was free to make my own friends; she had such a big heart, and she was always giving me hugs. She was artistic, and she stencilled bright purple tulips with green stalks on the walls of my new cream kitchen, and helped me paint my bathroom turquoise, my living room pink, and my bedroom a soft lilac colour. Ruth gave me a second-hand TV with a video player in it as a housewarming present, so I could watch videos on it; rom-coms like *Notting Hill*, where everything ends happily ever after.

Despite my friends' best efforts, though, the new flat didn't quite feel like happy ever after. For a start I really struggled with having to look after me – just me. After years of running round after Mum and Adam and the animals, I found it very hard not having somebody else to care for; I felt selfish, and I found being alone horrible. I didn't know what I was supposed to do with myself. I didn't even know who I was as a person, and all of a sudden I had to find out what I wanted to do in life; but with my future so uncertain, and Mum's case still ongoing, I couldn't make any choices, even if I'd known what I wanted to do.

I didn't feel safe, either. I told the police about my mother's card at the hospital, and warned them she would come after me.

'No, no, no,' they said, 'she wouldn't be so stupid as to do that.'

She did, of course. She started leaving pictures of Jet outside my flat, with bloodstains all over the photos, marking his black doggy face bright red. I came home to find bunches of dried dead flowers on my doorstep: the desecrated remains of yellow freesias and pink, pink roses. She knew nobody else would know what they were, but I knew: dead flowers from my sisters' graves, dead flowers for the dead.

And then, one Tuesday, as I made my way out of the flat to attend a meeting at the Kingdom Hall, the day I'd been dreading came.

Mum's white Volvo was parked outside my flat.

CHAPTER THIRTY

The car was empty. She could have been anywhere, waiting for me, watching and waiting. I took a photo of it from my kitchen window, because the police said they needed evidence to do anything about her continual harassment, and I phoned Jill to come and help. It was a relief when she said she recognised the car, too: confirmation that it wasn't just in my head.

The police arrested Mum, and released her – and then she went after my brother. I got a letter later that year, though, saying they weren't going to prosecute her for witness intimidation. It didn't make me feel safe at all.

I started having nightmares: violent, scary nightmares about my mum coming to find me, and about the old abuse. Her chanting, counting face, and the slam of the stick on my feet, and not being able to scream because my mouth was jammed full of hard, stabbing wood, pressing down on my tongue. I'd wake up in the night, in my new clean lilac bedroom, with that familiar feeling of a cold clamminess around my thighs. At least my mother wasn't around anymore to beat me for wetting the bed.

I went to my doctor, and he prescribed me antidepressants. I also tried to get some counselling, and was referred to a group who specifically helped survivors of child abuse, but they told me I couldn't receive counselling until after the court case was over, because I had to look like a victim for the trial. I'm telling you now that not everyone I saw was professional. It was such a severe case of abuse, it had gone on for so long and so many different agencies had failed to spot it, that lots of professionals, rather than helping me to come to terms with what had happened, instead took the opportunity to quiz me on how she'd got away with it for so many years, their eyes bright with academic interest.

At least I still got to see Adam, but it was with mixed feelings. It was usually at the Jehovah's Witness meetings, and also in attendance was my nan. She'd sit on one side of the hall and I'd sit on the other, and it messed with my head. We wouldn't talk to each other, and what hurt the most was Nan's studied indifference. I knew, in my heart, that it wasn't her fault, and that she did love me, really; my mum had just manipulated her. And not only for the past two decades, but even after I'd left; she had told my nan that I'd stolen that bank card, and she said I'd stolen all of her money. Even though it was my account, and I took the card for ID, not cash, in Mum's head it was *her* money, and she'd genuinely been robbed. So when the police had come to Nan's to take Christopher into care, and they told Nan that Mum had been arrested, she'd shrieked, 'It's that autistic twit's fault! She's stolen all of Eunice's money and driven her mad!' She still blamed me now.

No one could handle Mum's manipulation, least of all her own mother.

The pressure started to get to me. I didn't want to go to the meetings anymore, I was finding it too much, but my friends would say, 'Trust in God, God will get you through it.' It was as if my life was suspended, waiting for the court case. I couldn't sleep, I couldn't eat; the weight dropped off me. I felt guilty for betraying my mum, because I still loved her, despite what she'd done. You can't just turn off love like a tap. So my love still flowed like dirty water, drenching me in my disloyalty each and every day.

I felt like I didn't deserve any of my newfound freedom – the new dentures I eventually got to fill in the gaps in my teeth; the new haircut I had done, where the hairdresser asked me if my last haircut had been done by a drunken boyfriend, because of the chunks of hair missing from my head; the new flat; the new clothes; the new me. Who was I, anyway? I simply didn't know.

There was only thing I knew of that would make me feel like me again, I thought. Late one night, in the flat on my own, I smashed a glass in my pretty tulip-covered kitchen. I pulled up my top, and I sliced the clear translucent shard along my belly.

Blood followed the line of the glass, pure and simple: my old friend.

There I was. There was Torrie.

I watched the blood shine red in the kitchen lights.

The self-harming gave me a release: a release from the confusion. Even though I liked people being nice to me, it felt so strange, and so undeserved. Whereas, I thought I did deserve to be hurt. If no one else was going to do it, why shouldn't I?

I kept my new scars hidden, under my jumper. After all, I was an old hand at that; it came as naturally to me as blinking. I tried to get on with my life. The simplest things were a challenge. I remember the first time I went shopping in Superdrug: I didn't take a basket, but blatantly put my toiletries in my own bag before going to the till. I just didn't know how things worked; I had to learn as I went along.

I got myself on a basic maths and English course, but I didn't enjoy learning. I may not have picked up much from Mum's 'lessons', but the one thing emblazoned in my mind was that I would be beaten if I got something wrong, and so I found it very hard to unfreeze the bit of my brain that had to pick things up. I'd panic, and think, *The teacher is going to go apeshit if I don't get this right.* For a long while after I left Mum, I still believed I was autistic, too. After all, I had an official diagnosis from Great Portland Street, and it was what I'd been told for nineteen years.

In September 2005, I managed to get myself on a basic hairdressing course. I decided to choose hairdressing because I remembered how much I used to like brushing out Mum's hair, back when I was a kid and we used to spend those weirdly peaceful evenings together with me as her mini-beautician. The pleasure might have come in part from her being unable to stand up and hit me, a pleasure derived from feeling *safe*, but it was pleasure nonetheless, and it was about the only thing I could think of that I knew I enjoyed doing. But getting on the course proved a bit of a rigmarole in itself.

'What qualifications have you got?' the administrator at the college asked me, looking quizzically at the nineteen-year-old woman before her.

'I haven't got any.'

'You must have something,' she insisted, 'even bad grades.'

'Nothing, sorry,' I apologised, dropping my gaze in shame.

'Where have you been?' she asked, with palpable curiosity.

If only you knew …

Eventually, the college allowed me on a preparation-level course, aimed at youths who had played truant a lot at school. That was a scary experience: sharing a room with lots of confident teenagers who were swearing and mouthing off, with no respect for education or a desire to learn. They moaned so much about the course that it frustrated me to be around them. *You don't know how easy you have it*, I thought, *don't throw this education back in people's faces. You don't know how lucky you are.* They were also the most ballsy teenagers I'd ever met in my very sheltered life; I stayed apart from them, and kept myself to myself.

I can remember clearly the first time I mastered a French plait on the course. One of our teachers was quite strict, and I couldn't pick the style up under her tutelage. I recall thinking, *Mum was right: I am thick.* But then another tutor came over, with a different approach, and within two goes, I'd got it: it looked beautiful, and I felt very proud of myself.

Six months into my course, the teachers called me into their office. My first thought was that I was in trouble – any time anyone called my name I thought I'd done something terribly wrong – but they sat me down and said, 'We think you're very good at what you do and we'd like to move you up to the Level 2 course.'

I felt a strange pride in myself. I remember going home and telling Jo, 'You've got to have grades to get on that course!' I'd spent my life thinking I was the most stupid girl on the planet, but here were educated people telling me I could handle this higher-level course. I barely dared to believe it. *Not bad for an autistic twit.*

All through this time I was going in and out of hospital: the surgeons were making adjustments to Colin, or examining the impact of the pins in my hips, which had been inserted to help with my walking, or conducting various other operations and investigations. For four years, after a car crash in which I'd so nearly died, my mother had restricted my access to healthcare that I desperately needed, and it was going to take a long, long time for me to be well. Each new development led to further complications. I could walk again – but my hips were now too weak. Colin was adjusted – but the surgical scar from my latest op would then become infected. I was still taking my cocktail of daily pills, too: antidepressants for my mental pain, and morphine for my physical. It was hard to keep going with the course with all this going on, but I battled on and I did it.

And then, into this brave new world of mine, with its shifting tectonic plates of self-disgust and self-esteem, came a brand new kind of earthquake.

CHAPTER THIRTY-ONE

Victoria Martell sat me down one day and said, 'Victoria, I think you ought to be aware, whenever your case comes to court, it will be national news. You've got to be prepared.'

I didn't even know what the word 'national' meant. She explained that the story would be in every newspaper, and she also told me, in one of our chats, that my birth parents were local. And I suddenly thought, *My real parents are going to see this story*.

I wondered how that might make them feel: Spry was a distinctive name, so it was very likely they would know it was me who was the little girl involved. *If they find out they've given up their daughter to someone like that, it's going to be heartbreaking for them*, I thought.

I was curious about my parents. For twenty years I'd not been allowed to dream, or even think, about them. But, since I'd got out, I'd found out that what Mum had told me – about them being murderers and drug addicts – was completely untrue. In fact, even more than that, I found out that they had tried to stay in touch with me when I was a baby. Countless times Mum had turned them away on the doorstep of George Dowty, telling them firmly, 'She's my child now.'

Without the threat of the imminent media coverage, I'm not sure I'd have had the courage to find them, not so soon after leaving Mum, at least, but the ticking clock of the court case spurred me on.

I went to social services, and they agreed to help me track them down. The mediator's name was Carol: a lovely, beautiful woman with short, coppery highlighted hair. I liked her from the moment I met her. She'd been adopted herself, so she understood. She had dogs, too – two Labradors, Sam and Ellie – and I immediately bonded with her over that.

The most difficult thing was getting the search started. Carol asked me to give her my adoption file, so she could begin work on my behalf, but Mum had never given me any such file; I'd never even seen one in the stacks of stuff at George Dowty. Perhaps she threw it out or burned it, just as she'd got rid of all of Christopher and Alloma's childhood photos, so they wouldn't remember where they came from.

Carol was angry about the missing file – angry for me. 'You have a right to know this information,' she said. She told me the file was supposed to say where I was from, and it was usually a book filled with pictures and all kinds of other details. Sweetly, she tried to make me one herself, belatedly, cobbled together with what information she could find, but all she could muster was a single sheet of paper. Still, it was better than nothing. It was more information than I'd ever had before.

More than my parents, though, I wanted to find my brother. I knew my parents had given me up, so I thought there was a chance they wouldn't want to know me; I just wanted to contact them so they knew about the case, as I thought that was the right thing to do. But I had hopes for my brother, that blond boy who had written his notes and sent his photos so diligently for a couple of years. I had hopes he might want to be friends.

Finding my real family took a lot of patience. Carol had to find them, and then check they were happy to be approached by me, and then hurl the Molotov cocktail of my childhood into their front room. That knowledge, of them having to know, was hard for me as well: I felt instantly I was a disappointment, a nuisance, attached to this horrific case, which I'd been told would be splashed all across the papers, as sordid secrets are. I felt as if I was walking into their shining lives and stamping all over them with my muddy boots of grime and filth.

Nonetheless, my brother agreed to see me. We sent cards at first, and pictures back and forth. I told him I loved dogs, and I was thrilled when I saw he was wearing a T-shirt in one snapshot that said 'Dog Rules' on it. That was my big brother. It felt so surreal writing 'with love from your sister' at the end of the notes. He sent me a present from his holiday, a little blue stone heart necklace, which I loved, and I sent him back a slab of Thornton's chocolate with a card on it, saying 'to my dear brother'.

We met for the first time in a Pizza Hut in Cheltenham, maybe six weeks after our first letters were exchanged. I was sat there with Carol, waiting for him to arrive. And in walked this beautiful-looking lad, with piercing blue eyes. He was really tall and good-looking. *Gosh*, I thought. It seemed such a contrast to ugly old me.

His parents came with him. They were in their late forties: a nice middle-class family. His mum was really upset by the whole thing. She reached across the table to me when she arrived and said earnestly, 'We wanted to adopt you too, Victoria.'

I thought it was just a throwaway comment; the kind of thing a polite woman would say. I didn't realise they had genuinely tried to adopt me, not until much later, when I read my medical notes. It turned out that Mum had told people at the time that she didn't want me to be moved to a new family – because it would have upset me. She made everybody believe I was better off staying with her. It's sickening, really, but perhaps it's best not to dwell on what might have been.

I stood up and hugged my brother when he walked in. We felt a bit awkward, but a big part of that awkwardness was my unfamiliar feeling that I finally belonged somewhere; that he was mine. Mine in a way that Adam never had been; mine in a way that Christopher and Alloma had had together, but I had never known. Growing up with Mum, I'd always thought, *Torrie doesn't belong anywhere; Torrie doesn't deserve a family.* But I looked at Tom and I thought, *Wow, this is it then! I do belong somewhere, after all.*

Carol had told him and his parents about the abuse. I still kept a lot back, though – it's not the kind of thing you can bring up over a pizza. In fact, during our meal, I became more and more aware that Tom had had a normal life: a stable and loving, Christmas-and-birthdays kind of life. I grew quieter and quieter. How could I contribute to this conversation? I didn't want to frighten him off.

I found my necessary silence very hard, and very upsetting. I felt I couldn't just be myself; that I had to protect him. Even though he was my big brother, I felt I had to be the grown-up and keep him safe. I found it hard to talk about 'normal' things, because then I wasn't being me. 'Normal' for me was punches and kicks and being drowned in the bath. It was all very confusing.

That meeting went better than the one I had with my parents, though. I had a lot of sympathy for them, at first. Come on, I was the girl who had spent years planning her own suicide, who even now was on antidepressants and secretly slicing up her stomach.

I knew all too well what depression felt like. I didn't blame them one bit for giving me up, none of this was their fault.

Carol tracked them down, and my dad wrote me a letter. That was so weird, holding a plain white piece of paper with my dad's handwriting on it. I'd never seen that before; I'd never even seen a picture of them.

Carol had told them about the upcoming court case – and maybe that explained why it was such an awkward letter. There were no specifics in it. No 'we love you to bits' or 'we're proud of you' or 'we can't believe you're all grown up'. There was nothing much in it at all – just words on a piece of paper, nothing emotional.

Carol went round to theirs and took their picture for me. It was so odd, looking at it. My mum and dad, sat on a sofa, ordinary as steak-and-kidney pie, yet as magical as the fairies used to be to me. These were the people who had made me and put me on this earth. This was where I came from.

My mum was just in her fifties. She had thick, short brown hair, blue eyes, and the most beautiful skin. Dad was portly, with dark hair and brown eyes. The weirdest thing of all was that I could see myself in them, especially in my mum, in those blue eyes. Carol told me they'd had two other boys, after Tom and me, and they'd kept them; they hadn't given them up.

We arranged a meeting, at Butler's Cafe in Cheltenham. It was just the most bizarre feeling, waiting for them to arrive. In a way it was so unnatural, preparing to meet my parents for the first time at the age of twenty. My stomach was in knots, and I was frightened: frightened the court case would put them off, that they wouldn't want to know me. Carol tried to reassure me. The time ticked on. They were ten minutes late, then twenty, then forty-five … and then I knew they weren't coming. They had stood me up.

I said to Carol, 'I forgive them for giving me up, I forgive them for all that. I am more angry at them for doing this. When they know that I am sat here, waiting for them, watching the seconds tick by.'

Carol rang them, and they murmured, not even that apologetically, 'We couldn't manage it, sorry, it's a bit too much for us.'

She arranged another meeting, and then another, and they did the same thing again and again. I understood it was difficult for them, but it was difficult for me, too.

Carol finally got them to agree to a fourth meeting, this time at a meeting place that was just around the corner from their house. It was in a community centre-type place, in a room that she had arranged.

I was already sat in the corner when they arrived; corners of rooms were still my favourite places to be, where no one could hit me as they passed. For the same reason I lived in hoodie jumpers, the hoods pulled up over my blonde hair, offering thin cotton protection should anyone choose to wallop me on the head. Some habits die hard.

My parents came into the room, with my youngest natural brother tagging along with them. Carol had told me the older boy didn't want anything to do with me; he said I wasn't his family. I took that on the chin and tried to understand and be understanding, but it still hurt like hell. My littlest brother didn't really acknowledge me; he went straight over to play with the toys that were laid out in the room. He was only seven, though, so I don't blame him for that. It was extraordinary seeing him there. He had blond hair, too; he looked like me.

I stood up as Mum and Dad walked towards me. They froze in the doorway at the sight of me. Mum looked at me, nodded once, briefly, and then went to sit in the corner. My dad followed her. There were no cuddles or kisses, no tears of joy. No emotion at all, they just sat there. My mum barely uttered two words the whole time we were together, and that was hard, because it was her I really wanted to hear speak. She hadn't written me a single letter so I had no sense at all of who she was.

They didn't ask me anything, and I didn't say much back to them. There didn't seem to be the opportunity to ask them any questions, even though I was bursting with things I wanted to know. I didn't feel I could warn them about the case, or even tell them that I understood why they had given me up, and that I blamed them for nothing. There was just my dad, talking about anything and nothing, and my mum sat there in silence. It wasn't a meeting we repeated. There were to be no happy family reunions with my real parents for me.

My reunion with my mum's mum – my gran – was lovely, though. She'd written me one letter before we met, on proper thick cream writing paper with beautiful handwriting. That made an impression. We met in Butler's, with her turning up right on time. She was wearing a dark coat with a red scarf, and I remember when she kissed me her cheek was really cold because it was frosty outside. She hugged me and it was the weirdest feeling: *This is my real gran hugging me.*

She told me lots about when I was a baby. That's how I know I lay in my cot all day, without anyone to care for me. She said she would come round and have to change me or put a clean Babygro on me. Seeing me left alone like that really upset her, but, when she found out my parents had allowed me to be adopted, she was even more cross. I think she felt they hadn't pushed themselves; that they just did what they wanted to at the time, with no thought of the future.

She told me about the rest of our family, too: I had relatives in Scotland. I just found that so fascinating. I was so used to not being part of a family, and not belonging, that it was really surreal to think that somewhere, on a genealogical map, ancestral lines linked little old me to relatives north of the border.

I didn't see my gran often, but she'd write to me a fair amount. I treasured those letters on her trademark thick cream paper, as well as my brother's hastily scribbled cards, which arrived from time to time. My family ... the strangest thing.

Our reunion came at a particularly good time because, in that spring of 2006, I stopped seeing Adam and Christopher regularly. They no longer came to the Witness meetings – I think their new foster parents decided it wasn't healthy, or perhaps the boys themselves decided not to attend anymore. For me it was one more tie cut loose.

And still the court case didn't come to trial. Mum was delaying it as much as possible, of course: chopping and changing her legal team and using other tactics so the dates had to be put back, again and again. I'd get myself psyched up for the case, and then Victoria Martell would phone and say it had once more been delayed. That was so hard. I was living my life in a state of constant anxiety while we waited for it to come to trial, it was like a dark cloud hanging over me – because I was the one putting my neck on the line. Mum had manipulated so many people, and not one person had stopped her, not until I had spoken out. So I knew who was going to be in for it if she got off. It was really frightening. No wonder I was still having vivid nightmares, and wetting the bed nearly every night. The only good news was that, finally, she was arrested for witness intimidation, and remanded into custody until the case came to court. At that I felt a huge sense of relief, knowing I wasn't going to see her car outside my flat again, or come home to any more coded messages. I felt I could breathe.

Later on in 2006, I had to quit my hairdressing course. It required me to stand for long periods at a time, and my hips just weren't up to the job, pins or no pins. In the September I switched to a childcare course, Level 2 again, and got on really well with that. I even achieved distinctions in some of my work, something I was amazed at.

I enjoyed the course. They said I was really good with the children; all my years of looking after Adam, and loving my dollies, finally paying off. I was always happy being with the children; I felt safer with them than with adults. I liked nurturing them and making them laugh. As part of the course I even performed a puppet show for them, with puppets I had made by hand: three Billy Goats Gruff and a bridge and a troll.

And then, that autumn, Victoria Martell phoned again. This time, she said the judge had put his foot down: Mum couldn't move the trial anymore. In the spring of 2007, more than two years since I had escaped her clutches, Eunice Spry would be in the dock, whether she liked it or not.

I felt a shiver run down my spine.

'Who's that trip-trapping over my bridge?' I had made the troll roar out.

Three little demon Billy Goats Gruff were about to get their day in court.

CHAPTER THIRTY-TWO

'I'll pick you up tomorrow morning, OK, Victoria?' DC Martell said to me on the phone. I thanked her and hung up. Just one more night until I faced my mother in court.

I was a bag of nerves. Already, the trial had not started well. Just two days into the court case, in March 2007, the police had phoned me to say, 'You need to sit down. Your granddad's died.'

My poor nan, I thought. And then: *The pressure of the trial has killed him.* Can you imagine dying like that, with your daughter facing trial? It was just as Mum had always said: I'd destroyed this family. And then, God help me, I thought, *Mum's going to get away with it now because her lawyer will use this to get her off, like a sob story.* And then I felt guilty even for thinking that.

The closer the trial had come, the more and more convinced I became that Mum was going to get off. DC Martell would say to me, 'Trust me, Victoria.' And I'd be like, 'I'm trying, but I'm sorry, I don't. I really want to, but Mum has always got away with it before. What's different this time?'

My evidence had been delayed in the schedule, which was also unsettling. It had been delayed because another witness had come forward: a woman called Sandy, who remembered me from when I was young. I didn't really remember her, so that was confusing in itself. *What has she said?* I wondered. *What did she see?*

It was a Tuesday night, so after Victoria's call I got myself ready to head out to my Bible study meeting at the Kingdom Hall. I really wish I hadn't gone. Now the trial was on its feet, everybody wanted to know what I was going to say, and exactly what my evidence against my mother was. It was hard putting them off, especially one woman in particular, who was a good friend of my mum's and extremely nosy. I found her interest very intimidating.

My friends sat behind with me after the meeting, trying to reassure me about giving evidence, telling me that I was doing the right thing. Even though DC Martell had explained it to me, I was still very confused by the justice system. I was convinced – absolutely convinced – that if Mum was found not guilty, then I was going to go to prison. Because if the jury didn't believe my evidence, that meant I was lying; and liars had to be punished, I knew that all too well. I was petrified.

Jo and her husband Stuart took me home and dropped me off. I remember that night clearly: I didn't sleep a wink. I was very sick instead, all through the small hours, throwing up vomit until my stomach ached with empty acid; my clammy hands on the bright turquoise walls trying to root me in reality.

All too soon, dawn filtered through the curtains. I washed my face, barely able to look at myself in the mirror. I chose my outfit carefully. I'd thought really deeply about what I was going to wear, because Mum had never seen me walk as a young woman. Also, I wanted to impress the jury; they had to see that I was telling the truth.

I pulled on the long black skirt I'd picked out, and slipped on my high-heeled, black Clarks court shoes. Over my head went a white vest top, over the M&S bra that Ruth had helped me buy when I first got out, and then I tied a red wrap top over the vest, fastening its long, looping ties around my skinny waist. It wasn't a new outfit; it was one I'd worn before, and people had told me I looked nice in it, so I'd decided to wear it for the trial. I felt almost confident in it, the red a vibrant colour to try to lift my spirits.

The phone rang, piercing the stagnant air of the flat. It was Jo, calling to tell me that they'd see me at the courthouse. 'You're going to be absolutely fine,' she said. She asked if she could watch me give evidence from the gallery, when the time came.

It was hard for me, but I said, 'No, thanks, I'd rather you didn't.' I felt bad for saying that – I felt bad for ever saying what I wanted – but there was something inside me that thought, *If you're going to do this, you've got to do it for you*. I didn't want anybody else giving me the strength to go through with it, I wanted it to come from within me.

I heard DC Martell's horn beep outside my flat, and I made my way downstairs with a heavy heart.

'Good morning, Victoria, how are you?' she said sunnily, as I slipped into the back seat of her unmarked police car. Her upbeat words jarred with me. *Please can you stop tarting this up*, I thought, *this is really scary*. But I knew she was only being polite, and trying to put me at my ease.

It was a forty-five-minute drive to the courthouse in Bristol. Always Bristol: where Mum and I had abandoned Alloma; where I'd convalesced after the car crash; where we'd seen the driver of the lorry sentenced. It was even the same courthouse we were returning to: the same modern, spacious building I'd visited when I was fifteen, when the driver had been sent down for killing my sisters, and I'd thought it should have been me in the dock. How different things were now.

I was completely wrapped up in my thoughts. *She's going to get away with it, she's going to get away with it*, rang through my head with every heartbeat. The nearer we got, the scarier it was. It reminded me of driving to the farm.

DC Martell had secured permission for us to use the back entrance to avoid the media scrum at the front. Even though she had warned me there would be media interest in my case, I was still shocked by the massed journalists and broadcasters I saw there, all scurrying about on the front steps, like ants advancing on a particularly delectable sweet treat. I was grateful not to have to walk through them, but even seeing the national press *en masse* wasn't as daunting as the experience I was about to face.

The male officer with DC Martell checked the way was clear for us and then ushered me out of the car into the underground car park, and then inside. My stomach was an aviary of butterflies, darting up to my throat and back. The police escorted me into a side room and told me that I would be waiting there until the court was ready for me to give evidence. Sandy was still on the stand.

I was so pleased to be able to have my friends there with me. Jo and Jackie joined me in the room for the long wait, as well as Carol, the adoption mediator, to whom I'd grown close. They had brought me gifts on this strange, unsettling day. Jo presented me with a flowery gift bag packed full of presents, and she said, 'All the things in here, they remind me of you.' I pulled out a fridge magnet with the slogan: 'The most beautiful smile I've ever seen'. Jo said I was always smiling, no matter what. She gave me a cushion with the motto: 'I can do anything if I've got the right pair of shoes on'. That was a bit of a private joke, because I really struggled to find shoes: my feet had been so destroyed by my mum's beatings, and by years of running around the farmhouse gravel barefoot, that I found it very difficult even to wear shoes at times. I also pulled out a bottle of perfume, called Beautiful, and there were even more things in there, each of them with a thoughtful, personal message behind it. Overwhelmed by her generosity, I gave her a long hug. She was such a kind friend.

Carol had brought me a stuffed toy giraffe. She said to me, 'I was going to get you a lion, because lions are very, very brave – just like you. But the lion didn't look cute enough, so I got you the giraffe instead.'

I lightened everyone's mood then by saying, 'Well, I suppose I have stuck my neck out.' And we all laughed.

And Jackie? Ah, Jackie. This lovely woman, who had so bravely asked Mum about the bruises when no one else would; who had helped me so much and often made me laugh until I cried – well, she never did what anybody expected. That's why she was so much fun to spend time with. She'd brought egg sandwiches, made with eggs from her very own range of chickens. Mothering me so kindly, as always.

But I found I couldn't eat a thing.

The court officers came in and asked me if I wanted to review my evidence. 'No, thank you,' I said, almost offended. I didn't need to run through my evidence: I knew what the truth was.

After a couple of hours in the poky, windowless side room, they came to collect me for court. Jo, Jackie and Carol all gave me a hug, and then I left them behind, and followed the court officer down the corridors and up the stairs. I was left outside the courtroom in a long glass corridor, while the officer went to check they were ready for me. I was proud of myself for not limping.

Walking wasn't what was really on my mind, though. What I really wanted to do was run – run as far away as possible. Because

I was the first child to have spoken up, I was child A: the first to give evidence. I found that very, very scary: sticking my head above the parapet again. In the end, though, it was the thought of my siblings, of children B and C, Alloma and Christopher, that drove me on.

You've got a responsibility here, I thought, *you've got a brother and a sister who need you. You've got to go in there and show them it's OK, even if it's not OK. This is your family: you've got to do it for them. Be strong for them.*

I was always better at doing things for others than for me.

The court door opened, and I was ushered inside. My eyes searched everywhere for Mum; I was terrified about being in the same room as her again. People had told me she wouldn't be able to hurt me, but they didn't understand. I wasn't frightened that she was going to leap up and hit me. It was the mental control I was afraid of; seeing those eyes again, and what those eyes might make me do, or feel.

But I couldn't see her anywhere. Then I remembered Victoria Martell saying that Mum would always be behind a screen so we couldn't see her, and vice versa, and that she'd be taken out of the courtroom when I was walking in and out. That reassured me. I remember trying to make sure I looked strong and confident in my black skirt and my red top as I walked across the courtroom. Even though I wasn't feeling confident, I knew it was critical to come across well to the jury. They *had* to believe I was telling the truth. So I was steady on my feet as I went up the two little steps to enter a small, carpeted box: the stand.

I was sworn in, and my trial – in every sense of the word – began.

CHAPTER THIRTY-THREE

'I'm going to ask you about your childhood now. Is that OK?'

Our barrister, the lawyer working for the prosecution, stood up first. He asked me questions – the same questions the police had asked me, and Mark and Duncan, back when I had first told. I stared at the jury, and I told the truth.

The whole time I was giving evidence, I focused on one man and one woman in the jury. They looked nice and normal, in contrast to the eccentricities elsewhere in the court: the grey wigs and red robes of the main court players. The woman had shoulder-length brown hair and wore a turquoise scarf; the man was quite thin and tall, and had short, greyish hair. They were sitting next to each other, and it was the woman I mostly looked at when I spoke. She looked infuriated; she looked shocked; she looked like she cared.

Cough. Cough. Cough.

That was my mum, from behind her screen, making her presence felt as I gave my evidence. In the end the judge told her that, if she wasn't quiet, he'd have to send her out. She was quiet then; the whole court was. While I was speaking up – speaking out – you could have heard a pin drop.

I gave evidence for two days. Talking to our barrister was bearable, but I found it very difficult when my mum's lawyer came to question me. He was shorter than our lawyer, with dark hair, and I found him a very odd job. I couldn't grasp how he could stand there and defend her; how he could stand there and try to make out I was lying. The thing I found most exhausting, and humiliating, about the trial was trying to prove myself, to prove that I was telling the truth. Not only had I endured the abuse, but I then had to go through that. It was awful.

Mum's barrister was always trying to catch me out.

'Your mum does love you, doesn't she, Victoria?' he would say.

I would hesitate at that. 'I don't actually know if she does or not. But if she does love me, she has a very strange way of showing it.'

'She does love you,' he would say, 'because she took you to Disneyland.'

I'd replied to that question somewhat defiantly: 'I'd much rather have had a cuddle than go to America!' I snapped back at him. His line of questioning had made me so mad, slinging out this statement, as if to say, *Well, if you've seen Mickey Mouse then you've had a perfect childhood.* Didn't he know what my mother was like, how she had striven to appear so perfect, but only ever on the outside?

Another time he said, 'You weren't made to stand up all night in the shed at George Dowty, were you?'

'Yes,' I said, 'I was. I did.'

'Ah,' he said, 'but the shed was too full of junk for that.'

But then later, when painting a picture of Mum's happy-go-lucky household, he told me that we'd played in the shed. I couldn't help myself: I answered back. I was so frustrated that, after all we'd been through, we weren't being listened to. All my frustration bubbled up inside me and I said: 'Well, if it's too full of junk, *sir*, how could I possibly play in there?'

The judge interrupted me at that point and told me off, albeit gently. 'Can you please not answer back?' he said. 'We have to ask the questions.'

Only once in the whole two days did I break down while giving evidence. I was telling them about an incident with Alloma, shortly before she was abandoned, when Mum had been kicking her around the kitchen floor. As I recalled it, I burst into tears – because there's nothing worse than watching someone be hurt whom you can't help. I'd just remembered her desperate screams, and it brought floods of tears to my eyes and staccato hiccups to my wavering voice. The judge sent me out to compose myself, but I wasn't allowed to go back to my friends.

There was one other exchange I remember with my mum's barrister, just towards the end of his cross-examination. He was trying to paint Mum as a perfect mother again.

'Your mum loved you so much,' he told me, 'that after the car crash, she bought you a canal boat, didn't she? Because she thought you were disabled and you couldn't walk.'

'No,' I said, concisely, following the judge's advice.

'It was a disabled canal boat,' he said, his eyes on me.

'It was definitely not for me.'

'That's not the way it was. She got that for you.'

'No, it was for my granddad. Because he was disabled.'

He tutted in disbelief: 'Come, how's your granddad going to enjoy it? He was old. That boat was for you.'

I fixed him with a glare of my own. 'The only reason she bought that boat,' I said, 'was because it was called *Charlotte*.'

She hadn't told him the name, I could see that; he shook his head and he just stopped dead. 'No further questions,' he said suddenly.

Our lawyer stood up again, for the final question before I was dismissed. 'Victoria,' he said, 'I have never seen you so angry and determined. Please explain to me why you feel so angry.'

I paused, my thoughts whirling in my head, trying to pick one out to explain this jumble of emotions. 'Because she's over there,' I said at last, nodding at the screen, behind which my mother sat. 'She's over there, and she knows what she's done.'

And then I added, 'I still love her, but she needs to get some help.'

The trial continued, but for me it was over. I wasn't allowed to watch my siblings give evidence, even though I wanted to. I'd only ever heard Mum's voice telling me what was what, and I think it would have helped me to hear other sides of the story. I wanted to do it for me and my future, but I wasn't allowed, so as usual I just did what I was told.

Once I'd come off the stand, I went to the bathroom at the courthouse to splash some water on my face. A woman came up to me there, in the toilets, and proffered her business card. She said, 'I know we're not supposed to do this, but I'm from the –' and she named a very respectable mainstream newspaper that should have known better. 'We'll pay you for your story; we'll pay you to drop your anonymity: we want to get the first exclusive on the case.'

It was so overwhelming – I just wanted to go home. DC Martell got me in the car and we snuck out the back way to avoid the media. I saw the photographers and reporters milled by the court steps, a sea of bustling figures and camera flashes, and I was told they were all waiting there for me, which was incredibly stressful.

I don't remember getting home that night, but I do recall waking up the next morning, finding myself lying on the sofa in my pale pink lounge. A noise had woken me up. A funny noise, like the letterbox was repeatedly flapping with missives coming through the door – but I rarely got mail, and the postman only came once a day.

I ventured into the hallway, and I couldn't believe my eyes. Stacks of letters had been posted through the box, and still more were coming through, even as I stared in horror at the mounting papers. They were all from reporters, telling me they'd pay more than the next newspaper, and I really must sell my story. When I peeked out the kitchen window, I saw the car park was jammed full of journalists. My phone rang, and it was Victoria Martell, passing me on to the police PR woman, who told me she was getting requests in from broadcasters, and did I want to go on national TV once the verdict was in?

No, I did not. I was in so much pain, I was so overwhelmed, I was so confused by my wild mix of feelings, that the one thing I definitely did *not* want to do was talk to the world about what had happened. It had been hard enough telling the lawyer in the courtroom; the last thing I wanted was to go over it all again, or have my face splashed across the papers. I felt traumatised, not triumphant; battered, not brave.

I stuck a handwritten note up on my door, using my still-childish handwriting to carefully craft the shapes of the letters. 'Please,' it said, 'I'm really upset right now. Can you please leave me alone?'

But it didn't stop them.

The case continued. Mum gave her defence. 'I sweated blood for these children,' she said during the trial. 'I've worked non-stop. I love them; I still love them. Anyone who met these three children would say they've grown up to be fine respectable adults.

That's what I aimed to do and that's what I think I did to them.'
She said the only physical punishment she had ever given us was
'a smack on the bottom'.

As for her defence regarding the masses of scars on our bodies
… we were naughty foster kids and had put the sticks down each
other's throats; it was nothing to do with her. DC Martell later
told me that her defence became almost laughable in the end,
because her answers were so ridiculous.

I wasn't allowed in court, so I didn't see how the evidence was
stacking up: not only from the three of us, and Sandy, but also
from the dentist's and doctor's appointments we'd attended over
the years, from the DNA-sodden sticks they'd retrieved from
the farmhouse – and even from my sister Becky. She testified
about the bedroom scene she'd found when she walked in on me,
and perhaps this was the most powerful evidence of all. For this
wasn't a 'naughty foster kid telling lies' – this was Mum's own,
natural daughter, and she was saying it was all true.

But I didn't know all that, not at the time. From my perspective, it was pretty much my word against Mum's, and I knew
how that had gone down in the past. I had nightmares she was
going to go free; every night I wet the bed in abject fear. Fear of
Mum, fear of going to jail myself, fear of what would happen
next. I started to think I would be better off dead.

My friends tried to keep me focused on the positive. Jo was
sweet as always, and one Friday afternoon in mid-March she
invited me round for tea. I liked going to Jo's – she lived in a very
characterful little place, with big beams and a rustic feel, and she
always had flowers everywhere. It was a peaceful place to be. And
peace was what I needed just then: the case had closed and the

jury had gone out to deliberate their verdict. I'd been told that we probably wouldn't hear anything until after the weekend. I felt like climbing the wood-beamed walls.

But then my mobile started ringing. It was Victoria Martell, and she had just four words for me.

'She's been proven guilty.'

CHAPTER THIRTY-FOUR

I felt grief-stricken. I collapsed to the floor, to my knees; and that was where Jo found me, tears streaming down my face.

I've just put my mum in prison.

Jo pulled me up into her arms and wrapped me in a big hug. She gave me a kiss and she said, 'Well done, I'm so proud of you.' Then she led me to the sofa, and we sat there, trying to let it sink in, both of us crying, while mad thoughts flew around my head.

I felt guilty – for so many reasons: because I loved her; because I'd betrayed her. Because she'd told me, long ago, that I had turned her this way – so really, all of this, this whole thing, all of it was my fault.

That was a lot to feel guilty about.

When I said I loved her, people would shush me. 'It's misplaced loyalties,' they'd say. But that felt like they were dismissing my feelings, telling me I was wrong, and thick with it. *You autistic twit.* I couldn't help the way I felt – I had loved her for decades, for twenty-one years now – and she was, for better or worse, the only mum I'd ever known.

Victoria Martell's words rang in my ears, like sombre church bells, tolling in the cool spring air: 'She's been proven guilty.' I just couldn't believe it. I'd never, ever thought it would happen. I'd never dared to dream. I thought about DC Martell, how someone had once told me that you'd have to get up very early in the morning to get past her, and I was suddenly glad that she'd been our lead investigator. I don't think we'd have done as well with the case with another officer. Those reserved eyes of hers had seen straight through Mum, and made a judgement, in a way that no one had ever been able to do before her.

I didn't phone my siblings after the verdict. We'd kept our distance, during the trial, not wanting to jeopardise the evidence, and I didn't feel the urge to ring them now. It felt intensely personal somehow. We'd all gone on our own journeys to get to this place, and I'd been with Mum since I was a baby. It was a lot to get my head round.

The verdict still hadn't sunk in by the time Tuesday morning came round and I returned to my childcare course at college. I remember walking into our classroom and the tables were filled with newspapers, and each and every one had my mum's picture on it. There were pages and pages about the case inside the papers, all spread out across the tables. Even though Victoria Martell had told me that the case would make the national news, I could never have comprehended the magnitude of the coverage.

Each picture sent another sucker punch of guilt slamming into my stomach. It was so strange, our story being out there. Until the trial had happened, I'd been told to keep quiet about it, so as not to endanger the case – and that was just fine; that was kind of what Mum had always told me anyway, that we weren't to tell anyone about what went on in our home – but this … her secrets were now spread out for all the world to see. It was such a contrast to our insular family, to the way we'd grown up. My brain couldn't quite cope with it.

My teacher came out and told my fellow students to put the papers away. She called me into her office.

'Are you OK, Victoria?' she asked me.

At this, I burst into tears. I was in so much shock and disbelief; I didn't feel an inch of pride, just this weird, debilitating mix of guilt and stunned astonishment.

'Sweetheart,' she said kindly. 'You've got to go home. Have you had any counselling?'

I shook my head. No, I hadn't received any counselling. No counselling when I came out, and no counselling was being offered now, either, to help me get over it.

'There's a counsellor here,' she said. 'Why don't you go up and have a little chat before you go home? Go and have a chat and see if she can help.'

So I made my way up to the counsellor's office, where she was sat behind her desk. I think she thought I was going to tell her I was pregnant, or had been caught shoplifting, or some other typical teenage dilemma.

I started to tell her, and of course she recognised the case straight away. And she said gently, 'I'm sorry, but I can't help you. It's just too big. It's so bad there's nothing I can do. Maybe your doctor can help you.'

I made my way home in a bubble of shock, chased by journalists the whole way. They'd snuck into the college, they'd loitered in the loos and the lifts, and now they were waiting for me around every corner, proffering contracts, business cards, scribbled notes of appeal in my direction.

'How does it feel to have won?' they shouted.

Won? I thought to myself. *What do you mean, won? I just feel safe.*

'Why did you stay with her for so long?' they screamed.

That was another thing that made me feel guilty, like I'd been really stupid to put up with her for all those years.

They didn't seem to understand that I'd been scared.

I had to hole myself up in my flat, because I couldn't walk down the street without being stalked. Before too long, I had to quit my college course. I agreed to one press conference – encouraged by the police PR team, who said, if I did it, the press would leave me alone – and Christopher and I faced a room heaving with reporters, as microphones were thrust into our faces (Alloma had gone back to Bristol so she wasn't there). I didn't renounce my anonymity, so the media weren't allowed to photograph me, but it was still an incredibly intimidating environment. And agreeing to the conference, I soon found out, didn't make them leave me alone in any way, shape or form. Give them an inch and they'll try to take a mile. Nonetheless, I turned every single media offer down; I didn't feel ready to share my story any more than I had already done.

My siblings were in a different place, though. They talked to the press: a choice they made, and I didn't resent it. I'd seen them tortured, made to do so many awful things against their will that to see them choose to stand up and be counted, to make their own decisions, to tell their story with courage, was something that, in many ways, made me proud.

In a perfect world, the day we all left Mum we should each have been able to do what we needed in order to heal, independent of the others. But we don't live in a perfect world. Regrettably, my siblings' courage prompted the cut-throat media to make my position ten times worse.

'You've got to stand united with your brother and sister!' the reporters would call through my letterbox. 'You're letting them down. You don't want to let them down, do you?' And then: 'Oh, you think you're better than them, do you? Snob!' And then: 'You're the whistleblower. We want to hear it from you!' And then: 'You can help other people with your story. Don't you want to help other people?'

When my mother was sentenced, on 16 April 2007, the pressure intensified again. I'd wanted to see her sentenced, but once more I was advised against it. I hadn't seen her since the day I'd left George Dowty Drive, and I think it would have helped me to be able to see her again, to see her sent down. I might even have found the strength to look her in the eye.

It was reported that the judge, Simon Darwall-Smith, told Mum in his summing-up that it was the worst case he had come across in forty years in the justice system. He commented: 'It's difficult for anyone to understand how any human being could have even contemplated what you did, let alone with the regularity and premeditation you employed. I could not fail to notice that during the five and a half weeks of the trial you showed no emotion, even when the jury returned their guilty verdicts.'

Mum was found guilty of twenty-six charges in total, including unlawful wounding, cruelty to a person under sixteen, assault occasioning actual bodily harm, perverting the course of justice and witness intimidation. It sounds so dry when you say it like that. It doesn't quite summon up the screaming agony of being beaten on your bare feet, or the caustic flavour of the washing-up liquid down your throat, or the sheer terror of being held beneath the bathwater.

She was sentenced to fourteen years in jail.

My friends responded to the sentence with delight. Ruth and Jo kept telling me, 'You'll be grown up then, Torrie. She won't matter to you by then.' And I thought they were right; I thought I was safe for fourteen years. I felt as if the judge was like one of those fairground machines they have, the ones that pick up cheap-looking toys with metal-fingered grabbers: at long last somebody had picked her up and put her away – and I could go and live my life.

A few weeks after the verdict, Duncan and Jackie came with me to a Kingdom Hall in Gloucester – to Mum's childhood Kingdom Hall. I was there to be interviewed by a panel of elders: a formal occasion. Because even though Mum had been found guilty by a court of law, God was above all that. Mum wouldn't be 100 per cent guilty in the eyes of many Jehovah's Witnesses unless she'd been disfellowshipped from the faith. And that was why I was being cross-examined one more time.

I answered all their questions, for a couple of hours. They took their job seriously: there was a sense of 'you might not be telling the truth, so let's go through this one more time and see what God has to say about it all'. Then we all went back to Tewkesbury to await this second verdict.

It was strange for me at my local Kingdom Hall after the legal trial was over. While many Witnesses had been supportive of the court case, others had not. I understood it, to a degree: they didn't want to think that this had been going on under their noses, for all those years, so it was easier to call me a liar than to look into their own hearts and see if they could have helped us. It was easier to spit at me in the street, tell me they didn't believe me, and they wouldn't unless she was proven guilty …

Well, there was a lot of humble pie being washed down by the cups of coffee in the Kingdom Hall these days, that was all I could say.

One Thursday evening, a few weeks after I'd been in Gloucester, the elders stood up for the announcements section, which always comes halfway through the night. And they said to the gathered congregation, 'We've got to announce that Eunice Spry has now been disfellowshipped from the Jehovah's Witnesses.'

They didn't make a fuss about it; enough of a fuss had been made already. But hearing that in the Kingdom Hall – in the hall where she had literally labelled me an evil child, where she had held so many people in her power, intimidating them until they looked away, and didn't once come to our aid – hearing that was so powerful.

Freedom. Justice. Truth.

And I thought, *It's over. It is done.*

PART THREE

A LEAP
OF FAITH

CHAPTER THIRTY-FIVE

Hello, there. I bet you're surprised to see me still here. But, yes, there is a 'part three' to my story. I know most books like this end on that last line, don't they? Ding dong, the witch is, if not quite dead, then at least banged up, so we can all live happily ever after.

But real life doesn't work that way, it's not as open and shut as that. All those headlines you see in the paper, proclaiming justice has been done for victims, so now we can all rest easy in our beds – well, you never hear what happens next, after the media circus has packed up and gone home, and the justice system has run its course, and those at the heart of the story have to pick up their lives and move on. You never hear what happens to them afterwards.

This is what happened to me.

When I think of my life immediately after the sentencing and disfellowshipping, it's best summed up by a golden, furry snout and a black wet nose: Ollie, my very own dog.

Ollie arrived with me one magical late spring afternoon at my flat. A couple of Witness friends from Hereford had got him for me; the housing association had agreed to move me to a ground-floor flat, so I could get a dog, and I was a week away from moving when my Ollie arrived.

Originally, I was going to get a female dog and call her Belle, after my heroine in *Beauty and the Beast*, but it was a boy who bounded into my flat, a porky little boy who had been rescued from a puppy farm in Wales: a five-month-old golden Labrador I thought was lovely from the moment I saw him.

I loved having someone to care for again. That very first night I gave him a bath and he was in a bit of a state from his rescue: fleas jumped from his fur coat into the water as I hosed him down. I took him to the vets the next morning – he was a big heffalump of a dog, but I carried him all the way down to the surgery myself, clutching him tightly in my arms.

Before he came, I'd often wondered, *Why am I here? What am I supposed to do with myself?* But now I knew – I was here to love Ollie. That's what he taught me: how to love, without any of the complications I'd felt about my nan, or my siblings, or my mum. He taught me how to love, simple as that.

Every night, he slept across my chest, with his head on my pillow. He was daft as a brush, and he was my best mate. Just a week after he arrived, I moved into my new, ground-floor flat, a clean, cream-walled place, where I had new carpets put in; I even bought some new furniture. I bought my first ever bedframe, a proper blond-wood frame to put my mattress on, and I hung a princess net over the top of it and scattered it with fairy lights and clip-on butterflies. And I ordered a brand-new wardrobe from Ikea. Oh, I thought that wardrobe was something else! It had compartments for all my different types of clothes, and was a world away from grubby black bin-liners lying on the kitchen floor.

I hoped life was going to be OK now. Everyone was telling me, 'It's over. It's finished. Move on and be happy.' I wanted so much to be happy – even though I didn't really know who I was, or what would, in fact, make me happy.

I found it difficult having no professional support. It was as if I'd been dropped like a hot potato after the court case, offered no guidance or help. As far as the authorities were concerned, I was, after all, an adult: twenty-one years of age, and surely able to support myself and go out and live my life. What help could I possibly need now my mum was safely in jail? For decades, I might have had her telling me I was stupid, and useless, and evil. She might have made me look in the mirror and say it, until I knew it was true. But now people said to me, 'Don't be so silly, of course that isn't true! Put it all behind you and move on.'

I knew what they were saying was right, but the message didn't really reach me inside, in my heart and mind. After all, I had no mother, no family, no guidance to help me; I had to find my own way. In my childhood, I'd become a chameleon, adapting to survive. Now, I had to do the same again. What did other people do? They got houses; they bought wardrobes. I did the same. And I was like, 'Yeah, yeah. I'll be happy. I'm going to give it my best shot. By popular demand, that's what I've got to do. Everything's going to be A-OK now.'

In truth, Ollie was a huge help in that. I loved having a companion and taking him for walks. He gave me a reason to get out of the flat every day, and with his funny little character he gave me a reason to smile, too. It was a long time since I'd smiled. Throughout the trial, and the two years running up to it, I'd found it hard to enjoy anything: food, a book, a rom-com movie. I wasn't living, just existing. I'd been diagnosed with post-traumatic stress disorder, anxiety and depression, and I was still battling with various health problems, and knocking back my cocktails of pills. Yet Ollie really helped with the depression:

his smell, his cuddles, his softness; those big floppy velvet ears. I loved him so much. And it was his love, in the end, that made me stop cutting myself and have a bit of self-belief. If he believed in me, maybe I could, too.

I tried not to think about Mum anymore. I had to think about the future – which might explain, perhaps, why I decided not to prosecute Uncle Phil for his abuse. That, and the fact that I didn't feel I had the emotional strength to survive another trial: more giving of evidence, more cross-examination from insensitive, intrusive lawyers. The police rang me and gave me a choice as to whether or not to prosecute him, because I'd told them all about what he'd done when I'd told them about Mum, and I said no, I couldn't. No, thank you. I couldn't go through it all again.

On Friday, 20 July 2007, it started to rain. Heavily, relentlessly. I woke up at three o'clock in the morning to hear screams coming from the caravan park across the way; they were hurriedly evacuating the residents in the face of the rising water. There was a helicopter flying above my flat, its blades beating the air: it was searching for a young man who had gone missing in the fast-swelling river (he later died). That Friday was the night that signalled the coming of the Gloucestershire Floods, the county's worst-ever peacetime emergency and a truly devastating natural disaster.

It was a disaster for my new flat, too. The water started to come up through the floor, while Ollie and I sat on the bed, me clinging to his soft blond fur. All the lights had gone off; the electricity was gone. It was a bit like the stories of Armageddon that my mum used to shout about in my face, blackheads greasy on her nose, as she described the end of days and how I was going to suffer.

And, oh, I did suffer. The flat was swimming in water: dirty sewage all over my new carpets, and my pretty bed, and my magical wardrobe. It was so traumatic to build a home and then, literally months later, to see it swept away.

I was rehoused in Gloucester, almost within the shadow of my mum's former Kingdom Hall. Gloucester was the last place I wanted to go: it was so far away from my friends, whose support I still relied on, and I felt particularly uncomfortable moving to Mum's old neck of the woods, where I felt people were more likely to disbelieve what had happened; where I'd perhaps find my harshest critics. But beggars can't be choosers, and the floods had made beggars of an awful lot of people.

I moved into my new flat on a Friday night, just as it was getting dark. Club music pounded from the bars on the street, as young people careered about, clutching bottles of booze that smelled off-puttingly of Uncle Phil. They were yelling and swearing and shouting at each other. It was a huge culture shock. I had grown up on the farm, and within the confines of George Dowty; my flats after my escape had been in little Tewkesbury (population: 10,704), just minutes from my friends' homes. Now, I was in the big city, with all the noise and dirt and faceless neighbours that implies.

I remember sitting in my new flat that evening, with what belongings I had managed to salvage dumped around me in the living room, and crying – not because of what had happened to me, but because I'd been moved to a flat with no garden for Ollie, and I felt like such a useless mother, because he had nowhere he could go for a wee.

Ollie didn't mind, though. He followed me about, his big brown eyes full of love and trust and good humour, and he didn't even bark when our upstairs neighbours started having a blazing row, every word of which I could hear as the walls in our block were paper-thin. When the pubs kicked out, drunks wandered past and knocked on my windows. *Rat-a-tat-tat! We know you're in there!*

I cried myself to sleep for the first week. There was no help available to me. The council was inundated with requests for assistance at that time, and, because I had a roof over my head, I wasn't a priority. My friends couldn't support me as they were so far away – they told me to go to the Gloucester Kingdom Hall and make new contacts there. 'Trust in God,' they said serenely.

In the end, I realised there was only one person who could help me ... and that person was me. I had to help myself. *You need to get a job, and you need to save up, and you need to get yourself back to Tewkesbury in a privately rented flat*, I told myself firmly.

I recalled a place in Cheltenham where I had worked during a placement on my childcare course: a day nursery where I'd been very happy. I phoned the owner up and she called me in for an interview. 'You're really good with the kids and the parents hold you in high regard,' she told me. 'You've got the job.' And so I worked as a nursery practitioner, looking after three-year-olds on what the nursery called the 'juggler's floor' (every floor, each with its own age group, was named after a different circus act).

I enjoyed my work. If I saw a child who was a bit quieter than the others, I would make an effort to spend a bit more time with them to make sure they knew they were special, too. Yet I managed to strike a balance in my concern. I knew not every parent was like my mum, and, just because I'd been beaten at home, it didn't mean every grazed knee I saw was evidence of abuse. That balance was self-taught, and I trusted my instincts. In truth, I found the staff room a trickier place; the casual break-time conversations were for me a bit like that meal with my brother Tom at Pizza Hut: a weird kind of endurance test, or a pantomime in which I had to pretend to be somebody else, simply because I didn't know how to have a 'normal' chat with people. So much of my normality was so extreme.

My contact with Tom had sadly subsided in the past few months. I think the media coverage of the case took its toll; once it all came out, and not just the sanitised version Carol had told him. I believe it was just a bit too much, and our letters dried up.

It was an exhausting time for me. I was up at 5 a.m. every day to take Ollie for a walk and to drop him at his dog-sitter's, and then I'd catch the 6.30 a.m. bus to Cheltenham and do a full day's work at the nursery. I wouldn't get home until gone eight in the evening. Meanwhile, I saved every penny I could; my only expenses were food and Ollie's sitter. During those intense few months, doing all I could to get out of my horrid flat, on that scary street, I also received a small payment from the Criminal Injuries Compensation Authority, which I could use for a deposit on a rented flat. Within six months, I'd pulled myself off the scrapheap I felt I'd been thrown on, and I was able to move back to Tewkesbury, under my own steam. I was so proud of myself.

Using the rest of the compensation money, I paid for a year of rent in advance – so when I moved in, in the spring of 2008, I felt debt-free and ready for anything.

But, as it turned out, I wasn't quite ready for anything after all. Not by a long shot.

CHAPTER THIRTY-SIX

It all started off beautifully. I moved in on a bright spring day, into a semi-detached house on a nice estate in Tewkesbury, with open fields and rolling countryside just around the corner. The house had two bedrooms and a garden, actual stairs, and even a conservatory. It was a proper family home, so I decided to expand my little family to celebrate. Ollie and I welcomed the irrepressible Milly into our band of troopers, a chunky chocolate-brown Labrador with big brown jelly-bean eyes. She had the most amazing character: she was a real clown, a very cheeky dog. You couldn't even cuddle her that much because she would just make you laugh. She and Ollie loved each other to bits and would chase each other round and round the garden.

The dogs were a joy in my life. My stoma bag, old faithful Colin, was causing me a lot of problems at that time, and I was really quite poorly, vomiting a lot and having to increase the dosage of the painkillers I was on. The injuries I'd sustained in the crash, in particular from the seatbelt jamming tight across my torso, had played havoc with my gut and resulted in a hernia in my stomach lining, which caused acid to rise up my throat again and again, making me ill. Although still working at the nursery, I was in constant pain. I dragged myself into work regardless because I didn't want to be pitied – and I didn't want to give up on this 'normal' life I'd worked so hard for, which I'd somehow managed to secure for myself.

On many days I couldn't eat, because it put too much pressure on my stomach. I grew skinnier and skinnier. Ollie was like a shadow; he'd follow me everywhere and sleep outside the bathroom as I lay on the tiled floor, trying to feel well. I'd limp out to the fields with them both and sit on this old bit of farm machinery while the dogs got their exercise, and it did me so much good to see them. Milly would sit with her back to me and keep guard while Ollie ran off, as though they were tag-teaming who was 'on duty' to look after me, and Milly did the shifts outside while Ollie shadowed me in the house.

I don't know what I'd have done without them. What was strange about this time was that, now I'd 'made it', now I'd done it – up on my feet, my battles won, Mum in jail and me living in a lovely home with my lovely dogs – now was the time when I suddenly started thinking about what had happened to me. It was as if I hadn't had time to really consider it before. There had always been another mountain to climb: walking again, my stomach operations, then the court case, the sentencing, getting out of Gloucester … But now that everything was settled – now I *had* my happy ever after – now was when the truth of what had happened hit me across the back of the head like one of my mum's old baked-bean tins.

I started having nightmares about my mum coming to find me. All the time I would hear her voice in my head, telling me I was worthless. I began wetting the bed again, every night. Although I was desperately trying to fit into society, my mind refused to cooperate. It was as if my head was a washing machine, crammed full of the dirty linen of my memories, stuffed so full, in fact, that it couldn't turn round anymore and just got jammed.

The only thing that eased the pain was looking into my dogs' clear, understanding eyes. But I couldn't do that day in and day out, especially not when I was working.

I went to my doctor for help – I had a new one now, a really good GP called Jeremy – and he referred me to mental-health services. But again and again, I'd go through all the rigmarole you have to in order to get seen, and then there'd be no real help at the end of it. I knew my little brothers – whom I didn't see anymore, sadly, though we were sporadically in touch by text message – had had counselling given to them when Mum was arrested, because they were minors, but in all this time I'd never had any meaningful professional support. Trying to deal with it on my own was overwhelming. It was as if what had happened was a splinter inside me. For many years now it had been festering, with no counselling to eke it from my skin, and finally that thorn beneath the surface was showing its ugly head, riddled with noxious infection.

Now I was back in Tewkesbury, my friends rallied round. The women at the Kingdom Hall were so concerned about my weight loss that they organised a rota to leave suppers on my doorstep. I started talking to Jo and Jackie about the depression I was feeling, and I told them more about what I had gone through as a child. And then, one night, I started talking to them about Uncle Phil and I just couldn't stop.

I hadn't ever really talked about it before and it opened up a whole new world of pain for me. I probably hated him even more than I hated Mum.

The world of Jehovah's Witnesses is small. I'm certain Jo and Jackie wouldn't have betrayed my trust, so perhaps it was his own guilty conscience that prompted it – but Phil started attending our weekly meetings. I think he was worried about what I'd said, or might say in the future, and he'd decided to keep his enemies close.

I hated seeing him, sitting across the aisle from me in the hall. That face … He'd had a stroke since I'd last seen him, but when I saw him sitting there I still felt fear. It wasn't fear of what he could do; it was seeing that face and knowing what that face had done to me. I'd cry with the other Witnesses and say that I couldn't come to the meetings anymore, it was too much, but they'd say to me in reply, 'No, you should come, Victoria. You can leave it to God, He will sort it out; have faith in God.'

Yet it was getting harder and harder for me to have faith in God – not least because, that same spring, Mum had her appeal heard. She had two years knocked off her sentence; now she would serve only twelve years for two decades of torture. As I understand it, the basis of her appeal was that other parents, who had also been convicted of abuse but in cases where their children had died, had received lesser sentences. Her lawyer argued that she deserved to serve less time because we weren't actually dead. So because she'd always managed to find that sweet spot in the drowning punishments, before we were too far gone to be brought back; because she'd always thrown us a scrap of mouldy bread before we starved to death; because she was too damn sadistic to let us die; it was like, oh, OK, that's not so bad then. And her sentence was reduced.

I was finding it more and more difficult to cope with the pressure. Out one sunny afternoon in Tewkesbury, I walked past Alison's Bookshop and saw my own face staring back at me through the window. My siblings had published books about their experiences with Mother, and on one of the covers was a picture of my sandpapered face, my cheeks bloody with scabs that had stretched painfully as I'd beamed at the camera, smiling out from my strange 'normality'; the same smile I'd given the nurses in Frenchay Hospital, when I was trying to be a good girl, always trying to please. My eyes had been blacked out in the photo to conceal my identity, as I was still anonymous to the media, but of course *I* knew it was me. I burst into tears in the street. My siblings hadn't come to me and said, 'I'm doing a book, is that OK?' No one had told me the books were coming out, or asked permission to use that picture. It just broke my heart.

Then Phil upped his game: he started sitting outside my house. He would come and find me when I was taking the dogs out for a walk; chillingly, I think he must have watched me and worked out my routine. He didn't talk to me. It was intimidation, pure and simple: *I know where you are. Don't you dare say anything, Torrie* … He'd just sit in his car and stare.

People started telling me stories about him. He was still an alcoholic, of course, and they would tell me how they had seen him go into Morrisons and buy a whole bottle of alcohol, down it in his car and then drive home. He would leer at the female staff until they were banned from serving him because he was harassing them so much.

Those stories triggered a lot of deep upset. His drink-driving disgusted me – I'd have nightmares that he was going to kill people, just as my sisters had been killed – but it was his slimy, whisky-breathed, sheer sense of entitlement to slobber over any woman or girl he wanted that made me feel sick to my stomach. I'd go home and cry after I heard the stories, feeling such a failure

– because I should have said something, I should have taken him to court. I felt I was letting others suffer simply because I was too cowardly to take him on. I was angry with myself and yet I also knew what a horrendous, exhausting journey it had been taking Mum to trial, and I just couldn't go through it all again. The pain ate me up inside … until there was nothing left.

In 2008, I tried to kill myself.

Not once. Not twice. But too many times to mention.

I used pills. Well, I had enough going around, didn't I? And not just the various ones I was taking for my stomach and my hips and my pain, but I would throw in some classic favourites like Paracetamol and Nurofen, too: the lemonade mixers to the more exotic ingredients in my extensive drugs cabinet. I was in and out of hospital that whole summer, crying to Jeremy, my GP, on the phone, trying to find a way through it.

The one bright light on the horizon was that the doctors had finally said they thought it was time to reverse my colostomy. The operation was scheduled for January 2009 – eight years after it should have been done, if Mother hadn't stopped them. It was weird trying to imagine a world without Colin.

I had to face up to a different world before that, though. A world that I had never known.

A world without God.

CHAPTER THIRTY-SEVEN

'But I'm just not sure if He's there,' I remember saying to an elder at the Kingdom Hall in the autumn of 2008.

I wanted desperately to believe in what they were telling me: to believe in an all-powerful, all-forgiving God, who would make everything all right. I, more than anyone, needed a deity to wave His magic wand and restore my soul. I really, *really* wanted to believe.

'You need to pray to Him to let Him tell you He's here,' I remember them saying. But that confused me, because the scriptures also said that if I prayed to God but I didn't believe, then He wouldn't answer me.

It was hard enough already attending the meetings and seeing Phil across the way, but to then be told that I had to ignore him and 'trust in God' … *Well, God isn't helping me at night when I wake up screaming from another nightmare, my legs sodden with my own urine*, I thought angrily.

I began to feel anger towards the Witnesses, too – anger towards my friends. It felt as if my feelings were being belittled and undermined, simply because they believed that all this, all the horror I'd been through, was somehow part of God's plan. I started to think, *How can you put so much pressure on someone who's been through so much? That man sitting over there touched me with his filthy, dry hands and he makes me feel sick and I'm just to ignore that?*

Then I'd feel guilty, and as if I was doing it wrong. *Autistic twit.* I'd look along the line of worshippers at my friends – at Jo and Jackie and Ruth singing their hearts out in song, and Duncan and Mark reading from the Bible – and I could see they all felt it, felt God's grace or something; but I felt nothing. Not only did I not believe, I didn't *feel* anything. And I started to think that I was being disloyal to them, because I was going along pretending that I believed – pretending we were literally all singing from the same hymn sheet – when my heart wasn't in it. Thoughts whirled around my head: *Am I staying in the Truth because I believe it, 100 per cent, and this is how I want to live my future? Or am I doing it because it's an easier option to stay, because all my friends are here?*

In the end, I loved my friends so much I wanted to be honest with them.

I wish I could have said goodbye in person, but even then I knew myself well enough to know that I would never be able to withstand their loving attempts to persuade me to stay. So I wrote a letter. I sat down and I wrote a letter to them all one chilly autumn day, thanking them for everything they had done for me, saying I would defend them to my death, that just because I was leaving didn't mean I wasn't so very grateful for their help … but I *was* leaving. It was a very distressing letter to write – because, in the Jehovah's Witness faith, if you renounce your religion, you are renouncing every single person in the faith, too. If you're disassociated, you can't have anything to do with each other anymore.

Every friend I had was a Witness. In my eyes, it is one of the most courageous things I've ever done, walking away from them. I knew, if I left, that I would have no friends, no help, no human support. But I thought, *You've got to be true to yourself.* For so long Mum had made me do things I didn't want to; she had controlled me like a puppet or a limp rag doll; she had done whatever she wanted to me. But now I understood: *I have choices*. And I was choosing to leave.

It was heart-breaking going. I loved my friends so much – I still love them, in fact; there are some people there I will always love – but I had to do it for me. I didn't believe anymore, and I'd spent too much of my life already living a lie. I wasn't going to do it for one more day.

I sealed the envelope and I posted my long letter through the box at the Kingdom Hall. Then I went home and waited for the knock on the door. It came – of course it came. Elders I didn't even know that well came round and offered to do Bible studies with me, to help me through my loss of faith. Friends came to persuade me to come back. Witnesses of all varieties knocked, and knocked, and knocked, until I stopped answering the door or even going out. The mental strength it took to resist them was exhausting. But I did it.

The dogs helped enormously. Ollie and Milly … and Alfie. A new addition to my new life. He was a rescue dog, like Ollie – like me, to a degree. Alfie was hard work to begin with: he didn't like men and would bark if anyone came to the door, and he was wary of cuddles for a long time, until he learned how to trust. He was a gorgeous black Lab – I now had one of each colour – and he was a handsome boy, about five months old when he came to us. Ollie and Milly welcomed him in and didn't bat an eyelid at their new brother. I might have had no family to speak of – my real gran had also stopped writing around this time, and I had no contact with any of my siblings – but *they* were my family. They were all I needed. More than any humans had ever done, they accepted me for who I was, and that love was more healing than all the drugs under the sun.

It was odd spending my first Christmas on this earth as a non-Jehovah's Witness. I had a very, very sweet neighbour, Emma, who was quite poorly herself, but when she heard my story, she invited me round for a Christmas celebration, a few days before she went away for the holidays. I took great pleasure in wrapping a gift for her, curling the ribbon around it; so much so that she said, when I gave it to her, 'How can I open that? It's a work of art!'

She gave me presents, too: a lovely silver charm bracelet that nestled in a black velvet box, and a little Eeyore, the size of my thumb. It felt really naughty and strange to take them from her, as if accepting forbidden fruit. I was very grateful to her for those gifts.

I spent my first Christmas Day on my own, wandering the streets like the Little Match Girl, smelling other people's Christmas dinners and watching kids out on their brand-new bikes, happy and buzzing. I felt lonely, but it wasn't long before Emma returned, in the New Year, and she had an even more special surprise for me.

On Sunday, 4 January 2009, I celebrated my first-ever birthday at the age of twenty-three.

Emma invited me round for tea that evening. Her partner was out, so it was just the two of us. I was so excited, because I knew that birthdays were specific days to celebrate people: so this was Torrie's day, and Torrie had never, ever had a day to celebrate her before. Emma made tuna steaks and chips, and she baked pink cupcakes and stuck a candle on one of them for me. That was the first time I'd ever had a cake with a candle on it and made a wish. So strung out on enthusiasm, I can't even remember now what I wished for.

Four days later, I went into hospital for the closure of my colostomy. It was goodbye, Colin, and hello, brand-new me. It was a major operation. Because I had eight years' worth of scar tissue in my abdomen, as well as other complications from the crash and various operations, they couldn't do keyhole surgery on me, so I was opened all the way up. I remember coming round and it was really very painful, even with the strong doses of morphine I was on.

I had no one to visit me in hospital. Emma was pretty much housebound, and we weren't close enough friends for me to be able to ask that of her anyway. Without the Witnesses in my life anymore, I had no one. At visiting hours, everyone else would have their loved ones come in, and I'd be sat on my own. That was hard. I felt so very, very alone.

I had the dogs to go home to, but I wasn't really well enough to look after them, so my dog-sitter took them for me, so they were cared for. She left one behind, Alfie, so that I wasn't too lonely, and she would come in every day to take him out. He'd always run straight back to the house as soon as she let him off the lead, because he wanted to be with me. I loved those dogs, and the feeling was mutual. They became even more important to me after the operation, because I had to stop work, and they literally became my world.

Time passed. I have a clear memory of looking in the mirror a short while after the operation, after my wounds had healed. I was standing in the spare bedroom, in just my bra and knickers, and it was the first time I'd ever seen my adult body without the stoma bag attached. I hadn't ever noticed my body as a body in that way before and so I was almost caught by surprise. I was in the middle of getting dressed, but I stopped stock-still and I thought, *I'm a young woman. How did that happen?*

Automatically my mind flashed back to Mum, her sewing scissors snipping in her hand as she said, 'You've got no figure, Victoria. You're not going to be very pretty at all when you grow up. You'll never be able to wear nice clothes like Charlotte. You'll never be a proper woman.'

Well, well, well, I thought, staring in shock at my reflection, *Mother was wrong.*

I could see my scars in the mirror, too. They were unmissable, really; I had so many of them. Silvery lines criss-crossing my skin: my ravaged belly and my ravaged feet, and all the other places Mum had hit me. I used to be ashamed of my scars; I would think I was a waste of space and that they meant I didn't belong anywhere. But, looking at them now, I just thought, *They're a part of me.* In a way, while I may not have had any exam grades or letters after my name, those scars were my qualifications.

When the doctors talk about them in the future, I thought, *from now on I will say, with my tongue placed firmly in my cheek, 'Can you not diss my scars? I worked hard for them, you know.'*

Sadly, the operation wasn't a success. By which I mean, it quickly became clear that I was in excruciating pain most of the time, couldn't eat properly and literally had to pull stools out of my body with my hands. They upped the dosage of morphine to try to help me cope – though, ironically, I found out later that high doses of morphine can actually make the reversal op more likely to fail.

It was evident that that silver-scarred young woman's body I'd seen in the mirror wasn't mine to keep. The surgeons were going to have to reverse the operation again, and bring back Colin. My body had been through too much trauma to do it straight away, though, so it was decided the reversal would happen the following spring.

My heart sank at the thought of another lonely hospital stay, with not one visitor to lift my spirits.

Little did I know that I was about to meet someone who would change all that ... forever.

CHAPTER THIRTY-EIGHT

It was a crisp, cool autumnal day, and the brisk wind was whipping pink roses into my cheeks. Pink roses – just like the ones I'd placed on Charlotte's grave a few weeks before. Every year I still went to pay tribute to her and Judith on the anniversary of their deaths. Having never attended their funerals, I felt like I was still saying my goodbyes.

I was out for a dog walk in the fields behind my house, Ollie and Milly and Alfie running in exuberant circles around me, their tails wagging ferociously. One of the nice things about having a dog is that there's a community around it, and I was strolling with a fellow dog-walker when a tall, tanned man lolloped up to us. He was wearing a green woolly hoodie and I noticed he had very gentle eyes.

'This is my son, Ant,' said the man I was walking with.

'Hello,' I said, my eyes barely meeting the stranger's.

'Hello,' he muttered back, keeping his gaze fixed firmly on the dogs.

Because the dogs were my family, I always watched very closely to see how people responded to them – and vice versa. I was a bit like, 'If you don't like my dogs, then I don't like you.' Ant loved the dogs. He was more interested in them than he was in me, I think – at least at first. Milly came up to his outstretched hand and within a few moments she'd rolled onto her back so he could tickle her tummy, his large palms smoothing down her fur. *You little floozy, Milly*, I thought. But it made me smile.

Ant was very shy, like me. He was also older than me, about twenty-seven, with big broad shoulders, which tapered down to two huge hands. Those gentle eyes of his were set in a clean-shaven face, topped by thick dark hair, and I thought he was very handsome.

After that first walk, we arranged to go out with the dogs again, just the two of us. His family had a spaniel at the time called Jack. We'd meet up to take the dogs out and we'd go round the fields, chatting about this and that. Ant was a very calm person to be around. He didn't work – hadn't, for a long time, and I think it had become too easy not to, especially as he lived at home with his parents so he didn't have to pay rent – so he had a lot of spare time to spend with me. As we got to know each other better, we talked quite deeply about things, and I liked him for that. We'd meet up maybe once a week at first, then every day. He'd walk me back to mine afterwards, but I wouldn't let him in the house. I liked him, but I didn't trust him; I was a very guarded person.

One afternoon, however, when he'd walked me back to my door as usual, he hesitated on the doorstep and then said carefully, 'Please don't worry. If you let me in, I'm not going to do anything untoward.' After that, he would come in for a cup of tea and a slice of cake after our walk, while the dogs lay at our feet, hoping for a stray crumb to fall to the floor.

I was very proud of my house; I kept it clean and tidy, and I found it was a pleasure to have somebody there to share it with. And I enjoyed our conversations more and more. In time, we became very close friends. I remember the first time he hugged me: he was so tall and broad-shouldered that when he wrapped his arms around me, I felt like I disappeared, and I loved that feeling. I used to call him my 'gentle giant', and I adored the feel of his big hands as he stroked my back or my hair. He had caring hands – nothing like Uncle Phil's.

One time, Ant left his jumper behind after our cup of tea. I remember picking it up and smelling it; his scent was so reassuring. After that, I'd sleep with his sweater every night, spread out across my pillow so I could drift off to sleep with my senses surrounded by him.

Once we'd known each other for a while, I told him what Mum had done to me. He was angry, heartbroken; distraught. I found that difficult, because I felt guilty for upsetting him. Whenever anybody got close to me, I felt like my secret was this big bomb about to go off; that I was about to ruin a life. It was as if I represented to people the cruellest acts that humans can do to each other, and often they would go away and leave me because they couldn't cope with that.

But Ant didn't leave.

I told him about Uncle Phil, too. I was conscious that our relationship wasn't very physical, and I was very nervous about all that because of what Phil had done to me. I said to Ant, 'If you care about me, you're just going to have to wait, I'm afraid.' I was quite respectful of myself in that way.

Yet Ant respected me, too. He waited, with not a whisper of pressure or dismay.

I could see his love for me. I could see it in the way he would defend me in any family tiffs, in the way he would give me lots and lots of cuddles, in his open-mindedness and in his kind, caring nature. He was the best friend I'd ever had.

I spent Christmas 2009 at his parents' house. His mum, Maria, was Italian and she kindly invited me into their home to spend it with them. It was lovely, though I felt a little as if two worlds were colliding. I found it hard to relate to them and they to me: that difference in my childhood 'normality' leaves a mark in so many ways. Nevertheless, not long after, Ant moved in with me. And he was just in time for a very special occasion: Milly and Alfie were about to have pups.

I was so proud of my girl. She had eleven puppies in total, all chocolate-coloured except for one black pup. Alfie was a doting father, but it was Milly who transformed herself. Overnight, this dizzy, scrumptious girl of mine turned into a fierce mummy, defending her pups if you picked them up, her eyes out on stalks, watching you. Ant and I saw all the babies being born, and it was an exceptional experience. We were both besotted with them.

Two days later, I went into hospital for my stoma operation. I felt for Ant about that. The nurse came out to talk to him about it beforehand and it could have been so embarrassing, but he took it all in his stride. It wasn't even a big issue for him when he saw the bag for the first time. What really upset him was the rest of me: they'd had to open me all the way up again, and I had big staples all across my stomach; I was black and blue with orange iodine everywhere. Not quite the look I was going for.

He came to visit me every day in hospital, with such a smile on his face. He'd tell me all about the puppies, how they were starting to open their eyes, and he looked so happy. Even in my doped-up state, riding the wave of morphine, trying to keep the sickness it caused at bay, I could see how thrilled he was. I couldn't wait to get home to them all – and, when I did, it was one of the best times of my life, one of the happiest times in our relationship. Ant and me caring for the puppies: those energetic masses of brown and black fur that we played with and cleaned up after and loved.

One evening, we came back from the cinema and I went to let the puppies out into the garden as usual. One of the chocolate-brown pups, once she'd had her wee, leapt straight up onto my lap for a cuddle. She was licking me frantically with her little puppy tongue. She had a big wrinkle on her forehead and her ears were almost too big for her, like she hadn't grown into herself yet. Her name was Berry and she was like a ball of love. It was extraordinary, that enthusiasm of love for me; I'd never known anything like it. There was just something she saw in me that she simply adored.

After that, whenever I came in, she'd be desperate to get to me. She'd whine and whimper until I picked her up for a cuddle. She wouldn't do it with anyone else, and it meant so much to me that she cared that deeply for me and me alone. I'd never had that before in my life: she wanted me, for me. Her little tail would start going and she'd nibble at me with pure affection.

After a few months, the puppies started going to their new homes. In some ways that was lovely because I saw how they transformed the families and children they went to. I knew how much dogs had helped me in my life, and I cherished the idea of Alfie and Milly's offspring spreading the love that they had brought me out into the world.

Ant and I hadn't planned to keep any of the puppies; I already thought, if I was being honest with myself, that having three dogs was one too many. But I had reckoned without the affection of one special little girl. Berry became so attached to me – following me round at every opportunity, love writ clear across her wrinkly brown face – that Ant and I decided we would keep a puppy, after all. As I said to him: 'Berry has chosen me.'

In that Christmas of 2010, it turned out that, so had Ant himself. It was a white Christmas that year, with the deepest snow I'd ever seen, and we took the dogs out in it for a walk on Christmas morning. I grabbed the camera and took snapshots of my family: the Labs looked so beautiful against the snow. Later, Ant and I went round to his parents' house, their front room dominated by a picture-perfect festive tree, strewn with multi-coloured fairy lights and traditional baubles.

It was in front of that tree, as Ant and I were sat snuggled in an armchair, me perched in his lap, that he pulled out a diamond engagement ring. 'Victoria,' he said to me, those gentle eyes of his that I loved so much fixed firmly on mine, 'you're my best, best friend. You're the only person who has ever understood me. Will you marry me?'

I said yes straight away, my insides all content, and he scooped me up in a classic Ant hug: all long arms and big hands and broad shoulders to bury my face in.

'I don't want to live my life without you,' he whispered in my ear.

In the months that were to come, I could only hope he would remember those words – and abide by them.

CHAPTER THIRTY-NINE

My doctor, Jeremy, sat beside the desk in his GP's office, trying to puzzle through my latest medical predicament. I'd been trying to come off the high doses of morphine I'd been on since my various operations, but the patches they'd switched me to just weren't working. They made me sweat so much that the patches would slide off, and then I'd sweat even more from the pain and the withdrawal. I felt like I was being twisted inside; ripped apart from the inside out.

'I'm going to refer you to the substance misuse department,' he told me. 'I want to make it clear, Victoria, that I don't mean you've been misusing anything, but anyone who's been as poorly as you have – whether in a car crash or through cancer, or some other health problem – well, there's a risk they can become addicted to drugs, to the morphine. This isn't your fault, understood? But let's see if we can get you off it.'

Soon after, in the spring of 2011, I found myself sitting in the substance misuse clinic, which was wall-to-wall with patients who would fit your more traditional idea of a drug addict, all struggling with their own problems. It was quite frightening. *I seem to have got myself in trouble*, I remember thinking, *but I don't know how I've done it.*

The doctor called me in. She was lovely and understanding. 'So,' she said, 'we need to treat you for heroin addiction.'

'What?' I said, shocked.

'Morphine is heroin,' she explained. I was so distressed when I heard that; I'd had no idea.

She gave me a pill to put on my tongue and told me to let it melt there, and then go home. It had a really sour taste to it. I remember walking to get my bus and it was like an out-of-body experience: I was me but not me. I had to cross the road and all the cars were beeping at me but I couldn't stop walking, even as I heard brakes squeal and angry voices shouting at me. When I collapsed onto the bus it was like all the energy had been sucked out of me; I felt so odd.

Somehow, I managed to get myself home and up the stairs. I fell onto the bed. Ant came in and looked at me quizzically. 'Are you OK?' he said.

I had no energy to answer him. He got onto the bed and just cuddled me. He put his weight on me, and with his weight and his warmth, I eventually fell asleep.

I was horrendously sick that night, the first night of many. That first time was the worst because my body reacted badly, but the withdrawal programme I was on was tough, very tough. I had to go to the chemist every three days to get more drugs, and I remember each time I did I felt so ashamed, standing in line to get my fix, desperately needing it. Ant's mum would sometimes come with me – she was struggling to understand what I was going through, but she did try. She cared. I had stomach cramps, sickness, sweats and hideous shakes.

But the worst thing of all – the worst thing by far – was that, without the morphine to buoy me up anymore, I started feeling other pain, mental pain, which, unbeknown to me, the drugs had been suppressing for a very long time. The little pill on my tongue was to try to get rid of the physical withdrawal symptoms. But there was nothing to help me deal with everything that was fucked up in my head.

Emotionally, it was as if I'd just been hit by a bus or a train, or a 24-tonne truck – and, believe me, I know what that feels like. All of a sudden, I was thinking about my mum again, in a terrifyingly visceral way. I became really tearful, and I had vivid nightmares about the torture I'd endured for eighteen sodding years, and about Uncle Phil. I dreamt about the sticks down the back of my throat – maybe because I had to put the pill on my tongue, and it reminded me of that. To my dismay I even started wetting the bed again. Ant was very good about it, but it didn't stop the shame creeping up my spine when I woke with that awful spreading dampness on the backs of my thighs.

It all felt so raw and frightening. I was awash with all these feelings. It was like my life up until now had been behind a filthy window screen, the morphine layering inch upon inch of dirt and dust upon it, until you couldn't tell it was a window screen at all, and now someone had just come along and cleaned that window and I was like, *Oh my goodness, I can see everything. I can see everything and it's just awful.*

Judith's body in the crash. Mum's screaming face and the sticks in her hand. The surface of the bathwater as she plunged my face right into it; the glistening cat food in its shiny silver tin; Uncle Phil's bloodshot eyes and his big dry hands and his filthy, filthy cock. It hit me all over again as if it had happened that. Very. Same. Day.

Oh my God, oh my God, oh my God. The pain.

I was in agony.

I didn't know how to rid myself of these feelings. I was constantly picturing Mum, Phil; the abuse. I stopped eating, I stopped washing; I wouldn't leave my room. I didn't know who

I was or where all this stuff was coming from. It was as if I was that little girl again, frightened and so very, very alone. Like somebody had lit a match to the buried memories in my head and my brain was now on fire; it was a forest fire, that raged and burned and convulsed and ate up everything inside my mind, until all I could see were those licking flames, and each one contained a memory from my past that I didn't want to see, I didn't want to see, but I couldn't put the fire out and so it burned and burned and burned and burned and burned.

And then, one day, I found a cool, clear liquid that dulled the flames. It didn't extinguish them, not completely, but it suppressed them.

Its name was vodka: evil, evil vodka.

I don't know exactly, now, what prompted me to try it. I had always been very anti-alcohol. I'd never drunk myself, not even when the younger Witnesses had urged me to try it, when I first escaped from Mum. I'd always been put off when I saw drunken people carousing in the streets, especially in my nasty street in Gloucester; and then, of course, there was my experience with Uncle Phil. That was enough to put anyone off it for life.

Nonetheless, I'd seen people use it here and there for pain relief: a bad toothache, say, or just a bad day. And I thought, *I wonder* … And so I went down to the corner shop and I bought myself some vodka. I tried just a few sips from a glass at first.

Ah … That first shot. It did the same thing the morphine had done, I realised. It stopped the mental pain, and the constant thoughts about my mum and my uncle. I felt normal again. I started with a little bit … and then another little bit … and then a little bit more. I would drink it and screw my face up. It was rancid, really, like drinking nail varnish. I'd hold my nose and drink it, almost forcing it down – but still I forced myself to do it because, to me, it was medicine. It was making me feel better.

At first, I hid it from Ant. I hid it all over the house – under the mattress in the spare room, in the bathroom, behind the sink. I'd hide a bottle in the garage, or the shed, or even in some bushes outside, and I'd nip out to sneak a shot when I needed it, straight from the bottle; or I'd lock myself in the bathroom and drink it where he couldn't see. To begin with, I could just carelessly throw a bottle in with the weekly shop, innocent as you like, and he'd think nothing of it.

But then it started to escalate. It was scary how quickly it spiralled – spiralled out of control. It got to the point where I would just try to down as much as I could. I was drinking a litre a day, but I wasn't addicted to the alcohol as such.

I was addicted to not feeling that hideous, horrible pain.

One afternoon, Ant announced he was off to the corner shop to get some dog food and I said casually, 'Oh, can you get me some vodka, please?'

He didn't say anything. He brought it back for me, and he put it high up on the Welsh dresser we had in the living room, out of my reach.

'What's all this about then, Victoria?' he said. He was angry, I could tell; it was like the penny had dropped, and he was fuming. 'I can see what you're doing. You're a pisshead, aren't you?' He pointed towards the bottle, so high up on the shelf. 'You're not having it. You need to go cold turkey and come off it.'

There's no manual for these things; he was doing the best he could. I don't think either of us realised until that afternoon just what a big problem it was. I think for Ant – well, no one wants to think the worst of people they care about, and he didn't want to think the worst of me. He'd had blinkers on, but they were coming off now. As for me, I had fallen so far down the rabbit hole I didn't know which way was up anymore. That afternoon was the moment I realised I was too far gone even to care.

I was lying on the sofa, with dirty, greasy hair, covered in a cold sweat. The dogs were lying by the sofa beside me, casting worried looks up at the raised voices in their home. I needed a drink; I needed a drink so badly.

'You're not getting it!' Ant shouted at me fiercely.

I started to shake. My body craved the alcohol so much. I shook and shook and eventually I passed out. Ant was watching me. I went bright blue and then I bit my tongue mid-seizure and blood started pouring from my mouth. Ant rang for help; he rang the paramedics. They rushed into the house and gave me the medical attention my body now required: it couldn't live without the booze any more.

When I came round, still lying on the sofa, I found Ant's eyes, and I locked onto them. 'I'm so sorry,' I said, 'I'm so sorry.' I took a deep breath, and when I closed my eyes I found tears were in them, sad and shameful. 'I am an alcoholic,' I said. 'I am, I am. I'm so sorry, Ant. I'm so sorry.'

I never denied what I was, after that.

But that didn't mean I could stop myself drinking.

Life isn't as easy as that.

CHAPTER FORTY

I heard the door slam from my pit on the sofa. The house was a mess, and so was I.

'Come on, Victoria,' Ant said. He lifted my hair out of the pile of sick it was resting in, and made me sit up. Then he changed my stoma bag for me. He was nurturing and sweet and kind.

Other times, he wasn't. He would be very angry, and yell in my face. He poured away my vodka, even though the doctor told him not to, because he said that the withdrawal could kill me stone dead.

From where I was sitting, barely propped up with vomit in my hair, that would be no bad thing.

What a fall from grace it had been. In my befuddled state, I could still remember people who used to say to me, 'You've done so well, given what you've been through.' It had become too much to cope with, though, trying to keep that perfect, jolly, happy life in place – a life that had been happy only on the surface. It had been too hard, trying to be with people who had lived a much more normal life than me: struggling to appear as ordinary and well adjusted as they were was just too exhausting. Well, I didn't bother with any of that artifice anymore.

Gradually, I stopped paying my bills. The council took over my rent but only on a temporary basis, they said. Because Ant didn't work, he was paying nothing towards the utility bills. The compensation money was long gone, sucked into payments to the landlord. I found Ant not working very, very stressful. He had never worked in all the time I'd known him. I felt like I was being used; that he wasn't paying his way. My neighbour, Emma, tried to help, but she didn't really know how, and her encouragement, kind-hearted as it was, was somehow not enough to get through to me. We didn't fall out, but I'd sunk so low her friendship didn't reach me any longer. I felt more and more isolated and alone. In the end, my money arguments with Ant were another thing I wanted to forget about; another thing the vodka dulled the pain of. I just wanted all my pain to stop, and the only way to make that happen was to drink the next bottle of vodka.

My GP tried to help me over the next year, in a number of ways, some of them absolutely incredible – he would clear his diary of appointments to come and see me, and even visit on weekends, just to check how I was – and others seemingly bizarre. He told Ant that he *had* to give me alcohol; he told the corner shop they *had* to sell it to me. Because without it, now, I would die: my body couldn't live without it. He tried to get me help for alcoholism, but the alcoholism team told me I should be cared for by the mental-health department; when I went to them, they sent me back to substance misuse. I felt like a sausage in a factory, that nobody understood. I felt I had no one to turn to.

When Ant poured away the booze, I'd end up in A & E with severe withdrawal symptoms. He and others thought that was the best place for me. 'If she's in hospital, she's safe,' they reasoned. But as my visits added up, the A & E staff grew more and more exasperated. 'You're a pisshead, you don't belong here, go home' – that was their attitude.

People told Ant to leave me. 'Stay away from her,' they said, 'she's scum. Leave her alone.'

But he refused to give up on me. 'No,' he would say, 'this is not the Torrie I know, this is not her.' He'd get me up and wash my hair. And he'd take the dogs for a walk for me, after I'd put down their food on the kitchen floor with a shaking hand. I was still managing to keep the dogs fed and watered, because I loved them so much, but everything else in my life was a mess.

I tried to come off the alcohol for him. 'Well done,' he would say, 'well done, Torrie.' I wanted to come off it so badly. I think I came off too fast, though, wanting to impress him, and I took ten thousand paces back. Sweats, shaking, seizures in the living room, biting my tongue, sometimes even losing my sight – it would fade out in front of my eyes. So, so scary.

It nearly tore us apart. I was barely there, just existing, really, a shell of my former self. But Ant looked inside that shell and he knew me, he knew. And he didn't give up.

'Leave her, she's not worth it! You've done your best for her, now let her go!' people would screech at him.

The more they shouted, the more I drank.

In the end, sometime in the spring of 2012, Ant did move out. I didn't blame him. He was only a young man, and he couldn't cope with watching someone he loved drink herself to death. It was fair enough.

I watched him go and I thought, if I could think at all, *That serves you right, Torrie. You have let everybody down. Just like your mother always said … you* are *the scum of the earth.*

I kept drinking after he left. Of course I did – I had to numb the pain. Every day, I'd drink until I was asleep, and then when I was awake I'd drink to sleep again. I didn't want to be awake; I didn't want to be alive. Over and over I would think about Mum, and then I'd raise that nasty bottle to my lips and try to drown her out with desperate mouthfuls of acrid, bitter booze.

I became a skinny girl sitting on the sofa, my blonde hair stringy and thick with grease, lying lank about my shoulders. I didn't bother putting in my dentures, so my mouth reverted to its natural state: dark gaps in my tooth-line where the vodka could flow through easily. And my hands? Oh God, my hands. They were dry, dry as dust from all the dehydration.

I knew of only one other person who had dry hands like mine: Phil. Uncle Phil. I was turning into the man I hated and that was just the most, the most awful thing in the world. I looked at my hands, and felt their calloused yellow skin, so familiar to me from when his drunkard's hands had touched my young white body, and I thought, *You're turning into him, you're turning into that man you detest.*

I reached for the bottle and I drank some more.

One morning in the May of 2012, a letter landed on the doormat with a slim, thin sound. It was from my landlord, telling me I was out: he was going to evict me. I tried to sober up, and I went down to the council offices to ask them to rehouse me, hopefully in a place with a garden or a nearby park, so the dogs would be OK.

But they said I owed them rent, and that as far as they were concerned, I had nowhere else to go. I qualified for a place on the street: no more, no less.

And I knew. Oh God, I knew.

I knew at that point I was going to lose the dogs.

Ollie, Milly, Alfie, Berry: my babies, my family.

I was the worst mother in the whole wide world.

'Ms Spry …' I heard a European accent from somewhere through the pounding fug of my head. 'Ms Spry …'

Opening my eyes, I squinted against the glare of the hospital lights. I was in A & E … again. I was always in A & E, having been picked up for being collapsed in the street; or Ant might have called 999 if he'd come round to walk the dogs and found me passed out in my bed. He did still pop in regularly, no matter what some of his friends – or even the doctors – said. He was still my best mate; it was just a very hard thing for him to handle. One out-of-hours doctor told him he didn't know why he bothered, though – 'You might as well leave her in her pit to die because some people you can never help.'

I tried to focus on the doctor before me now. He had a German accent. I could hear beeping machinery, and the occasional glug of drips as they pumped vitamins into my arms, replenishing my battered body.

'Ms Spry, time to go home now, yes? Nurse, take the drips out. If she wants to go home and drink herself to death, we might as well let her.'

And I was unceremoniously chucked out of bed. I nearly fell down the stairs on my way out; I was shaking so much from the withdrawals.

A lot of the nurses and doctors felt like that about me. In many ways, I didn't blame them. I went to A & E nearly forty times in eighteen months. Nurses would tell me in disgust, 'I wouldn't spit on you even if you were on fire,' or 'An old lady just died up there because people like you are taking up beds.' I felt so guilty about that. More murders to add to my conscience. More reasons to drink myself to death.

The problem was, if you break your leg in society, it's all plastered up and people can see it, so they'll leap to their feet to help you: they'll offer you a seat, or go to fetch a glass of water. But with mental ill health, especially a case like mine, where I had decades of anguish eating at my soul, it's an invisible affliction, and you can't see it, so no one offers you a way to take the weight off your figurative feet. I don't want this to make me sound like a victim because the drinking *was* all my fault, and I admit that, hand on heart, but I felt so awfully misunderstood at that time. I wasn't trying to cause trouble; I was just trying to take my pain away. I'd ended up in this fucking pit and I didn't even know how I'd got there … it was truly terrifying.

Some of the nurses were nice, though. Some of them would say gently, trying to get through to me, 'You're going to kill yourself if you go on this way.' But I'd think, *So?* I didn't love myself, so I didn't care. I couldn't understand it when they, or Ant, would get angry with me. My reaction was, 'Nobody cares about me. Why are you getting angry? No one has *ever* cared about me. Why should you?' I couldn't see Ant's love, anymore; I could only remember my mother's hate.

I'd be released from A & E, over and over, and I'd go back home. I reverted to how I used to live, back when I was a child: the curtains drawn against the world, living in filth and squalor. My only routine was that of caring for the animals, for my precious dogs. In the end, there was no heating in the house, no running water; no loo that flushed. The place was a tip. I ended up living in a place as dirty and messed up as I was.

But … I couldn't stay there forever. The clock was ticking. *Tick-tock. Tick-tock.* Louder and louder, no matter how much I tried to drink to make it stop. If I was asleep all day – I reasoned, in my illogical, drink-addled state – did it mean that day hadn't happened? If I drank enough, would the day never come when I would have to say goodbye to my beautiful dogs?

Of course it didn't. *Tick-tock. Tick-tock.* And, too soon, far too soon, that horrible, desperate day dawned on me. And I knew, in the bottomless pit of my soul, that I was doomed.

CHAPTER FORTY-ONE

It was a glorious summer's day, on the worst day of my life. Friday, 29 June 2012 dawned bright and clear, a summer scorcher. Through my closed curtains I couldn't see the sunshine, but the bedroom felt airless and stuffy as I pulled out the vodka bottle from under my mattress and reluctantly swigged from it. I hated every mouthful that passed my lips, but I knew my body couldn't cope without it – my body or my mind. I was hooked, no matter how much I hated that fact. My 'medicine' taken, I padded downstairs.

The dogs twisted about my feet and tried to lick my dry hands, but I pulled my palms away from them. Ever since I'd got the letter from the landlord, I'd tried to keep my distance from them. I felt like I'd failed them, just as all the adults in my childhood had failed me; I hadn't protected them. They were loving someone who didn't deserve it; best not to lead them on.

It didn't stop them, though. They would still sleep with me, up in my tip of a room, and Berry would lie on me and lick my face until I came round from one of my drunken stupors. Ollie would look at me with those wise brown eyes of his, as though to say, 'It's OK, Mum, I'm here. I'm always here for you.'

I had rare visitors that day: a social worker, Ant, and a woman I'd never met before. Her name was Belinda. She worked for a local Labrador rescue group.

I can still see her now, striding into my living room in her Dubarry leather boots. Very posh and well spoken, she was tall and wiry, with practical, short hair. She was there to talk to me about rehoming the dogs, because the landlord wanted me out and I was going to have to move soon – no matter how many times I buried my head in the bottom of a bottle, trying to keep time standing still.

It was my GP who had found me somewhere else to live, in the end. He'd helped to organise these multi-agency meetings and eventually they found me a room in Cheltenham in a place called Belroyd House. It provided assisted accommodation for people with mental-health problems. Pets were banned.

Jeremy had begged for me, though. He'd said, 'She lives for those dogs; you've got to let her keep a dog.' And, after all his efforts, they relented. 'One dog,' they said. I could keep just one dog.

Belinda was only there to talk to me that day, to give me the lowdown on how she could help. The Labrador group she worked for was a special kind of rescue service – the dogs remained in the charity's care for life, even after they were rehomed, so I knew transferring ownership of the dogs to them would mean my family would go to good, safe homes, that they were guaranteed to be well looked after. If Belinda took them, they wouldn't just be abandoned in a cage in an anonymous animal shelter, their future happiness left to chance. I felt I couldn't let her walk out of my front room and risk that, so I raised my shaky voice above the hubbub of conversation in the room and I said, 'Can you take them today, please?'

Ant and the social worker protested – 'No, next week, next week would be fine' – but I raised my voice again and said, 'Please, this is killing me. I want them to go now. Please let them go now.'

It was too much for me to have their fate hanging over them for one day more. Belinda sized me up with her no-nonsense eyes. She nodded briskly, and then went out to make a few phone calls. When she returned, I was sitting on the sofa, watching the dogs gambolling about my feet. She came over and perched on the arm of the sofa next to me, and she wrapped her strong arm tightly around me.

'I can tell from the way you spoke just then,' she said, 'and the way you took control, that you really love these dogs.'

I nodded wordlessly, tears streaming down my face. I was so distressed at the thought of losing them. My heart was breaking before her eyes.

'I've rescued a lot of dogs,' she told me firmly, 'some of them are scared and fearful, but your dogs are not like that. Your dogs are loved.'

She gave me some forms to sign then, transferring ownership of my babies to her charity. I signed them blind, blinded by my tears, my hand scribbling out a shaky signature that I could barely see through the sheets of salty water that fell from my eyes.

And then she said six words that chilled me to the bone. 'I'm ready to take them now.'

I called the four of them to me and they came running up obediently, as they had always done, dutifully responding to their mother's cry. I didn't make much of a fuss of them; I didn't want to upset them. Wiping the tears from my wet face to try to hide my sadness, I bent down to their level. I kissed each of them on the top of their beautiful heads.

'Thank you,' I said, 'thank you for everything you've done for me. I will always, *always* love you.'

'You can keep one, Torrie,' Ant reminded me. There was a tremor in his voice: he was cross at me. He was sad to see the dogs leave so suddenly, for he had loved them, too. 'You *must* keep one.'

'But how can I choose between them?' I cried. 'How? *How*?'

He shrugged. It was a decision only I could make.

In the end, I chose Berry, because she had chosen me. It was very, very hard saying goodbye to Ollie in particular, because he was the one who had taught me how to love. I'd never known true love until I met him. He was mine and I was his; but Belroyd House was a tiny place with strict rules, and I was worried he would bark and get thrown out. Berry was still young enough to be taught new tricks.

And then they went. Belinda had a Jeep parked outside. She took them out the front door, and the three of them leapt into the car, very trustingly, just as I'd taught them. I didn't watch them go; I couldn't.

After they'd gone I lay down on the stairs, and I sobbed and sobbed and sobbed. *I don't deserve dogs*, I thought. *I don't deserve Berry. I am a vile piece of muck. I got myself my babies and I've not looked after them. I am horrible, worthless, evil scum.*

I reached for the bottle, the bane of my life, and I swallowed and swallowed and swallowed, as hard as I could, until I couldn't remember anything more.

Beep. Beep. Beep.

Ah, I knew that sound. Bleating machinery reminding me that I was still, somehow, alive, despite all my best efforts. I opened my eyes. Hello, institutional ceiling tiles. Hello, hospital.

I didn't know what had happened, but I could guess. I'd been found on the street outside my house, vomiting blood. In the few days since the dogs had gone, I'd drunk two litres of vodka every day, and my body had finally given up.

I looked around me. There was another patient in the room, a woman in her early thirties. She had a cloud of dark hair around her pretty face, but that face looked awfully sad.

'Hey, are you OK?' I called across to her. Whatever was going on with me, my heart still reached out to those in need.

She tried to smile, but it didn't reach her eyes. 'Yes,' she said. 'I'm just missing my girls, but they'll be in later.'

She told me she had two little daughters. She was in for a heart condition, a problem she'd had since she was a girl herself. We chatted about this and that, trying to keep her mind off things. She was very well spoken and well educated.

'Why are you here?' she asked me at one point in our conversation. 'You look so young.'

I burst into tears, too. 'I'm an alcoholic,' I confessed, 'and I don't know how in hell I've got here.' And then I found myself telling her my story: about my mum, and the car crash, and the trial, and the dogs. She listened so carefully, and we talked for hours – until visiting time, when her husband and her two little girls arrived, with a rucksack full of things she'd asked for. It was lovely to see her with a smile on her face.

The porters came to move me to a different ward, but she stopped them momentarily, so she could hobble over to me to say goodbye. She was clutching something in her hand, an item from the rucksack that her husband had brought in.

'I want you to have this,' she told me. 'I've had this for as long as I can remember. It's brought so much love and happiness in my life, so much good luck. And if anyone deserves a bit of that, it's you, sweetheart.'

And I thought, *For her husband to have remembered to bring this in for her, it must mean a great deal. But she's giving it to me…?*

She pressed it firmly into my palm and wrapped my fingers round it. 'You take it,' she told me. 'You will get there, I promise. I can tell you're a fighter. You're going to be absolutely fine.'

As the porters wheeled me away, I opened up my fingers. In my hand lay a rose stone, a sparkly pink stone about the size of a golf ball with a rough texture to it. It was very solid, and very real, and it gave me something to hang onto.

I had a visitor myself at the hospital, not long after that. It was Ant, loyal Ant: my best friend. He didn't visit the hospital very much, but he came that day, because the nurse had asked him to bring me in some clothes. He brought me an envelope, too – an envelope that had been posted through my home front door.

Inside was a card: a card covered in cute coloured cupcakes. It was a note from Belinda, the woman from the Labrador rescue group, and it was the most powerful and beautiful letter I had ever read.

She told me the dogs were absolutely fine. She told me *I* was going to be absolutely fine. She said the dogs had loved me. 'I go to so many places to rescue dogs,' she wrote, 'and, sometimes, the dogs don't come out like yours did. Some of our dogs are terrified, and untrusting, but yours were clearly loved. They are quite clearly happy dogs.

'Don't listen to what anyone else says. You're not evil, you're not bad. They're just dogs, at the end of the day, and they're going to be fine.

'You go off now, and you live your life. Be free. Love Berry. Be strong.'

I slept with that card under my pillow every night. It was as close as I could get to my babies.

I had a third encounter in hospital at this time. Not on the same visit, oh no – I went back to the house, and I couldn't cope with seeing Ollie and Milly and Alfie's things everywhere, so I fell straight off the wagon and straight back into A & E – but it was an encounter that, in the long run, changed everything for me.

Three visitations: the rose-stone woman, and Belinda, and my third mystery guest. If I was still religious, you might say it was like the three wise men at the Nativity, bringing precious, priceless gifts. If I was still a nursery nurse, maybe they'd be the three Billy Goats Gruff – but instead of skipping happily over the bridge, trip-trapping mindlessly on their way, this time they reached a hand down to the unhappy, ugly troll, and they brought him up into the sunshine and the fresh green meadows, and they taught him how to run again in the clean mountain air.

'My name is Lauren,' said the woman in the bed next to me.

And Lauren was the woman who would save my life.

CHAPTER FORTY-TWO

Lauren had a Labrador, too. So that was it: we were friends for life. She also had a hilarious sense of humour, and she was a great listener. She listened to me tell my story, and I heard hers in return. And Lauren, well, she never gave up on me. She point-blank refused to. Sometimes you need a champion to show you the light through the dark.

We swapped numbers in hospital. And one day, after I'd been discharged yet again, and had returned to my lonely house with my bottle of vodka – for I was still waiting for the room at Belroyd to become available – there was a knock on the door and it was Lauren. She came in and she cleaned the entire kitchen; she even laughed about the mess. She was so relaxed and easy-going that I didn't feel embarrassed about it. Lauren was one of those people who just accepted you for who you are. She already knew my difficulties, and she wasn't there to judge: she simply wanted to help.

After she had finished, she came upstairs, to where I was begrudgingly swallowing down my 'medicine', grimacing at each and every shot, tears on my cheeks at how dependent I had become on this evil drink. Ant had just walked Berry and let her in to see me, so my little girl was there. I called her and she jumped up onto the bed and groaned and cuddled into me. I smiled my gappy, toothless smile, and Lauren said it made her happy to see me happy. She persuaded me to have some of the Fortisip the hospital had sent me home with, which is a special nutritional drink, and she patiently traded the booze for the liquid vitamins with me until she thought I'd had sufficient. Then she and Ant took Berry for another walk, and I guess they traded stories – there were certainly a lot to share.

I've said it before, but life isn't easy. Lauren's friendship wasn't a sticking plaster that suddenly made everything A-OK. I'd swear I wasn't going to drink again, but then I'd end up so depressed that I just started necking from the bottle. Countless times after we met I fell off the wagon, heading back into hospital with my tail between my legs, just like Berry after some mishap, but Lauren didn't seem to care. So many times before, no one had visited me in hospital – and I accepted that, I thought it was what I deserved – but Lauren came in again and again, bringing me magazines and fresh food and clothes. I thought I was such a bad person, so it was a genuine shock to see somebody who cared that much. What struck me in particular was that she had met me at the worst point in my whole life, and yet she saw something in me that she loved. That touched me. I started to believe in myself – but only because she believed in me first.

There came a day that turned out to be my last day in hospital. I was looking at Lauren, at her blonde curly hair and her gorgeous smile, trying to cheer me up, and I made a decision. People say that when you stop doing something like drinking, you have to do it for yourself. But I didn't – I did it for her. Because she'd actually gone against the grain and was really loving me: she'd put her neck on the line and I kept on letting her down. Finally, I reached a point where I really, really didn't want to do that anymore.

My empty house was a trigger for my drinking, and I was very lucky when Ant's parents said I could move in with them until the room in Belroyd became available. Ant and I spoke a lot in the time I was staying there. He was still very raw about us losing the dogs – raw about everything. I attribute a lot to Lauren with my recovery, but that's not to say Ant wasn't there for me, too. It had been an incredibly fraught time, to say the least, but I felt, at last, that we could both see the light at the end of the tunnel now. I was going somewhere safe, where I could get the help I desperately needed. He was still my best friend, my boyfriend, my fiancé, and I still loved him. Luckily for me, he still loved me, too.

Two days before I moved into Belroyd, I went back to the house to pack up. I was surrounded by pictures of my babies, and their smell, and their blankets, and it was all too easy to find a stash of vodka and sample its sourness. But I didn't drink it all. I knew there was help for me now, if I asked for it, so I called Lauren, and she came and picked me up. I was shaking, I felt I'd let everyone down, but she soothed me and bathed me and dressed me in a pair of pink fleecy monkey pyjamas, with little grey primates printed all over the legs, and she tucked me into bed. Her guest room had buttery magnolia walls and smooth wooden floorboards, and the bed was made up with thick cream sheets, with cosy red blankets spread over the top. I felt so blessed to be slipping in between those sheets, to have people who loved me.

Ant came with me, and he gave me a big Ant cuddle in his lovely, long-limbed arms before I went to sleep. That night, I finally dared to dream that everything would be OK.

I never went back to my house again. Lauren and Ant's mum and my social workers packed for me. It was a massive job, because I was downsizing from a house to a single small room; but then again, material things had never been important to me. I trusted them to do it, and I was simply grateful for their help.

In August 2012, I moved into Belroyd House. Lauren drove me there. It was a large white building with arched windows, double glass doors and an office at the front. My room was a ground-floor studio flat, with a tiny bathroom off to one side. There was a cream carpet, and a single strip of lino in the kitchenette. I had a brown sofa, a table and chair, and a single bed.

My key worker, Faye, was there to greet me; a condition of the place was that you had to see a key worker every week. And she said to me, 'Where's Berry?'

'I'm not having her,' I said. I'd been told by people I didn't deserve her, and I believed it. Ant's family had been looking after her while I was in and out of hospital, and I thought she was going to stay with them: not my dog anymore.

'What?' Faye said in surprise. 'Jeremy has fought tooth and nail to get that dog in here.'

'But I've been naughty,' I explained.

'You've not been naughty,' she replied, gently. 'You just need a bit of help. And that's our job, to make sure you're all right, and to make sure Berry's looked after. Give yourself a chance, Victoria. Berry is your dog. Don't you worry, we'll sort this out.'

And she did. The next day, Ant's mum brought Berry to me. My little girl came bounding into the room; Maria had to let go of her because she rushed straight for me. Her lovely floppy ears became her happy ears and they just flew back on her head as she ran into my arms. Her soft velvety head pushed upwards for a cuddle, and she jumped up at me and licked me and loved me, as she'd done ever since she was a baby.

'Welcome home,' I told my gorgeous girl, barely able to believe my luck. 'Take a good look around. This is our new home.'

*

It was a week later. Lauren had stayed the first night with me, Ant the next. They'd tag-teamed – but now I was on my own. It was selfish, I know, but I thought to myself, *I've just been dumped here and now they've all gone.*

It was overwhelming being in the new place. I wasn't allowed to drink – in fact, it was a condition that I had to be sober to stay there – because it was a place for people with mental-health problems, and not alcoholics; as though the two could be neatly divided like that; as though the world was black and white and not a murky grey. I felt frightened and unsure of myself. When I'd first moved in, only the week before, I'd had a sense of a fresh start … but I wasn't so sure now that I was quite ready for that. I felt that maybe my mum had been right all along – for look at who I was, and what I was, and where I was: an alcoholic, in a halfway house. *The devil's child, the scum of the earth.* I'd turned out just as she had predicted.

Quietly, I slipped out to the shop, and then I came back home. Berry was on the bed, curled up asleep. I sat next to her on the mattress, careful not to disturb her slumbering form, unable to look at her. I unscrewed the bottle cap. I drank straight from the bottle.

There was a sharp tap on my door. 'Come in,' I called, tucking the vodka under the bedspread. Faye came in, and she shut the door behind her. There was CCTV at Belroyd House, and she knew exactly where I'd been on my little excursion, and what I'd brought home.

Faye paused, and she looked at Berry and me curled up on the bed. 'That little girl thinks the world of you,' she said gently.

I nodded, having no words, not trusting myself to speak.

'Time to have a sandwich now, Victoria,' she said, matter-of-factly. 'Why don't you get Berry out, too? She needs a walk. It would do you both good.'

I couldn't believe it. Why wasn't she shouting at me? Why wasn't she grabbing my hair and pushing my nose in my filthy mistakes? But no, she was just really calm. It was like she understood and this, in turn, had a calming effect on me.

I reached out a hand, my dry, yellow, alcoholic's hand, and I stroked Berry's soft fur coat. I thought to myself, *Faye is right. This dog loves you.* That meant more to me than anything else. *Stop thinking about what the world thinks of you, when she thinks the world of you. She chose you. Stop thinking you don't deserve her, just because people have said it. People will always look down on others; they'll always have opinions. You've got to be true to Berry, and be true to yourself. Just because you've made mistakes, it doesn't mean you're an evil person.*

That was such a staggering thought I told myself it again.

Just because you've made mistakes, it doesn't mean you're an evil person.

I kept the sob in my throat inside, snug and tight. I wanted to prove to everyone who had doubted me that they were wrong; that I wasn't just a waste of space, that I did have a heart.

That I could look after Berry.

My girl raised one eyebrow at my touch, and then lifted her heavy Labrador head and rested it in my lap, letting out a snuffly doggy sigh as she did so. A pink tongue briefly passed her lips to lick my hand, and then she fell back to sleep.

And I thought to myself, *Enough's enough. This has got to stop.* Once and for all, it did.

EPILOGUE

I lived at Belroyd House for a year. It wasn't an easy year, but it was a year I had to live. In a way, there was something liberating about having lost everything: my home, my dogs; my dignity. It stripped me back to basics – but now I had a second chance.

Every time I went to the shops, I was a bag of nerves; the colourful bottles lined up on the shelves a painful reminder of everything I'd been through. It had become so normal to me to cast one into my basket with a horrifying *clang*, like a jail door slamming shut, so imprisoned had I been in my addiction, that it felt like someone had chopped my arm off when I came out of the shops without buying booze. I would phone Ant and tell him: 'I haven't bought any vodka, I've been so good.'

Ant was brilliant. He didn't live close to Belroyd, but he'd come over and stay regularly and – day by day, week by week – we grew stronger together.

Faye gave me an enormous amount of strength, too. Wary to the end, I didn't trust her at first. I found I could talk to her quite openly about my past, about the bare-bone facts of what had happened to me as a child – but telling her how I felt inside? That was hard. Twenty years of being told your opinion doesn't count makes it hard to volunteer that kind of information.

Berry was the key to our breakthrough; that dog really did save my life. Faye would let me bring her to the office for our weekly meetings, and as I sat and stroked Berry, and learned how to open up, the barriers between us slowly broke down. I started to let Faye help me. By the end, it felt like I had a big sister just down the hall in the office, a moment away if I needed a chat, or someone to help me sort out train tickets, or respond to a formal letter. It was lovely. I'd never had that before: someone to look after me. Faye helped me to tackle my debts; she got me back on track.

I made another friend, too, in Belinda, the woman from the Labrador rescue group. I was struck by how she had seen good in me at my lowest point; she'd known nothing about my childhood when we met, she simply saw an alcoholic who was giving up her dogs, but, nonetheless, she had seen something in me that had made her write that incredible note, and that meant a great deal to me. I tracked her down through the charity, because I wanted to say thank you, and she became another of my champions, just like Lauren.

It was Belinda who persuaded me to have my teeth fixed again. I was so self-conscious about my smile; I used to try to stretch my top lip over my teeth to hide the gaps, but it meant I couldn't smile properly. Belinda took me to the dentist so they could give me a brand-new, full-mouthed smile.

It was a tough experience. Can you imagine? Being lowered back in the dentist's chair, completely at his mercy, while he asked me to open my mouth wide and then poked around inside; my tongue sensitive to every prod and touch; my mind racing with recollections of my mother's spiky sticks. Belinda held my hand throughout, as the tears flowed freely down my cheeks, but it was worth it. I walked out of that dental surgery with a great big smile, beaming from cheek to cheek in a way I never had before.

And there was so much more to smile about, these days. Not least my beloved Berry, my beautiful girl. The two of us went for walks every day. She really was an exceptional dog. And she grew up in Belroyd: I saw her change from a mad little puppy into a responsible, protective adult dog. She looked after me; she kept me sane. Berry would hang back on our walks to pad alongside me as I struggled at a slow pace, hampered by the painful pins in my hips; her smiling face, looking up at me, seemed to say, 'You're not alone, I'm here.' I would take my camera out on our walks so I could capture her joy at life and her delicious doggy face, and I took so many shots that I ended up setting up a Facebook page in her name, so I could put the images online. That led to me making new friends via the website, with lots of equally enthusiastic dog lovers.

Faye told me my pictures were really good – so often and so fervently that, eventually, she persuaded me to enrol on a photography course at the local college. I liked being behind the camera, showcasing others' beauty, yet creating something myself.

For Berry's third birthday, in the spring of 2013, I arranged for the two of us to have our picture taken by a professional photographer, as a record of how far we'd come. The photographer – as everyone always was – was struck by my gorgeous girl's face, and he asked if he could enter Berry in a national dog-portrait competition, for the prettiest face. I said yes, but didn't think any more of it – so you could have knocked me down when we found out she had won. There was even an article about it in the local paper, and I read it and thought, *That's my girl*. I was so proud of her.

While still at Belroyd, I got another dog. Although Berry had flourished with the one-to-one attention, I noticed she became lonely once I started college and was out during the day. Faye got permission for me to have another dog, and I knew that two was my limit. I will never have four dogs again: it was too many, and I can see that now.

I went to the Forest of Dean to pick up Noah, a black Labrador rescue dog, from a puppy farm that had been raided by the RSPCA. He was sat in the corner of a dark shed when I first saw him, shaking like a leaf. The RSPCA man placed him in my arms and I said, 'I'm having him, I'm taking him.' I wanted to get a rescue dog because I knew how grateful I had been when other people had rescued Ollie and Milly and Alfie for me, and I wanted to give something back.

Belinda gave me updates on my lost family, something I was grateful for. They all went to separate homes, where they were happy. Alfie went to a gardener; Ollie to an old lady who had an enormous garden; and Milly to a young couple, where they wrote that she had her own 'personal trainer', something that made me laugh so hard. That was so Milly – always a little madam, she would have loved that.

I never thought about trying to get them back. They were settled now, and so was I. Nevertheless, I will always, always love them.

Noah took time to adjust to his new home. I can remember rolling a ball towards him at Belroyd House, and he would back up into the corner of the room at the approaching toy, really frightened. He reminded me of myself, in a way – how I used to back up into my corner cubbyhole in Mum's kitchen, hoping not to be hit. As with all scared creatures, patience and love were what saw him through. Berry and I slowly convinced him he was safe now, and he began to trust us.

Berry loved him – she was like a bossy big sister, showing him the way – and what I loved was that Noah's arrival heralded a different dynamic in her. She let go of some of the adult responsibility she'd assumed when we first moved into Belroyd, and she had some fun. The two of them would race across the fields and tag each other, and Noah's name seemed to me even more apt. I'd named him Noah because, after the catastrophe of the great flood, Noah survives and everything is calm and back to normal. After the drama of the past few years, I wanted that serenity in my own life, too.

As it happened, I became a big sister myself again at that time – when Adam and I were reunited. Ant and I ran into him on the street one day; one Saturday afternoon when we were out walking the dogs. Adam was then about twenty years old, with long, scruffy hair.

It was strange for me, seeing him so grown up, but in many other ways he was still very young. He still had that loud, nervous laugh he'd always had. He didn't have a job when we met; he'd gone to a mainstream school after we were rescued, but when you start your education at the age of thirteen, when you can't tie your own shoelaces and you've been taught to think you're better than all the other kids, well, 'being on the back foot' doesn't really cover it.

He put his arm around me when he saw me and gave me a soft little punch to the shoulder. 'All right, kidder,' he said, with genuine affection. He still had that good heart I'd always seen in him, and he and Ant really clicked, sharing a similar sense of humour.

After that first meeting, he'd often call round to Belroyd House to see me. I'd take his shirt and wash it for him, and give him a meal from time to time. I was glad we were in touch again.

We didn't ever talk about Mum; it was too much. But we didn't need to say anything: we both knew the truth. I looked him in the eye and I saw his pain and his sadness and his soul, and we both knew. Flying horses wouldn't stop me from loving him.

In July 2013, the time came for me to leave Belroyd. Faye helped me find a new place, but I organised the move all by myself. I thanked her for everything she had done for me, but she said, 'No, thank *you*. We don't have that many successes, Victoria. You and Berry made it a joy to come to work.'

Belinda and Lauren helped me paint my new home. It had a garden for the dogs, and we painted the lounge a lovely duck-egg blue and my bedroom was princess pink. Belinda treated me to a pair of new curtains for my room – beautiful pale-pink curtains with big roses on them. It's crazy when you think about it: my curtains are a gift from the woman who took my dogs away from me. Funny how life works out.

Ant didn't move in with me, not at first. I told him he had to get a job, so we were both pulling our weight: a team, the two of us against the world. One month later, he came back and he'd got himself sorted, got himself a good job, and I could see, from the off, that he was instantly a happier human being.

The two happy human beings closed their front door, shutting themselves inside their snug new home. And I thought, *Life begins right here. Right now.*

The letter landed on the wooden floorboards in our hallway with not a blast of fanfare or ceremony, just a silken whisper of paper on wood. I picked it up with the rest of the mail and took it through to the kitchen, telling Noah and Berry to calm down as they twisted with excitement and affection around my legs.

Dear Ms Spry, we are writing to let you know that your mother, Eunice Spry, is scheduled for imminent release …

It was February 2014. My mother had been due to serve twelve years in jail from 2007. They were letting her out five years early. She had served just seven years for what she did to me – and to Alloma and Christopher. Seven measly years for trying to destroy three children's lives.

The early release wasn't because she had been rehabilitated. In fact, she never once confessed her guilt, or owned up to what she did. My liaison contact, Penny, told me Mum could, in fact, have been let out even earlier had she chosen to apologise and admit she was wrong. She never had. So that wasn't why she was being released 'early'. The sad fact is, pretty much all prisoners are. The British Government's own Sentencing Council website says, 'For sentences of a year or more, an offender will serve half their sentence in prison and serve the rest of the sentence in the community on licence.' It's standard protocol. If a judge says fourteen years, it only ever means seven on the inside.

Penny came round to my house to talk to me about it all on a wintry February day, following up on her letter. We both sat on my big grey sofa, one at either end, and Berry waited attentively by my side as we both watched Penny get her papers out of her bag, running her fingers through her short grey hair as she prepared to discuss my mother's case.

317

'As you know,' she began, 'Eunice will be released in July. At the minute, the plans are to move her to Worcestershire.'

My jaw nearly hit the floor: Worcestershire was only a short distance away. Not only had everyone told me that she would be jailed for twelve years, they'd also said, when she did get out, I'd never have to see her again; that never, in a million years, would they allow Mother to be close by me again. Now, she was going to be moved just down the road!

I gave Berry a stroke along her soft brown back, and I took strength from her. 'What do you mean, Worcester?' I asked Penny, looking her straight in the eye.

'She's done her time, Victoria,' she told me firmly. She was sympathetic but it was clear she felt there was nothing more she could do. 'Now, we need to keep this very quiet about her release, because she could be in danger of being harmed. Whatever you do, don't talk to your brother about this.'

'Why not?' I asked.

'Because if he goes to the media, there could be a problem.'

Christopher had done TV and press interviews after the trial, as well as writing his autobiography. I guess his confidence in talking to the media had been noted by the powers-that-be.

'What kind of problem?' I asked, stroking Berry over and over.

'Well,' she said, 'if the people in her new area get wind of what she's done, they will put pressure on the council not to home her there, and that will make things very difficult indeed.'

'Can I ask you something?' I said. 'Do the people who are rehoming her know that I was nearly dead two years ago? Do they know that I nearly died? And that I'm only down the road from Worcestershire and that, you know, I might not be able to cope with her being there?'

'No, I don't think that matters,' she said smoothly. 'The release meetings are only about Eunice: her safety and her rehabilitation; making sure she won't reoffend and harm the public.'

She might not harm the public, I thought, *but what about her victims?* But Penny didn't have anything else to say; she packed up her papers and left.

For days on end, I thought, *Is that what I do then? Just keep quiet, tell no one, be a good little girl?* It was messing with my head. *Am I letting Mum win by being bothered by her at all? Or am I not protecting my own back by doing what I'm told?*

I tried to speak to people about it – I wanted to talk to the people who had the responsibility of rehoming her, to look them in the eye and make them understand. I'd seen my mother manipulate people for twenty years, and I knew how easily she could convince them that what *she* wanted was what *they* wanted. I wanted to warn them to be on their guard.

But no one would give me any names. No one would let me attend any meetings. Everyone told me only one thing: I had to move on.

'This is all about Eunice now. She's out of prison, she's done her time,' they would say.

'But you're letting her out when she's not sorry!'

It was that, more than anything, that made me worry. If she admitted she was guilty, I wouldn't have given her headspace, but if she wasn't sorry then she still thought she was right – and, therefore, that I was wrong. And I knew what Mum did to people when she thought they were in the wrong. I *had* to take my concerns seriously. How could I move on when she hadn't? But no one would listen.

'She's banned from Gloucestershire,' the authorities told me. 'You should count yourself lucky, to have that. We don't normally do that even for murderers. It will be a condition of her release: she won't be able to step foot in Gloucestershire.'

'And you think she's going to listen to you? You think she's not going to cross the border? She's never listened to anyone but herself.'

Someone actually told me I should go to karate lessons, to get some strength and martial arts awareness. One of the police officers – someone who had actually worked on my case – told me, 'When I got married, my husband told me I needed to stop going on about my ex not paying maintenance. I think you need to stop going on about Eunice.'

I couldn't believe it. 'You're comparing Mum to your old boyfriend?'

'Move on, move on', that was their mantra. And all the while I was thinking, *I have moved on, that's exactly what I have done. But this could jeopardise everything.*

I managed to get a multi-agency meeting convened, attended by some of the official departments who had helped me when I was drinking. But the meeting was about me, about how they could support me and help me cope, rather than about my mother. Here was an idea: how about they moved her away from me so I didn't *have* to 'cope'? *Why can't I just live my life, instead of simply having to survive?* I wondered. I was tired of fighting all the time.

At the meeting I said: 'I don't want to see her, I'm frightened about seeing her. I'm fighting never to see those eyes again. I don't want to see her face ever again.'

'You've got to move on, she's done her time now,' I was told.

'But when is *my* time done?' I asked. 'When will it stop for me? I'm not asking for much, I'm not asking for a million pounds and a mansion. I'm asking you, please, to say she can't come to Worcestershire, for her to be rehomed in a place where I won't bump into her. She wants to come here for a specific reason. Please put her at the other end of the country.'

'Victoria, you do realise you can't have everything you want,' they'd say.

'I know that,' I'd reply, with bitter comprehension. 'I didn't have everything I needed for nineteen years.'

That meeting couldn't help with the central issue, of course. Even though there were official departments in attendance, I knew all too well that one hand of the government body didn't talk to the other. 'It's not our area,' they would say. It was just like when I was a kid, and the dentists who saw me with my teeth smashed out didn't talk to the doctors who examined my sandpapered skin, and they in turn didn't talk to the teachers who saw my mum humiliate me, or the education inspectors who came round to observe our non-existent home schooling – and no one spoke to the social workers who had registered grave concerns about my adoption. No one was communicating; nothing had changed.

My nightmares started again, as did the bed-wetting. I heard from liaison officers – people who later told me that they shouldn't have said anything; that I wasn't supposed to know – that Mum had started paying people to do jobs for her on the outside. A scrap of information here, a titbit of knowledge there … I heard she was intrigued by the fact that I hadn't told my story, when my siblings had. Knowing Mum, she thought there was some wiggle room there, potential for manipulation. She was unrepentant, she was unashamed; she hadn't participated in any rehabilitation. Prison hadn't broken her. She was still my same old mother, playing her sick games once again. And I was so, so worried.

In a way, I have my drinking to thank for what happened next. Because, in the end, I thought to myself, *I have fought so very, very hard to get back on my feet. You have to fight for this, Torrie: you have to fight for this life you have made for yourself. You cannot back down this time. You didn't go through all that just for her to mess up your life again. You need to finish this, once and for all.*

I decided I would start a petition, arguing for my mother not to be rehomed near me, seeking for her county ban to be extended so she could come nowhere near me. It was a very challenging thing to do, because it turned out you practically needed a law degree to be able to word the petition in the correct way that was needed. My body might have been covered in countless scars from my mother's beatings, but those qualifications wouldn't help me here.

I was so grateful when I found help from a man online, Chris Wittwer, who dedicates his time to helping victims of abuse, and he did it all for me. I even cried when he sent it through. I had to write a statement to go with it, and I wrote how everyone had said, at the time of the trial, that it was the worst case they'd ever come across. If this was true, I argued, then how, in the next breath, could they all be telling me to just move on?

Alloma and Christopher added their names to the petition in support, so we could stand united, but it wasn't something they felt impassioned to campaign about in a major way. With her usual feisty flair, Alloma would say to me: 'Why are you letting her destroy your life? I'm not scared of the old witch.'

With the petition wording sorted, I pondered how I could make a real impact with it. A blank petition floating out in cyberspace wasn't going to get my mother rehomed elsewhere, I needed to get people behind it, to ask them to lend their voices to my campaign. I remembered what Penny had told me on my sofa: *'If Christopher goes to the media, there could be a problem.'*

Her words gave me an idea.

It took me a couple of months to reach a decision. I fretted: was I doing the right thing? Would it upset people? Would I be penalised for this? I was genuinely frightened. Then I thought, *Right, you're just going to have to close your eyes, pinch your nose and take a leap of faith – and hope it works out.*

When Lauren had packed up my house for me, back before I'd moved into Belroyd, one thing she'd kept for me were the files and files of letters that the journalists had sent me, straight after the trial. I looked at them, in that May of 2014, and I thought: *Can I play them at their own game?* I'd been so proud not to give my name away to the media when I'd been under so much pressure to do it, immediately after the trial. But now, I wanted to.

I wanted to do what I thought was right.

Ant was worried for me. 'Are you sure about this?' he asked me. He knew as well as I did that you can't just pluck self-esteem out of the air. Could I really be confident enough to stand up and speak out for myself – and not suffer any consequences?

What was driving me on was my desire not to lose everything I'd built up, not to lose the home we'd built together. I was happy – and I wanted desperately to stay that way. 'Not really, love,' I told him, with brutal honesty. 'But if I don't take the leap, I'll never know.'

I went to a media agency, who arranged an interview with the *Sun*. After that, I gave interviews to magazines. I went on *This Morning*. What was hard was that often, just at the last minute, I'd be told I couldn't mention the petition, due to 'legal reasons'. My whole reason for telling my story was to bring the petition to people's attention, so that was very frustrating. Most of all, I didn't want to look like a victim. The media concentrated on the horror of what I'd been through, when the message I really wanted to communicate was: 'I'm fighting back now. Help me to help myself by signing my petition.'

Happily, bit by bit, people *did* sign. Within the first day we had over 1,000 signatures. I was overwhelmed by the support, especially from my friends in the online dog community, who shared the link to the petition on their social-media pages, over and over and over again. They took the campaign to their hearts and that initial number of signatures ballooned – until we'd gone way past 10,000 names, which was the magic number I'd been told I would need to hit. I found it incredible, everyone pulling together: so many human beings working to counteract one evil one.

There was space for people to leave comments next to their signatures, and I took a lot of strength from the overwhelming kindness of strangers in their messages of support. The amount of times I cried and wanted to hug people at the other end of the

Internet … And the more signatures I got, the more confidence it gave me.

My going to the media didn't go down well with the powers-that-be. I'd crossed the line as far as they were concerned, by not allowing my protests to be heard through the 'proper channels'. Never mind the fact that when I'd asked to have a voice at my mum's rehoming meetings, I was told they didn't mix the two sides, and that I'd only ever gone to the media in the first place because I wanted to feel safe. I felt officials tried to patronise me. 'You're a vulnerable adult, you shouldn't be putting yourself out to the papers,' they told me. When I criticised the lack of communication between government departments, and called their efforts 'wishy-washy' several times, my unvarying vocabulary was commented upon. 'You like that word, "wishy-washy", don't you?' one of the team sneered. And when I mentioned that I'd written about my campaign to my local MP, seeking help from anyone I could think of, I was told I was a 'bit of a name-dropper'. But I didn't let that bother me. I kept my head held high, I fought back – and I won.

For, after I went to the media, I finally managed to secure a meeting with the MAPPA officials. MAPPA stands for Multi-Agency Public Protection Arrangements. It brings together the police, the prison service and the probation service, and has responsibility for serious offenders. At long last, I got to speak to the people who would be rehoming Mum. It was what I had wanted more than anything – because, before this victory, I had just been a name on a piece of paper to them; I'd been so conscious of that. Now, they would have to talk to me face to face.

To begin with, they tried to placate me. 'Miss Spry, you've got to realise we didn't know what was happening with your mother back then. We didn't know what she was like. We do now.'

'But if that's true,' I argued, 'why on earth are you trying to put her down the road from me, if you know what she's like? This isn't just a random stab in the street. She did this over years, over decades. She manipulated everyone. To my mind, she's now doing it all over again.

'People tell me,' I continued, 'that this is the worst case they've ever come across. If I was in your shoes – if I was doing your jobs – I would do everything in my power to help the children she hurt go to bed at night, safe. That's what I'd do.'

They went quiet at that, because there was nothing more they could say.

I won several battles in that meeting, including the right to a panic alarm in my home – where before I'd been told I was foolish for even wanting one. And I won the right to write a letter to my mother's probation officer, which the MAPPA people promised me they would read out in their next multi-agency meeting.

That was an emotional letter to write. I had to beg them, from the bottom of my heart, not to rehome her in the county next door. I said, 'I've just built my life up, after this woman trashed it. Trashed it from almost the moment I was born. And I am fighting now not only for my life – because I want to settle down, I want to have children. So I am fighting not just for me, but for my future babies. Because I want them to grow up free from harm. I don't want to feel like I'm on the run with them, that I'm always looking over my shoulder. I just want to feel *safe*.' I sent the letter with a summary of the serious case review of my case, which had been conducted by the Gloucestershire Safeguarding Children Board after the trial and listed, in bullet point after bullet point, how my mum had got away with her abuse for decades: by manipulating and intimidating the authorities. *Please don't let her do it again*, I thought, as I sealed the envelope and sent it off.

They told me later that, when the letter was read out, the whole room was in tears. By that stage, so was I: tears of joy. Whether through the petition, or the MAPPA meetings, or my going to the media – and in so doing making Worcestershire an unsafe place for my mother to be – I achieved my mission: impossible. I was told she wouldn't be moved to the county right next door, and she was still banned from Gloucestershire.

I was so proud of myself. And I thought, *You've done this, Torrie – and you've fought her by yourself. No one can take that away from you. You've done that. You*. And I felt genuine pride in myself for going to the police in the first place, all those years ago, for perhaps the first time ever. I felt pride that I'd put her away, and I felt pride that I'd finished the job properly, now, in making sure she couldn't harm me again.

It was so strange, when July came round: knowing she would be coming out. What was frustrating was that they wouldn't tell me exactly when it was happening. Every day, for thirty-one days, I wondered: *Is this the day? Is this the day she can walk down the street, ponytail bouncing, flick-flicking its tail on the end?*

I have wondered what I would do if I saw her again. Her liaison officers talk to me about *her* safety, but I don't think I'd hurt her, if our paths did cross; I'd be too worried she'd hurt me first. I've told Ant that if ever I saw her again, I'd have to walk away with my fingers in my ears because I know, with her snake's tongue, that she could whisper poison that would eat me up. I've heard enough of her words to last me a lifetime.

I think she wanted to return to Worcestershire because I think that's where my nan lives now. I think, I don't know; because anything I hear about that family comes on a Chinese-whispers grapevine. Several years ago, I heard that my old dog Jet had died. Poor, loving Jet: Nan had taken him after my mum was jailed. There was a bit of me that had always hoped we would one day be reunited, so I could thank him for all he did. Now, we never will be, but I hope he knows how very much I loved him.

I've heard rumours on that same grapevine that my nan has dementia, these days, and that makes me sad. I would love to see her again, to see those twinkling eyes that were the bright spots of my childhood, but I would never go to visit her. Because I know that, if she was of sound mind, she probably wouldn't want to see me, and I respect that.

I also heard that Uncle Phil died, a couple of years ago now. The way I heard it, from a neighbour, he passed away in his mother's home, and Nan was so far gone with dementia that he lay dead on the sofa for three days without her noticing. He'll never face justice for what he did to me now. But, having lived the hell of an alcoholic's life myself, I like to think that maybe, just maybe, he suffered in his own way before he died. I take strength from the fact that I proved myself stronger than him, in the end: far, far stronger. I dragged myself out of my pit; he died enmeshed in his.

I have my campaign to thank for a lot of my strength today. Through it, I turned what could have been one of the worst years of my life into one of the best. Because I'm now talking to social services, and sharing my story to try to help other children, to improve officials' understanding of the psychology of abused kids. I've sat down with the head of my local social services, Duncan, and gone through the serious case review of my case, highlighting to him what I believe still needs changing; where lessons can still be learned. It's such a good feeling, to think that my past isn't a wasted childhood, and that I can use it to help others. For I can remember so clearly sitting in my wheelchair in Mum's kitchen, year after year, thinking, *Why don't they want to save me? Where is everybody? Why does no one want to help?* And Mum using it to her advantage: 'Nobody loves you, Victoria. They don't care.'

I don't want that ever to happen to another child.

I'm trying to show people, through my case, how they can help kids like me. Some social workers think they can go into a room and ask a child once if they're being abused. The child, with terrifying threats hanging over their head, will say no; and the social worker may think, *Great, no problem there.* Over and over I'm told there isn't time to talk to kids, but that is the central problem in getting children to open up, and ask for the help they desperately need.

It's about trust: building trust. Having a key worker who gets to know a child, and builds a relationship with them. Trust is what makes the difference. Trust is what saved my life. Trust gives a child a choice.

For there will always be Eunices in this world. There's not a fairy on this planet – much as I'd like to believe there is – who could wave a magic wand and rid the world of every child abuser.

But with better training, training that I now hope to be a part of in the future, we can close the net on them. We can encourage agencies to talk to each other, challenge each other; to fit the puzzle pieces together and realise what's really going on.

None of this potential would have happened if I hadn't hit rock bottom, through my drinking. But because I lost everything, I learned to fight against the odds. I'm grateful, in a weird way, to have lost it all, because a new me rose from the ashes of that forest fire that burned so wildly in my brain: a new-born phoenix, a brand-new start.

The best thing of all, though, is that the new me … is just me. It's Victoria, a little girl who was tortured as a child, but lived to tell the tale. And so, if you saw me in a coffee shop today, I'd be the blonde girl sitting in the corner, taking comfort from the walls that have my back; a hoodie jumper raised above my hair, its thin cotton protection still a comfort blanket I can't quite give up. I'm the girl who says to my fiancé in the supermarket, when we're in the washing-up-liquid aisle, 'Don't get the lemon flavour!', the girl who is always saying 'sorry' out of habit. I'm the woman who, this September, didn't visit her sisters' graves for the first time, to lay yellow freesias on Judith's plaque. As time has gone on, I'm not sure she deserves them.

Ant and I take Noah and Berry out for a good long walk every day, the wind whipping through our hair as we throw balls for them to chase. Berry comes racing back and drops her gift at my feet, her tail wagging and her big brown eyes looking up at me with such love. My dogs were the first people ever to accept me for who I am. They made me think: *If they love me, why shouldn't I love myself?* Thanks to them, I have now accepted me for me. I used to want to fit in with people, with society, and so I tried desperately to do anything I could to make that happen. But, increasingly, I'm now proud to be someone who stands out.

I even have hopes for the future. The future ... There once was a time when I couldn't even imagine one for myself. Now, I hope that Ant and I will be able to start a family together. I worry that I won't be able to – after all, I did have a 24-tonne truck drive into my pelvis – but that's what I want, more than anything. And if I'm lucky enough to have it happen, I will love my children for who they are, from top to toe, every single hair on their heads.

I don't want a perfect life. Someone said to me the other day that they were a bit of a perfectionist; I'm anything but: because we're not perfect. We don't live in a perfect world. There are bumps along the road and you've got to accept that and just do your best.

This book is the story of my bumpy road so far. I'm going to put this book on the shelf now, a cardboard cover keeping its secrets safe, and I'm going to walk away. And I'll keep on walking down my road, into my future. I know some days will be rainy and others bathed in glorious sunlight. Yet every single day, come rain or shine, will be mine. Mine to spend how I wish.

So, I want you to close your eyes and imagine. Imagine me walking my dogs, Berry's brown tail going nineteen to the dozen. Imagine Ant and me cooking up a supper together in our bright, clean kitchen. Imagine me with a camera to my face, taking a snapshot of my family.

Welcome to my world.

THANK YOU FOR READING ...

My story. I would like to ask something of you all. If you feel angry or upset at the way my mother treated me, or the way the authorities dealt with my case, then please, please channel that emotion into helping other children.

Because it's too late for me now: tears and vitriol can't turn back time and change what's happened; it's just life. I don't feel sorry for myself; what I feel is that I want my story to make a difference. Please, let's all use the power of our feelings by channelling them in a positive, proactive way.

So, if you're reading this, and it's sparked a thought in you about a child you know; if you're sitting there worrying that something isn't quite right in a family in your life, then please take action. Don't leave it for someone else to make that call. Because that's what happened in my case: everybody thought it was somebody else's responsibility. But we're all responsible for each other. Please make that call.

If you're worried about a child, you can phone the NSPCC helpline on 0808 800 5000, text on 88858 or email help@nspcc. org.uk. They're open 24 hours a day, seven days a week. If you wish, you can remain anonymous, and you don't have to wait until you're certain there's a problem before calling. If the hairs are standing up on the back of your neck and your instincts are telling you something is wrong – then please, make that call.

Thank you.

ACKNOWLEDGEMENTS

To Alloma, Christopher and Adam: I love you. Thank you for being you. As with roots to a tree, our roots will never change, even if our branches grow in different directions. We were very different people growing up, with very different characters, but sadly the road we walked together will always remain the same. You all inspire me in your own different ways. Alloma, you are so artistic and intelligent; Christopher, you have such a generous soul; and Adam, you are such an honest soul. Adam, you will always be my little man, and I will always be your little mummy. You will always have a place in my heart.

Alloma, Christopher, Adam: we may not have the same blood running through our veins, but my loyalty to you all and my memories of you mean you will be forever in my heart and part of my family. When we look at each other, we don't need to utter a word: we know the pain, but also the strength each one of us possesses, because we've been there together. Please know that I will never abandon you as people did with us. If you ever need me, you know where I am. I will never turn you away. I will always love you, understand you, defend you, care for you and ultimately be here for you, no matter what life throws at us. Be happy, be free. You can achieve anything in life you want to. I wish you all the happiness and love that you all so rightly deserve xxx

To my dear nanny Katie and granddad John. Nanny, my only true and sincere happy memories of my childhood are those that you made for me. You stood up for me when I was a child, which many were too scared to do. I know you were under Eunice's hypnotic spell, but at least I have some special memories with you as a little girl. I will always love you and Granddad. Thank you for my cuddles as a little one.

To my beautiful and precious fur-babies, Berry and Noah. Berry, you are probably the first soul on this planet who has loved me for just being me. As a puppy you chose me and refused to leave my side. Later on, you saved my life; you gave me a reason to fight. You showed me all that was beautiful in the world and pulled me out of a very deep and dangerous depression. Thank you, my little Bambi. I saw you born and your little paws grew into bigger paws that walked across my heart and beside me through life's journey. Noah, my beautiful, funny, gentle boy, you're Berry's buddy, Mummy's little man: thank you for making us complete. I love you both more than I can ever describe.

To my dear Anthony, my very best friend. My goodness, what a journey! Thank you for never leaving me. You've never given up on me throughout some horrendous times. To remain so loyal to a person who at times wasn't very lovable takes a special type of man. When you wrap your arms around me, it's like nothing else matters. You've defended me and never let anyone speak badly of me. Whatever happens in life, I know we will be best friends till the end. I love you!

A big thank you too to all of Ant's family: Neil, Maria, Phil, Rich, Jack and Jessica. Thanks for all your help.

To Lauren: thank you for your friendship and for fighting my corner. I will never have enough words to thank you for what you did for me. We met as strangers but we will be lifelong friends. You're amazing!

Also my gratitude goes out to the lovely lady I met in Cheltenham General Hospital, who talked to me when I was at my lowest: a beautiful, kind-hearted stranger who told me to stay strong and who gave me her rose stone. You have no idea how much that meant to me. I took that stone to every hospital appointment for that following year. I would go to meetings to rebuild my life and hold that stone tight in my hand. If you're reading this, thank you for your faith in me. You were right: I was strong and I got there in the end.

To Belinda Filmer. Thank you for taking care of my fur-babies. As we've discussed many times, it's clear we met for a reason. You released me from the chains of condemnation. You saw the good in me, you understood me. My love for you will never leave my heart; you are so precious to me. A surrogate mum! I love you and look up to you so much – thank you. I never thought I could love the lady that took my dogs away as much as I love and respect you.

Thank you to Sandy Young. You did what so many people were too frightened to do: you stood up to Eunice, challenged her and stuck up for me. You fought for me as a little girl. You're an amazing woman with so much strength and love.

I'd also like to thank the following people for their support throughout everything. To all the doctors and nurses who've helped me, especially those at the Barbara Russell children's ward in Bristol Frenchay Hospital, Ian Nelson and Mr Livingstone. To the two incredibly brave off-duty police officers who got out of their cars and approached such a horrific car crash scene on the M5 motorway in 2000; to the air ambulance service in Somerset, Dorset; to JC Woods; to Rob Lorenzo (the paramedic who kept me alive on the side of the road for forty-five minutes), you're one of my heroes. Thank you for saving my life and my brother's life. James Wheeler, thank you for all your hard work trying to put me physically back together; you're an amazing surgeon. To Jill, my lovely stoma nurse in Cheltenham, and Dr Andrew Green, such a devoted and understanding doctor. Carol Endal and staff at Yorkleigh surgery; and all at the Jesmond House practice. Finally, to Jeremy, an amazing doctor who fought for me and supported me through some very dark times. You got me through so much. Thank you – and thank you to everyone who's been involved with my medical care, so very many of you have helped me.

To those Jehovah's Witnesses who saved my life and supported me: Mark, Ruth (I love you so much and always will), Megan, Dave and Maeve Tyler, Duncan and Jacqueline Costello, Neil Bebbington, Jolene and Stuart Kurtain, Anne Romeo, Bob, Judy, Ben, Alison and Amy Lockwood, Lucy Swift, Nikkie Lewis and Chloe Bone. Many more of you helped me – you know who you are. I will be forever indebted to you. Thank you.

Thanks also to Carol Bull (and Sam and Ellie). I'm so grateful it was you who supported me down that very difficult road to find my biological family. Every time I look at my toy giraffe and elephant I smile fondly, remembering our time together. Roger, Lesley and my biological brother: you're my 'proper' family. I will always love my beautiful brother.

Sue Wilson, an amazing boss and now friend for life, it was a sheer joy to work at your nursery: thank you for giving me that chance; I came into my own there. Thank you too to the ladies who worked on the 'juggler's floor' when I worked there. It was hard but I loved it. Lucy, you were so encouraging and I greatly enjoyed my job because of your unwavering support at the time. Trina, Emma, Faith, Poppy: such a great team of girls to work alongside.

My eternal gratitude to my neighbour Emma, a special person in my life who gave me my first ever Christmas and birthday presents. I treasure my tiny Eeyore and my charm bracelet. Thank you for all that you did for me.

A very special thank you to Faye Kelsey – you are so good at your job! Thank you for breaking down my trust barriers, and for showing me that I was a person and that I mattered. You told me it was OK to make mistakes and that I wasn't a bad person. I hated going to Belroyd, but when it was time to go because I no longer needed it I didn't want to leave. You did something for me that no one else had ever done before. You didn't judge me or force your opinions on me. You listened properly to how I was feeling and respected my opinions and my dreams. Berry and I will always love you. Also a big shout-out thank you to Tammy, Nick Stevenson, Julia, Frankie (from Isis) and Rita Wood; and to the staff at my local CostCutters at Walton Cardiff, Tewkesbury: thank you all for your support through that very difficult time. Your help and care during my dark days – when so many in our community turned the other cheek – made a huge difference to me.

To Ken Goodwin, thank you for going above and beyond the call of duty to help support my petition in the summer of 2014. And to Chris Wittle: you helped me get that petition up and running. You're a selfless human being who cares – thank you so, so much for all your unwavering support. I simply couldn't have done it without you!

Special thanks to Julia Douglous, Louise Goode, Jessica Levy, Marc and Corra Lantham: amazing, courageous people. Sarah,

Duncan, Cathy, Jodie and Isabelle from the County Council – thank you for helping me to understand my past and for enabling me to have a voice for future children.

Victoria Martell: I will never forget that day when I finally found the courage to tell you the horrors of my childhood. You were the first person I'd ever truly confided in. Thank you so much for believing me and for setting me free from Eunice.

Christine Morrison Hughes, I've not yet met you. You live on the other side of the world but sometimes I have felt closer to you than someone sat right next to me. Thank you for your love, care and mummy wisdom.

A very big thank you to all of our friends on Berry and Noah's Facebook page for all your love, fun and support. So many of you tirelessly kept my petition in newsfeeds and tweeted every day until I had reached 12,000 signatures; you've all supported me and been with me through so many highs and lows. Berry, Noah and I would like to thank Linda Jackson, Linda Parker, Kimberley Stonlake, Genevieve Connatty, Michelle Long, Lynn Ede, Becky Blissitt, Herbie Dog, Hugo Huggins, Wizz, Frankie and Wilfy, Tonia and Wiggins (Noah's brother) King, Victoria Newport, Rose Bridge, Lynda Foster, Anne and Ole Lovell, Wendy Bird, Lesley Bowen, Georgina Apari, Sonya Epperson, Brinton, Valerie Harrison, Myles Harrison, Lauren Henderson, Georgina Toomer, Maggie Pine, Carl Thompson, Sarah Murphy and the gorgeous Milo Murphy, Alyson Wonderland and the beautiful Sage, Alison Clews, Buggerluggs and Jack Clews, Sally Victoria, Fraser Edge, Kate and Teddi Maloney Stelljes, Emma Handley, Annee Shelton-Mathews, Beverley Dickinson, Becky Williams, Kim and Maxi Ware, Joelle Hargreaves, Karen

Johnson, Alastair Hilton's Lulu Hilton, Carolyn Plumb, June Harvey, Jenny Shimmin, Mandi Grech, Tom Rennie, Victoria Oatham, Jenna Kemp, Patricia Kleinbrook, Sarah Kibble, Marsha Crocker-Hazel, Carolyn Silcocks, Eric, Ernie and Bailey, Victoria Filmer, and Hayley Lanciano.

To Sara from Ebury Press. Thank you from the bottom of my heart for giving me a chance to do this book and have a voice. I've enjoyed doing it and it's been such a cathartic experience. Kate, my dear ghostwriter, I am so pleased it was you I worked alongside to make this book happen. You were a joy to work with – very professional and empathetic. Thank you for bringing my words to life.

I know I will have forgotten someone in these acknowledge-ments. If I have, I've not forgotten you because I'm not appreciative – it's because so very many of you have supported me and my little family; I'd have to write another book just to list you all. The fact is, though, that I simply can't thank you all enough. You're all amazing. If you're reading this and you've helped me through hard times in my life: thank you. Since escaping Eunice, I have met so many wonderful people. I wouldn't be here today without you.

Victoria Spry, 2015

Me with Noah and Berry on my
twenty-ninth birthday, January 2015.

The dog who taught me how to love:
me with my beautiful boy Ollie.

Berry as a puppy. She chose me.

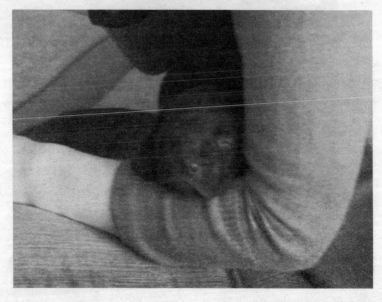

They will always have a place in my heart.
From left to right: Milly, Alfie, Ollie.

With my family, Berry and Noah, on a walk.

Welcome to my world: with Berry and
Noah (top left), and with Ant (bottom).